The Hiker's Guide
to WASHINGTON

by

Ron Adkison

FALCON PRESS

Helena, Montana

ACKNOWLEDGMENTS

Numerous individuals contributed immeasureably to the production of this book, and I'm indebted to them for their generous help and support.

Many thanks to Bob Arrington; my wife, Lynette; and Rick Marvin for their welcome company on several hikes, as well as their important suggestions and corrections.

I also wish to extend my appreciation to Linda Harris and my wife for typing the manuscript.

Many government employees politely and energetically answered an endless barrage of questions and allowed access to the copious information in their files.

Finally, I wish to express my appreciation to the publishers at Falcon Press for allowing me to undertake this project.

Printed in the United States of America.

Library of Congress Catalog Card Number 92-054611

Falcon Press Publishing Co., Inc.
P.O. Box 1718
Helena, MT 59624

Illustrations by Steve Morehouse.
Maps prepared by Ron Adkison.
Cover photo by Cliff Leight of Ptarmigan Ridge trail in the Mount Baker Wilderness.

Adkison, Ron.
   The hiker's guide to Washington / Ron Adkison. — 2nd ed.
      p.   cm.
   ISBN 1-56044-166-6 :
   1. Hiking—Washington (State)—Guidebooks. 2. Washington (State)—
   Guidebooks.   I. Title.
   GV199.42.W2A35   1993   92-54611
    917.97'0433—dc20   CIP

 Text pages printed on recycled paper.

MAJOR GEOGRAPHIC REGIONS

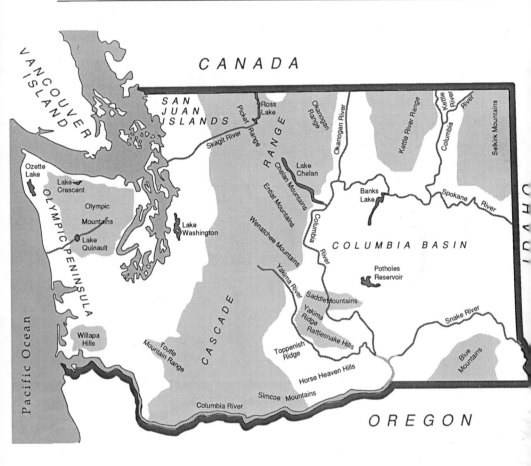

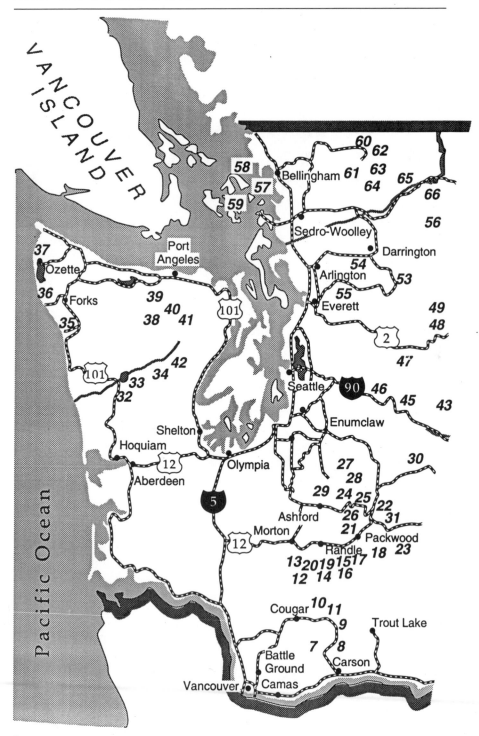

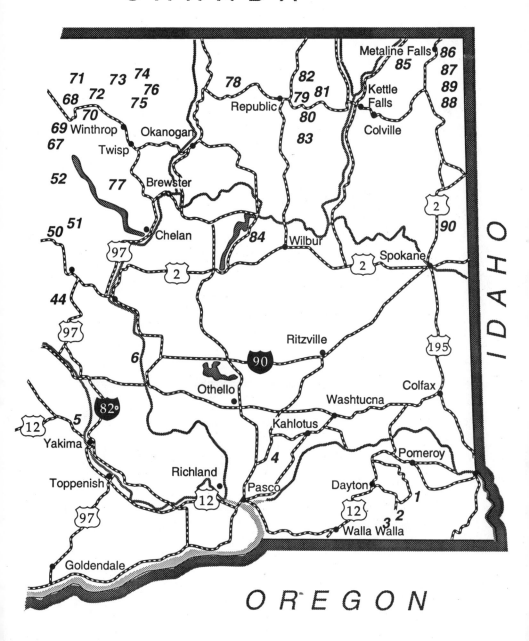

CANADA

Metaline Falls 86
85 87
71 73 74 78 82 89
68 72 76 79 81 Kettle 88
75 80 Falls
70 Republic 83
69 Winthrop Okanogan Colville
67 Twisp
52 Brewster
77 2
50 51 90
Chelan 84 Wilbur
97 Spokane
2 2
44
97 195
6 Ritzville
90
Othello Colfax
82° Washtucna
12 Kahlotus
5 Pomeroy
Yakima 4
Richland Dayton 1
Toppenish Pasco 3 2
12
97 12
Walla Walla
Goldendale

OREGON

IDAHO

v

CONTENTS

HIKING IN WASHINGTON, AN INTRODUCTION

Washington is a land of superlatives. It's a land where mountain peaks soar above dense forests and deep river valleys...a land where vast wheat fields thrive in what once were parched deserts...a land of abundant rainfall and drought...a land of mountains and rugged coastlines...a land of deserts and forests.

Washington is so varied that it defies description. You can stand along the sea coast and stare in disbelief at the ethereal presence of giant volcanoes perpetually clad in white. You can stand on summits that see only a few weeks of spring a year and view distant deserts where summer lingers on and on.

A land of diversity

Diversity may best describe the landscape of Washington. Half the state is mountainous, cloaked in some of the finest coniferous forests in the nation. In their honor, Washington has been dubbed "the Evergreen State." But much of the eastern half is bunchgrass steppes and parched basalt-rimmed coulees—transformed almost overnight into one of the nation's breadbaskets. The mighty Columbia River supplies precious water to irrigate this region of little rain.

One third of Washington is federally owned—that is, it's public land that belongs to each and every U.S. citizen. More than four million acres are federal wilderness, which will be left in their primitive, undeveloped state for the benefit of those who choose to explore them or those who simply need to know that wilderness exists. Large blocks of roadless land remain, and they must legally be designated wilderness if they're to be preserved.

The most familiar geographic feature in the state is the Cascade Range. The southern half, a region that sees more loggers than hikers, is heavily forested and punctuated by volcanoes. The northern half boasts some of the most rugged, spectacular mountains in the nation.

Nearly all of the Cascade crest north of Snoqualmie Pass has been designated federal wilderness. In the south, scattered parcels of pristine country, sandwiched between logging operations, have been protected. East of the Cascades, much of the Rocky Mountains and Blue Mountains lies within national forest land, but only two wilderness areas have been set aside.

To people who tend to judge value in terms of economics, wilderness may seem a wasteful folly, "locking up" resources that are "worthless" unless exploited. But the protection of wilderness affords direct economic benefits. These areas are the source of clean air and abundant oxygen, the source of clean water and subsequently generated electricity, and the last stronghold of wildlife.

Only experienced climbers, who can safely negotiate hazards such as deep crevasses, should venture onto ice fields. Kevin Duck photo.

of strenuous activity in a primitive setting, wilderness is everything. Indeed, we need these "wastelands" to survive. Their promise keeps us going from day to day.

The chance to hear a mountain's story

Hiking is for everybody. Look at your fellow hikers next time you're out on the trail. Representatives of every age group are enjoying wilderness and public lands to the fullest. They're also exposing themselves to a great learning opportunity.

As you hike along, keep your eyes, ears, and mind open. Be receptive to the silent story the mountains tell. Rocks reveal a mountain's history, from its advent below the ocean floor to its upheaval far above the earth's surface. Vegetation reflects the conditions under which it grows, and the trained eye can visualize the processes that created specific habitats.

By virtue of their size, mountains dramatically influence the distribution of plants, animals and weather patterns over large areas. The Columbia Basin, for instance, owes its extreme dryness to the moisture barrier of the Cascade Range. An experienced hiker knows that vegetation is sorted by elevation, with each life zone adapted to the climatic conditions created by the mountain's great relief. While foothills bake in 100-degree heat, temperatures on alpine peaks only a few miles away may be forty degrees cooler.

Within certain climatic and life zones, tiny "microclimates" often occur, influenced by the availability of moisture and sunlight and other factors. These microclimates may harbor plants and animals characteristic of life zones normally found great distances away.

There is much to see, do, and learn in our wildlands. As we roam the mountains, we step back in time to a simpler existence, uncomplicated by the workings of man. When we enter the wilderness, we become independent of the outside world. Nature's schedule is tied to the seasons and the rising and setting of the sun, not to the time clock.

John Muir's words are as appropriate today as they were when he uttered them years ago: "Climb the mountains and get their good tidings. Nature's peace will flow into you as sunshine flows into trees. The winds will blow their own freshness into you, and the storms their energy, while cares will drop off like autumn leaves." □

Marmots are found throughout the Cascades. Cliff Leight photo.

UNDERSTANDING THE HIKE DESCRIPTIONS

The Hiker's Guide to Washington presents ninety hikes in the Evergreen State. See the maps on pages *viii* and *ix* to find their locations. Nine to ten categories of information describe each hike: 1) the general description, which is a brief synopsis of the hike; 2) the elevation gain and loss, which indicates how strenuous the hike is; 3) the trailhead elevation; 4) the highest elevation reached during the hike; 5) the maps which will be needed; 6) the best times of year in which to undertake the hike; 7) the availability of water; 8) permit information (if a permit is required); 9) instructions for finding the trailhead; and 10) the description of the hike itself. Most of these categories are self-explanatory, but additional explanations of certain entries will help you get the most from each hike.

A detailed map accompanies each hike. Intended only as a general introduction to the trails, terrain and features of a given area, these maps should never be substituted for the United States Geological Survey (USGS), Forest Service, or national park maps recommended for each hike. See page nine for a complete list of the symbols used in the maps in this book.

General description

Three basic types of hike are described in the general description: the round-trip, the loop-trip, and the point-to-point hike. For a round-trip you travel to a particular destination and then retrace the same route back to the trailhead. On a loop-trip you arrive at a particular destination and then follow a different route back to the trailhead. The point-to-point hike begins at one trailhead and ends at another; it requires you to hitchhike back to the initial trailhead, have someone pick you up, leave another car at your destination, or perhaps split up your group and begin from opposite trailheads, exchanging car keys in the backcountry.

Hikes are also described as day hikes, backpacks, overnighters or a combination of these. Generally, day hikes are either too short for backpacking, lack adequate water or campsites, or are in areas restricted to day use. A backpack or overnighter either covers too much ground to be comfortably completed in one day or boasts attractions, such as fine scenery or fishing, that dictate a leisurely pace.

A hike listed as a day hike *or* backpack can be completed in one long day or broken down over two or more days. It may have special features that may entice some hikers to extend their stay.

Elevation gain and loss

The elevation-gain-and-loss figures, generally accurate to within 100 feet, indicate the rigors of a particular hike. For round-trip hikes, the elevation gain and loss is given going one way. For example, a round-trip hike that gains 1,500 feet and loses 250 feet would lose 1,500 feet and gain 250 feet on the way out. For loop or point-to-point hikes, the total elevation gain and loss is listed, with a minus sign indicating elevation loss. Only one figure is listed if the hike is either all uphill or all downhill.

A single figure listed for a loop trip, for example 3,500 feet, indicates that hikers gain 3,500 feet and also lose 3,500 feet (usually not all at once, since many ups and downs are encountered in the backcountry).

Consider this example: If a hike gains 1,200 feet, then loses 500 feet, then gains another 1,000 feet, and then loses another 300 feet, the elevation figures would be +2,200 feet and -800 feet. These figures help indicate the difficulty of a hike more accurately than would the difference between elevation gain and loss (in this example, 1,400 feet).

Maps

Under the heading "maps," three types of maps are discussed: USGS topographic quadrangles and Forest Service and national-park maps.

Each national forest and park offers maps of the areas it covers. These maps are not particularly useful for hiking, but they can be invaluable for locating trailheads and obscure forest roads.

Many of the larger wilderness areas in Washington are detailed in individual maps that feature contour lines and show most trails. Some of these maps list elevations and distances in meters, which can be frustrating for diehards who refuse to convert to the metric system.

These wilderness and national forest maps are currently $2 to $3 each and are available at most ranger stations. National-park maps are free and available at visitor centers and park entrance stations.

USGS topographic quadrangles are preferred for backcountry hiking. These maps depict contour lines that allow hikers, with a little practice, to visualize the landscape and identify landmarks such as peaks, lakes, and creeks.

The 7.5-minute USGS quads usually have contour intervals of forty feet, cover areas of approximately nine by seven miles, and are based on a scale of 1:24,000, meaning that one inch on the map is equivalent to 24,000 inches on the ground. The 15-minute quads usually have contour intervals of fifty, eighty, or 100 feet, cover areas of approximately fourteen by seventeen miles, and are based on a scale of 1:62,500. Each national park in Washington is covered by a topographic quadrangle, but these maps are presented on a different scale and some are metric. They condense a large area onto a comparatively small sheet, thus losing much detail.

Unfortunately, many USGS quads are out of date and don't show recent features, such as roads or trails. But the landscape hasn't changed, and so even an out-of-date map can be useful.

The maps in this guide are accurate and up to date, showing the correct location and configuration of important roads and trails. They're designed to complement the quadrangles listed for each hike.

Topographic quadrangles are available at most sporting goods and backpacking-supply stores, or you can order them directly from the USGS. To do so, simply list the maps you want in alphabetical order and indicate how many of each you need, which state they are for, the desired scale, and the price. Be sure to specify the correct title as it appears under "Maps" in the hike description. Map orders are frequently delayed or returned if the name of a map requested isn't accurate. Standard quads currently cost $2.50 each, while national-park quads are $4. Include a $1 handling fee for orders under $10.

Send map orders to U.S. Geological Survey, Box 25286, Denver Federal Center, Denver, Colorado, 80225. An index of Washington state quads is available free upon request.

Topographic quadrangles of Washington are also available at the Public Inquiries Office of the USGS, located at the U.S. Courthouse in downtown Spokane: Earth Science Information Center, U.S. Geological Survey, 678 U.S. Courthouse, W. 920 Riverside Ave., Spokane, WA 99201.

Season

"Season" listings indicate the optimum season in which to undertake a particular hike. Since conditions vary on a yearly basis in the backcountry, these listings should be considered general guidelines and are by no means imperative.

Season listings for high-country hikes generally refer to the time of year in which the hiker is least likely to encounter snow and storms. But early-season hikers should anticipate lingering snow or high water, and late-season hikers should plan for the possibility of autumn snowstorms and hunters.

The seasonal suggestions for lowland hikes that receive little or no snowpack are still aimed at helping the hiker to avoid rainy winter weather.

All-year listings indicate that there are no special seasonal problems to prevent hikers from traveling easily. However, storms can make an area temporarily inaccessible. Always check weather forecasts before venturing into the wilderness, and be prepared!

Finding the trailhead

"Finding the trailhead" tells you how to find the point at which to begin a hike. Some trailheads are along interstate highways, while others lie deep in the mountains at the ends of rough, seldom-used dirt roads. Use the general-location maps in this guide, a state road map, and the pertinent national-forest or national-park map to locate the trailhead. Be prepared for a variety of situations, not only in the backcountry but also en route to and from trailheads. Always be sure your vehicle is in good operating condition; check your brakes, have a full tank of gas, and carry some basic survival equipment. A shovel, axe, saw, about five gallons of water, tire chains, blankets, extra clothing, and food should enable you to deal with emergencies. To avoid the possibility of theft, never leave valuable items visible in your vehicle. Trailheads where vehicular vandalism is a problem are usually posted as such.

The hike

In the descriptions under "The hike," there are frequent references by number to mountain peaks and lakes—for example, "Peak 7065" or "Lake 5350." These indicate the elevations of unnamed peaks and lakes.

This guide wasn't intended to lead hikers to campsites, but they're mentioned in most hike descriptions. Occasionally, waterless campsites are discussed. These dry camps, which usually have water nearby, have many advantages over fragile streamside or lakeshore camps. In general, they're in more durable locations; thus, hikers don't create a lasting scar to degrade the landscape. Dry camps are a logical choice for hikers who desire solitude. And, perhaps best of all, they tend to be comparatively free of insects and are usually much warmer than low-lying campsites near water.

Occasional mention of cross-country routes indicates that special skills are required—skills that many hikers have yet to develop. Don't attempt a cross-country hike unless you're a seasoned hiker who can find the way without the benefit of a trail.

Class 2 or class 3 climbing routes are also not for everyone. These off-trail routes involve skills beyond those of the average hiker. Class 2 routes are generally scrambles over rough, steep terrain, often involving boulder-hopping or scrambling on unstable slopes, where it may be necessary to use your hands to keep your balance or latch onto a hold. If you have some cross-country hiking experience, you should have no trouble on class 2 routes, but you should wear sturdy footwear with lug-soles.

None of the hikes in this guide require travel on class 3 routes, but trips to nearby peaks or other interesting side trips may. Class 3 routes entail basic rock-climbing skills, employing hand and foot holds. These routes are often rather exposed, and novice or unsteady climbers in a party may want to use ropes.

You're likely to encounter various trail or route markers in the backcountry. Most common are the "i" blazes carved into the bark of trees. These are especially useful if the trail is faint or buried in snow. Piles of rocks known as "ducks" or cairns mark cross-country or very obscure routes, often in rocky or alpine areas.

Be sure not to blaze trees or build ducks or cairns in the backcountry. These markers are already plentiful, and an over-abundance of them is unnecessary and detracts from a hiker's wilderness experience. Other hikers can find their way as you did, and if some hikers need more ducks, cairns, or blazes to point the way, they shouldn't be traveling off the trail in the first place. Bear in mind that trail signs are semipermanent fixtures in the backcountry and that mileages listed on them are often inaccurate and contradictory.

Keep in mind, too, that it's not mandatory—and, for some hikers, not advisable—to take a given hike in its entirety or in the described direction. Study the information presented in this guide, and then let your desire and ability tell you which trail to take and how far to go. Ultimately, enjoyment of the outdoors is what will bring you to the backcountry time and again. □

The beautiful Canadian dogwood. Cliff Leight photo.

MAP LEGEND

Interstate	**00**	Described Trail and Trailhead	⊖--→
U.S. Highway	(00)	Alternate Trail and Trailhead	⊖--→
State or Other Principal Road	(000)	Cross-Country Route	·······→
Forest Road	0000	River, Creek, Drainage	∿↗
Paved Road	▭▭▭	Falls or Rapids	—//
Dirt Road	= = = =	Meadow or Swamp	⁂
Locked Gate	= =¦= =	Springs	♂
Bridge	⋈	Lakes	
Pass or Saddle	‿	Dry Lakes	
Power Line	▪-▪-▪		
Mine or Tunnel	≺		
Building	■	STATE BOUNDARY	
Ranger Station	♟		
Peak & Elevation	X 0000		
Camp site	△		
Glacier			
Depression			

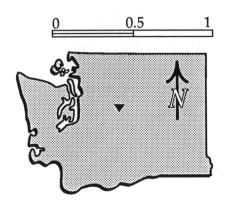

Map Scale and Trail Location Symbol

WILDERNESS BOUNDARY

BACKCOUNTRY RULES AND WILDERNESS REGULATIONS

When you hike in the backcountry, you have a responsibility to travel lightly on the land and leave no lasting impression of your wilderness visit. Familiarize yourself with the rules and regulations of each backcountry area *before* setting out. When in the wilderness, employ techniques to minimize your impact on the land as much as possible.

Many heavily used wilderness areas or wildland zones have special restrictions that may vary from year to year. These restrictions are usually posted at the trailhead. The following list of regulations and suggestions for low-impact traveling are, for the most part, common-sense rules. Study the list before venturing into the backcountry to ensure a safe and enjoyable trip and to minimize your imprint upon the land and the natural community as well as on other visitors.

Mount Rainier, Olympic, and North Cascades national parks

• **Firearms are prohibited in all national parks.** However, hunting and trapping are permitted in accordance with Washington state laws in the Ross Lake and Lake Chelan national recreation areas, as well as in all national forest areas.

• **Dogs and other pets are not permitted on trails, except in the national recreation areas and on the Pacific Crest Trail, where they must be controlled and on a leash at all times.** Dogs are permitted in national forest areas unless otherwise posted, but the Forest Service doesn't encourage dogs on trails. They can annoy other hikers and harass wildlife, pollute water sources, and foul campsites. It's best to leave your dog at home.

• **Backcountry permits are required for camping in national park or recreation area backcountry, but they aren't required for day hiking in those areas.** Permits for Mount Rainier National Park backcountry are required only from June 15 through September 30 each year. The permit system is intended to limit the number of hikers entering trailheads each day, thus preventing overcrowding and allowing visitors the opportunity for solitude and a rewarding wilderness experience. The permit system may seem like a hassle, but it's quite effective in preserving the qualities that visitors seek in the backcountry. Since permits are issued on a first-come-first-served basis, have a flexible itinerary in case the quota for your original destination has been filled for the day.

• **Collection of natural features such as rocks, plants, driftwood, and antlers is prohibited.**

• **Backpackers may camp anywhere in Olympic National Park as long as they employ minimum-impact techniques and camp at least 100 feet from lakes and streams.** In North Cascades and Mount Rainier

Fresh trout sizzling in the pan reward a long day on the trail and an evening of fishing.
Bob Arrington photo.

national parks, hikers must camp at designated trailside campsites or establish their own cross-country camps at least half a mile from maintained trails and one mile from designated campsites.

• **Fishing is allowed in accordance with Washington state regulations, but hunting is prohibited except in the national recreation areas.** Disturbing or molesting wildlife is always prohibited.

• **Campfires are restricted to established campsites and may be temporarily prohibited during periods when the danger of forest fire is high.** In Olympic National Park, all areas above 3,500 feet west of the Elwha and North Fork Quinault rivers are closed to open fires, and all areas above 4,000 feet east of the Elwha and North Fork Quinault rivers are closed to open fires.

National-forest and national-park backcountry

• **The three national parks and most wilderness areas in Washington limit to twelve the number of people hiking or camping together.** In areas that don't have a group size limit, large groups of hikers should consider splitting up into smaller units and camping and traveling separately, since larger groups invariably have an adverse impact upon campsites and trails.

• **Mechanized and motor vehicles, including mountain bikes, are prohibited in all wilderness and national-park backcountry.** Some roadless areas not officially designated as wilderness may also have motor-vehicle restrictions in effect.

• **Where terrain permits, camps should be a minimum of 100 feet from lakes, streams, meadows, and trails.** Keep in mind that campsites located away from water sources are generally warmer and comparatively insect-free. Carry a supply of water to camp for drinking, cooking, and washing to avoid beating a path to the water source and trampling delicate vegetation. Fragile streamside and lakeshore vegetation may take years to recover after being trampled by too many hikers. If possible, use pre-existing sites. If you must camp on a previously unused site, choose a durable spot in the forest on sand or rock slabs. If you clear your spot of any rocks, twigs, or needles, be sure to spread that material back over the site before leaving. Never uproot or damage vegetation, dig trenches, or perform any excavation at any campsite. Leave the site as pristine as you found it. Also, respect the right of other visitors by camping far from occupied campsites (at least 500 feet) and avoiding excessive noise and boisterous conduct that is out of place in the wilderness. Most visitors seek wild places for peace and solitude, so be a good neighbor. Also, camping is not permitted within 200 feet of the Pacific Crest Trail.

• **The use of backpack stoves is encouraged in the backcountry.** During the summer dry season, in some fragile timberline areas and in areas that are heavily used, campfires may be prohibited. This restriction will be posted at the trailhead. Campfires leave lasting scars upon the land. If you must build one, keep it small, build it on bare mineral soil, never leave it unattended, and douse the fire with water—never bury it—before leaving camp. Make sure it's cold and completely dead. Never build a fire in subalpine or timberline areas where dead and fallen wood is obviously scarce. Trees in this high-elevation environment have a short growing season and endure the harshest of weather conditions. Twisted, wind-sculpted snags are aesthetically appealing, and no visitor, except perhaps during an emergency, can justify burning the meager amount of fuel available from these silent, enduring sentinels.

• **Hikers should refrain from shortcutting switchbacks and walking out of the established trail bed.** Doing so can cause an erosion problem that in some cases is difficult to correct. Moreover, the rugged slopes between switchbacks actually require more energy to negotiate and may not save any time at all.

• **Storing or caching equipment in the wilderness is prohibited.**

• **Any destruction, injury, or defacement of natural features is prohibited.** Avoid disturbing trees, shrubs, wildflowers, grasses, etc., which are interrelated segments of the natural community. Do not blaze, carve initials or drive nails into, cut boughs from, or otherwise damage live trees or standing snags. Damaged trees are vulnerable to insects and disease.

• **Hikers should refrain from collecting plant or animal life, minerals, or other natural or historic objects.** Don't pick wildflowers. They usually wilt quickly, so leave them in their natural setting for others to enjoy. Allow flowering plants to complete their life cycles, thus perpetuating the beauty of the landscape.

• **All unburnable refuse should be packed out, including that thoughtlessly left behind by others.** Plastics and aluminum foil don't burn and must be packed out with any bottles, cans, and unburnable garbage—never buried. The plastic-coated, airtight foil packages commonly used by backpackers don't actually burn, so be sure to pack them out. Wild animals will quickly dig up buried food scraps. Don't disrupt the natural foraging habits of wildlife by offering food or leaving scraps behind. This also creates future animal problems at the site for campers who follow.

• **Littering the trail should be avoided.** Since even little bits of trash

Named for Captain William Clark of the famed Lewis and Clark Expedition, the beautiful clarkia is one the state's most interesting flowers. Bob Arrington photo.

detract from a wilderness experience, put all trash into your pocket or pack while on the trail. Even biodegradable items such as sunflower seed husks or orange peels don't belong in wild country, and they take a very long time to break down into the soil.

• **Smoking is discouraged, especially in dry, windy weather.** Smoke in a safe location free from any flammable material, and never crush out a cigarette on a log or stump. Be sure all matches and burning tobacco are out dead before leaving the area. Take your butts with you.

• **Hunting and fishing are allowed in accordance with state game laws.** Target practice in wild areas is discouraged and disrupts the peace and quiet of other visitors. Hunting is prohibited in national parks.

• **Water quality should be protected.** Camp at least 200 feet from water sources. Some backcountry areas have toilets; if so, use them. If toilets aren't available, bury body wastes in a shallow, five-to-eight-inch-deep hole in the biologically active layer of soil that will quickly decompose it. Carry a small, lightweight garden trowel for this purpose. Locate a spot at least 200 feet from trails, campsites, and existing or potential water courses so that runoff won't contaminate water supplies. Fish entrails should be burned whenever possible and should never be discarded into water sources. Keep all wash water at least 100 feet from water sources, and don't use soap or detergents in or near water sources or potential water courses. Even "biodegradable" soaps contain pollutants that can contaminate water. Next time you're in the backcountry, consider using sand or gravel to clean your cookware; it's often much more effective than soaps.

• **Pack stock have the right-of-way on backcountry trails.** To avoid conflicts with pack stock and packers, stand well off the trail, preferably on the downhill side, and talk to the packer in a normal tone of voice to let the animals know you're there. Some pack animals are easily spooked by sudden noises and movements.

• **In the Enchantments area of the Alpine Lakes Wilderness (see Hike 44), there are special regulations in effect:** Dogs are prohibited on trails, campfires are prohibited, group size is limited to six people, a two-night camping limit is in effect at campsites, and, from June 1 through September 30, wilderness permits are required for day or overnight use. Three-quarters of these permits can be reserved by mail anytime after March 1 each year. A reservation fee of one dollar per person per night is required. However, hikers must still drive to the Leavenworth Ranger Station to obtain their reserved permits. The remaining quarter of the daily quota of overnight permits is available on a first-come-first-served basis. In other backcountry areas throughout the state, sign in at trailhead registers where provided. This information helps the Forest Service meet the needs of hikers in wilderness areas and may help locate lost or injured hikers.

• **Any construction altering the natural character of the land, such as rock walls, fire rings or large fireplaces, tables and benches, shelters, bough beds, rock or wood bridges, or trenches, is not permitted.** Make an effort to leave little or no trace of your passing.

This long list of rules and regulations may intimidate or seem too restrictive to some hikers. But it's become necessary to preserve the wild character of the land, to minimize the imprint of visitors, and to provide a rewarding outdoor experience for those of us who feel the need to spend time in pristine country—country that in today's world has become a precious commodity. □

An inquisitive Columbian ground squirrel inspects a hiker's pack. Michael S. Sample photo.

INSURING A SAFE WILDERNESS EXPERIENCE

No one expects to become sick or injured in the backcountry, but it does happen. Washington's wilderness areas are exactly what the name implies— wild country, where the processes of nature continue as they have from the beginning of time, untamed by the works of man.

The following list of potential backcountry hazards is intended to rekindle a sense of awareness of what to expect in Washington's wildlands. Awareness and good judgment are a hiker's best insurance for a safe and enjoyable trip.

• **Carry a good first-aid kit, and know how to use its contents.**

• **Study an area before setting out.** Read books, study maps, and obtain as much information as possible from the ranger station nearest your destination. Rangers can tell you about a variety of potential problems, such as bears, high water, lingering snow, bad weather forecasts, etc. You frequently pass ranger stations en route to trailheads—an excellent opportunity to gather last-minute information.

• **Leave a detailed travel plan with a responsible person before setting out.** Let him or her know exactly where you're going, your route of travel, and when you expect to return. Then stick with that plan faithfully. If you fail to return, that person should contact the county sheriff or district ranger in your travel area so that a search can be initiated. If you return later than planned, be sure to notify those agencies so that any search can be discontinued.

• **Never enter the backcountry unprepared.** Carry a topographic map and a compass, and orient yourself frequently as you proceed, observing and locating peaks or other prominent features. This is particularly important when hiking cross-country (which should, of course, only be attempted by experienced hikers). Some hikers might be surprised at how different country can look once they've turned around to travel in the opposite direction.

• **Take along proper equipment.** Good, sturdy, comfortable footwear (preferably lug-soled boots), a dependable shelter, warm clothing (wool, fiber-pile and polypropylene are the logical choices for Washington's wet weather, since they maintain much of their insulating value when wet), and plenty of food should be the basic components of every hiker's gear. Equipment should be lightweight, with as little bulk as possible. Consider carrying a tent and other gear that blend in with nature's colors. Numerous fine books are available to aid beginning hikers in selecting outdoor equipment.

• **Don't overextend yourself or members of your group.** Choose a hike within the capabilities of all the members of your party, and stick together on the trail, particularly toward nightfall.

• **If a storm is imminent or darkness is descending, make camp as soon as possible.** Bear in mind that darkness can come quickly to the mountains. Never hike at night.

Properly equipped campers enjoy winter in the backcountry. Michael S. Sample photo.

• **Carry an ample supply of drinking water, particularly on hot days.** Remember that you can become dehydrated on cool days as well, since cool weather tends to distract you from your thirst. For strenuous activity during hot weather, allow one gallon of water per day per person. Experts believe that hikers should drink whenever they're thirsty and not ration their water supply.

• **Avoid hiking alone, particularly while traveling cross-country.** If you choose to hike solo, leave a travel plan with someone and stick to it.

• **Never take unnecessary chances in the backcountry.** Don't be too proud to turn back if high runoff or snow blocks the route or if a member of your party becomes ill or injured. Since the mountains will always be there, take the necessary precautions to insure that you can return to enjoy them.

• **Know the limitations of your body, your experience, your equipment, and the members of your party.** Don't exceed those limits.

• **If you think you're lost, stop at once, sit down, remain calm, and decide what to do.** Study your map and try to locate landmarks that will help orient you. Don't proceed until you're sure of your location and certain you can get back on course. If you left a travel plan with a responsible person, and if you followed that plan, a rescue party will be looking for you soon and should have little trouble locating you. In many backcountry areas, following a creek downstream eventually will lead you to roads and civilization, but in some larger wild areas, this may lead you deeper into the backcountry. Be sure of your route to avoid compounding the problem.

Use the universal distress signal—a series of three shouts, whistles, flashes of light, etc. If you must build a signal fire, do so only if it can be done safely. Rescuers will be directed to you by the smoke, not the flames. Keep in mind that you may be held financially responsible for expenses

Hikers can't always depend on the convenience of bridges in the backcountry, so they must be prepared to ford creeks and rivers when necessary. Bob Arrington photo.

incurred during a rescue operation—additional incentive to play it safe in the wilderness.

• **Use extreme caution when crossing waterways.** Among the more frequently encountered hazards are swift-moving rivers and streams. Some water courses are bridged, but many are not. Moreover, many bridges wash out on an almost yearly basis during spring runoff or wet winter storms. Don't underestimate the power of fast water; it can and has quickly swept hikers to their deaths. Search up or downstream for a log crossing or for boulders to hop across, but remember these can be slippery. If you can't find a crossing, you have two choices—either turn back or ford the creek. During spring runoff or if you're confronted with a glacial stream, the water will be at its lowest during the morning hours, since cool overnight temperatures slow the rate of snowmelt.

Have a plan before entering the water. Are there sandbars or waterfalls downstream? Search for a level stretch of water, perhaps where the stream has divided into channels. Enter the water at a spot where you and your gear will wash up onto a sand or gravel bar in the event you lose your footing.

Cross at a forty-five-degree angle downstream. You can use a stout staff or pole on your upstream side. Since bare legs create less friction with swift water, remove your pants and socks, but put your boots back on for better footing. Unhitch the waist strap on your pack and be prepared to unload it if you slip.

• **Acclimate yourself to the elevation if necessary.** Washington's mountains aren't excessively high in elevation, but hikers traveling from low-lying areas might need to adjust to the reduced oxygen at higher altitudes, particularly noticeable above 8,000 feet. A rapid change to a higher elevation can result in altitude sickness, characterized by headache, insomnia, loss of appetite, nausea, fatigue, and shortness of breath. Rest, liquids (no caffeine),

The final stage of growth of a cummulonimbus cloud, a thunderstorm, generates lightning and rain, snow, or hail. National Weather Service photo.

and high-energy foods, such as dried fruit or candy bars, can help relieve these symptoms. If they persist, however, descend to a lower elevation. Regardless of elevation, take it easy the first few days on the trail.

• **Always carry reliable shelter.** You might enjoy beautiful, dry weather, but storms can hit at anytime. Even in summer, snow is possible, usually above 4,500 feet. East of the Cascades, summer thunderstorms are a threat to hikers. In addition to a reliable tent (which can also shelter you from sometimes intolerable hordes of insects), carry good rain gear and clothing that will maintain its insulating properties when wet. Check extended weather forecasts before setting out, and watch the sky, being alert to changing conditions. Anticipate the possibility of a storm and be prepared.

Pacific storms can last for two or more days, but thundershowers are typically brief. If you notice the buildup of cumulonimbus clouds and hear thunder, avoid ridges and mountaintops, solitary trees, open areas, rock overhangs, and bodies of water. Seek shelter in a dense grove of small, uniformly sized trees if possible. Stay away from anything that might attract lightning, such as metal tent poles or pack frames. Also, beware of flash floods or rising water. Never camp close to streams or water courses that you think might rise substantially during heavy rainfall.

• **Hole up during inclement weather rather than flee the mountains and risk hypothermia, a potentially deadly lowering of the body's internal temperature.** A hiker who's wet, tired, and exposed to the wind is in danger of developing hypothermia. Since it can occur at relatively mild temperatures, many hikers simply can't believe they're being affected. Observe members of your group. If symptoms such as shivering, fumbling hands, stumbling, slurred speech, and drowsiness are present, immediate treatment is necessary and indeed may save the victim's life.

Remove the victim's wet clothing. Give warm liquids—but not coffee, tea, or anything containing caffeine—to warm him internally. Then place him in a sleeping bag next to someone or between two other people. Skin-to-skin contact is the most effective way to provide warmth. The Forest Service has abundant information on the causes, symptoms, and treatment of hypothermia; it's available at most ranger stations.

• **Carry an effective insect repellant.** Insects are an almost constant source of annoyance during summer in the mountains. Nearly all backcountry areas have varying amounts of mosquitoes in early summer and biting flies in late summer. Natural repellants containing citronella can turn a potentially miserable outing into an enjoyable one.

Wood ticks are common during spring in wooded, brushy, and grassy areas. All ticks are potential carriers of Rocky Mountain spotted fever, Colorado tick fever, and tularemia (rabbit fever), diseases transmitted through the bite of infected ticks.

Cases of Lyme disease have been reported, particularly in moist areas of western Washington. Lyme disease infection usually displays three stages of progression. The first indication often occurs two to three weeks after a bite by an infected tick as an enlarging circle of redness. Later, there may be headache, stiff joints, and fatigue. The heart and nervous system can be affected, with paralysis of facial muscles and irregular heartbeat.

When traveling through tick country, a few minor precautions can help to insure a safe outing:

(1) Wear clothing that fits snugly around the waist, wrists, and ankles. Layers of clothing are most effective in preventing ticks from reaching the body.

(2) Use a strong insect repellant to deter ticks. They don't always bite right away but often crawl around on a potential host for several hours before finding an ideal place to feed on the victim's blood.

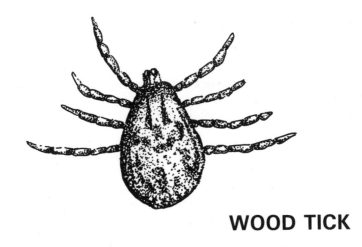

WOOD TICK

(3) Examine yourself and your pets frequently while in tick country. If you find a tick, have it removed or remove it as soon as possible. Let a physician remove a tick to avoid infection and the possibility of leaving the tick's head under the skin. If you must remove a tick yourself, protect your hands with gloves, cloth, or a piece of paper. Tweezers are the best tool for the job; use a steady pulling motion, but avoid crushing the tick. The application of tincture of iodine may induce the tick to let go as well as reduce the chances of infection. If the tick's head remains embedded in the skin, a secondary infection may develop. In that event, see a physician to have it removed. After handling a tick, wash your hands and apply antiseptic to the bite.

(4) Symptoms of diseases transmitted by ticks usually appear two days to two weeks after a bite. They include severe headaches, nausea, chills, fever, and pain in the lower back and legs. See a physician immediately if you notice these symptoms.

• **Purify potentially contaminated water before drinking, brushing your teeth, or otherwise ingesting it.** Remember the days when you could drink from mountain streams without a second thought about the purity of those waters? With an increasing number of visitors to Washington's wildlands, the question of water purity is a major concern to hikers. Despite the media attention given to *Giardia lamblia* (a single-celled, microscopic parasite) in recent years, diseases contracted from water sources have been a problem in certain areas from time immemorial. A variety of other germs, in addition to Giardia, are present in backcountry surface waters throughout Washington. Most hikers who drink untreated water probably won't contract any symptoms of intestinal illness. But to be safe, hold suspect all backcountry waters and take appropriate steps to purify it.

Rapid boiling for five to ten minutes is a sure way to kill water-borne microorganisms. But since water boils at a lower temperature at high elevations, boil it for at least ten minutes to be safe.

Other purification methods include adding tincture of iodine or a saturated solution of iodine to drinking water. Various purification tablets are available at most backpacking and sporting goods stores. These methods may not be as effective against Giardia as boiling, but they're quite effective against a variety of other water-borne organisms. There are also a number of filters on the market that are an effective but expensive means of purifying water. When purchasing a filter, choose one with the smallest pores in its filtration element to ensure removal of the tiniest microorganisms.

Carrying water from home may be the safest alternative, but it's impractical for extended hikes.

When you must use water in the backcountry, choose a source upstream from trail crossings and campsites. Better yet, use spring water, which is more likely to be safe, particularly at the spring's source. If you become intestinally ill within three weeks of a backcountry visit, see a physician.

• **Take precautions to avoid encounters with bears.** Much of Washington's backcountry is ideal bear habitat from the coast to the mountains. By and large, these animals remain well-hidden in the dense forests. Occasionally, though, they're tempted by careless backpackers who bring odorous foods into the backcountry or leave behind food scraps.

Check with the ranger station nearest your hiking area about bear problems. In any event, anticipate the possibility of encountering bears on your

The common black bear has become so accustomed to people and so willing to eat camp provisions that it presents a serious problem to backpackers. The grizzly bear (inset) is extinct over most of Washington, but a few may remain in the Selkirks. Larger than the black bear, the grizzly has three-to four-inch claws, a shoulder hump, a "dish" face, and yellowish-brown fur, frequently tipped with white. Michael S. Sample photo.

visit and suspend your food from a tree. This also protects food from marauding rodents.

Grizzly bears range through the northeasternmost corner of Washington and the Pasayten Country, but they're rarely seen. Black bears, however, are common throughout much of the state, except for the Columbia Basin.

Parts of North Cascades and Olympic national parks have their share of bear problems. Since the animals there are protected from hunting, they eventually lose their fear of man and begin viewing hikers as walking smorgasbords.

Suspend your food via the counterbalance method—the safest way to hang food in a tree. Put all food and any other odorous items, such as toothpaste, soap, or garbage, into two evenly weighted stuffsacks and hang them from a sturdy tree limb, ideally fifteen feet above the ground (use a long stick) and ten feet from the trunk. The stuffsacks should hang no more than five feet below the tree limb and no less than ten feet above the ground. Leave packs

Frequently seen far above timberline, mountain goats are also readily found in spruce and hemlock forests in the Olympic Mountains, throughout the Cascades, and in parts of the Selkirk Mountains. Michael S. Sample photo.

on the ground with the pockets unzipped to minimize damage by a nosy bear or rodent.

Give bears a wide berth, particulary sow bears with cubs, and if a bear retrieves your food, don't even consider recovering it. Simply learn from your mistake and try to insure that it won't happen again. Report any bear activity to a nearby ranger station after your hike.

• **Also beware of mountain goats.** These typically docile creatures aren't direct threats, but they're on a never-ending search for salt. During the hiking season, you represent a potential source.

Boots, shoulder straps on backpacks, sweaty clothes, and urine all attract mountain goats to high-country campsites. Protect your gear from being eaten by goats, and keep your distance from these potentially dangerous animals.

• **Drive with care in the mountains.** Driving to trailheads in Washington often involves negotiating narrow, one-lane paved or dirt roads, often heavily traveled by logging trucks. If you're unaccustomed to mountain driving, drive with caution and exercise common sense. Stay on your side of the road, watch for turnouts, and use them if you encounter oncoming traffic. Be prepared to stop your vehicle within less than half the visible distance ahead. One vehicle should always stop when meeting another on narrow, one-lane roads. Also keep an eye out for cattle and logging trucks on mountain roads. Mishaps can be avoided by driving with care and attention.

• **Be sure to carry the "ten essentials" on any wilderness outing to insure safety and, perhaps, survival:**

(1) A topographic map of your travel area and a compass, as well as a working knowledge of their use.

(2) Water and means of purification (a minimum of one gallon per person per day in hot weather).

(3) Sturdy, comfortable footwear and extra layers of clothing.

(4) A signal mirror.

(5) Dark glasses and sunscreen.

(6) A pocketknife.

(7) Waterproof matches and fire-starter.

(8) A tent, tarp, or some type of emergency shelter.

(9) A first-aid kit.

(10) Plenty of food.

Most importantly, always bring a healthy dose of common sense, since the most important factor insuring an enjoyable outing is safety.

If you'd like to learn more about backcountry hazards, their causes, and how to deal with them, you might want to consider taking courses in first aid and outdoor survival, offered in many communities. At the least, study one or more of the many excellent books on these subjects. □

Ancient North Cascades glaciers, finding weaknesses in otherwise resistant bedrock material, have gouged and plucked out depressions on their downward journeys. Such depressions later filled with water to become spectacular mountain lakes. Ron Adkison photo.

Hiking with children

With the birth of a child, some new parents might think their hiking and backpacking days are over, at least until Junior is old enough to walk several miles and carry a pack. But parents who forego hiking trips during a child's formative years are not only missing out on some of the most rewarding and memorable experiences to be enjoyed as a family, but the kids will also miss a tremendous learning experience in which they will gain confidence and a growing awareness of the world around them.

Kids can enjoy the backcountry as much as their parents, but they see the world from a different perspective. It's the little things adults barely notice that are so special to children: Bugs scampering across the trail, spiderwebs dripping with morning dew, lizards doing push-ups on a trailside boulder, splashing rocks into a lake, watching sticks run the rapids of a mountain stream, exploring animal tracks on sand dunes—these are but a few of the natural wonders kids will enjoy while hiking backcountry trails.

To make the trip fun for the kids, let the young ones set the pace. Until they get older and are able to keep up with their parents, forget about that thirty mile trek to your favorite backcountry campsite. Instead, plan a destination that is only a mile or two from the trailhead. Kids tire quickly and become easily sidetracked, so don't be surprised if you don't make it to your destination. Plan alternative campsites enroute to your final camp.

Helping children to enjoy the hike and to learn about what they see, always point out special things along the trail. Help them to anticipate what is around the next bend—perhaps a waterfall, or a pond filled with wriggling tadpoles. Make the hike fun, help kids to stay interested, and they will keep going.

Careful planning which stresses safety will help make your outing an enjoyable one. Young skin is very sensitive to the sun, so always carry a strong sunscreen and apply it to your kids before and during your hike. A good bug repellant, preferably a natural product, should be a standard part of the first-aid kit. Also, consider a product that helps take the itch and sting out of bug bites. A hat helps keep the sun out of sensitive young eyes. And rain gear is also an important consideration. Kids seem to have less tolerance to cold than adults, so ample clothing is important. If your camp will be next to a lake or large stream, consider bringing a life vest for your child.

Parents with young children must, of course, carry plenty of diapers, and be sure to pack them out when they leave. Some children can get wet at night, so extra sleeping clothes are a must. A waterproof pad between the child and the sleeping bag should keep the bag dry, an important consideration if you stay out more than one night.

Allow older children able to walk a mile or two to carry their own packs, too. Some kids will want to bring favorite toys or books along. These special things they can carry themselves, thus learning at an early age the advantages of packing light.

Kids may become bored more easily once you arrive in camp, so a little extra effort may be required to keep them occupied. Imaginative games and special foods they don't see at home can make the camping trip a new and fun experience for kids and parents alike.

Set up a tent at home and consider spending a night or two in it so your child can grow accustomed to your backcountry shelter. Some kids will be frightened by dark nights, so you might bring along a small flashlight to use as a nightlight. Kids seem to prefer rectangular sleeping bags that allow freedom of movement. And a cap for those cool nights will help keep the young ones warm.

Weight conscious parents of very young children can find an alternative to baby food in jars. There are lightweight and inexpensive dry baby foods available, and all you do is add water.

Children learn from their parents by example. Hiking and camping trips are excellent opportunities to teach young ones to tread lightly and minimize their imprint upon the environment.

Thus, important considerations to keep in mind when hiking with the kids are careful planning, stressing safety, and making the trip fun and interesting.

A springtime stroll across wildflower-decorated slopes in eastern Washington delights parents and children alike. Jan Kemp photo.

There may be extra hassles involved with family hiking trips, but the dividends are immeasureable. Parents will gain a rejuvenated perspective of nature, seen through their child's eyes, that will reward them each time they venture out on the trail.

All or part of the following hikes are suitable for family day hikes or backpacks. Carefully read each descriptions and prepare for any hazards that may be present. After the number and name of each hike, you will find suggestions for destinations.

Hike No. 1: Tucannon River Trail; Ruchert Camp, or any of several campsites along the trail. **Hike No. 6:** Gingko Petrified Forest. **Hike No. 8:** Falls Creek Falls. **Hike No. 9:** Cultus Creek Loop; Cultus Lake area. **Hike No. 10:** Spencer Butte. **Hike No. 11:** Lewis River to Bolt Camp. **Hike No. 12:** Norway Pass. **Hike No. 26:** Snow Lake. **Hike No. 29:** Carbon Glacier. **Hike No. 31:** Deep Creek to Tumac Mountain; Twin Sisters lakes area. **Hike No. 33:** Quinault Loop Trail. **Hike No. 34:** Enchanted Valley; Pony Creek Bridge area. **Hike No. 36:** Rialto Beach to Chilean Memorial; campsites near Hole-in-the-Wall. **Hike No. 37:** Cape Alava Loop; Sand Point campsites or Cape Alava. **Hike No. 48:** Forest Road 9030 to Island Lake; Talapus or Olallie lakes. **Hike No. 49:** East Fork Miller River to Lake Dorothy; campsites along shores of Lake Dorothy. **Hike No. 59:** Boulder River to Boulder Ford Camp. **Hike No. 62:** Mountain Lake-Mount Pickett Loop; Mountain Lake Trail, loop around the lake. **Hike No. 64:** Obstruction Pass Beach. **Hike No. 68:** Baker River to Sulphide Camp. **Hike No. 71:** Panther Creek to Thunder Creek; Thunder Creek Trailhead (Colonial Creek Campground) to Thunder Creek or Neve campsites. **Hike No. 73:** Rainy Pass to Snowy Lakes; Cutthroat Creek Trailhead to Cutthroat Lake. **Hike No. 75:** Cedar Creek Falls. **Hike No. 81:** Tiffany Lake. **Hike No. 89:** Northrup Canyon Natural Area to Northrup Lake. □

Mushrooms and other fungi are common in the damp coastal forests. Cliff Leight photo.

COMMON TREES OF WASHINGTON

DOUGLAS-FIR 100-250 ft.

WHITEBARK PINE 50-60 ft.

stunted form

WESTERN HEMLOCK 125-175 ft.

PONDEROSA PINE 150-180 ft.

MOUNTAIN HEMLOCK 75-100 ft.

WESTERN REDCEDAR to 200 ft.

WESTERN WHITE PINE 100-175 ft.

ALASKA YELLOW-CEDAR 70-100 ft.

coastal form
25-30 ft.

LODGEPOLE PINE 75-80 ft.

BIGLEAF MAPLE to 100 ft.

PACIFIC MADRONE to 100 ft.

WESTERN JUNIPER 20-60 ft.

WESTERN LARCH to 150 ft.

RED ALDER 30-60 ft.

LYALL LARCH to 150 ft.

SITKA SPRUCE 150-200 ft.

GRAND FIR 125-150 ft.

ENGLEMANN SPRUCE 100-125 ft.

timberline tree

SUBALPINE FIR 40-100 ft.

THE HIKES

HIKE 1 *TUCANNON RIVER TRAIL*

General description: An easy 8.2-mile, round-trip day hike or overnighter along a shady Blue Mountain stream in the Umatilla National Forest.
Elevation gain and loss: 520 feet.
Trailhead elevation: 3,560 feet.
High point: 4,080 feet.
Maps: Panjab Creek and Stentz Spring 7.5-minute USGS quads; Wenaha-Tucannon Wilderness map; Umatilla National Forest map.
Season: May through mid-October.
Water availability: Available along entire route.

Finding the trailhead: Follow directions given in Hike 2 to Tucannon River Road, 31.4 miles from U.S. 12. Turn left onto this sometimes narrow and rough dirt road for five miles to its terminus at the trailhead. Since a sign near the end of the road indicates ''no parking beyond this point,'' you'll have to park between here and Sheep Camp, a quarter mile back down the road.

The hike: A fine mountain stream shaded by huge old-growth timber characterizes this leisurely stroll along the northern boundary of the Wenaha-Tucannon Wilderness. Fishing for rainbow trout can be productive, and you may even hook a salmon. If you do, don't keep it; the state is trying to re-establish a viable salmon fishery in the Tucannon River drainage.

Two trails begin at the trailhead: a streamside trail, closed to motor vehicles, and an upper trail, open to trail bikes. Both trails join within a half mile. Thus, there is a possibility you'll encounter one or more of these noisy, trail-eating machines during your outing.

Begin your hike on the lower trail, an old, closed logging road under a forest canopy dominated by grand fir and including western larch, ponderosa pine, Douglas-fir, and lodgepole pine. After the upper trail joins your route, you leave the roadbed, continuing on a narrow trail. The small, shrubby tree growing in the deep shadows cast by the towering forest is the western yew. Distinguished by its rough, scaly, reddish bark, green to red berries, and sharp, flat needles, the western yew is typically found in shady canyon bottoms and along stream banks.

Other plants that thrive along the trail include prince's pine, the beautiful calypso orchid (an endangered species), queen's cup, violet, and false Solomon's seal. Other wildflowers you'll likely notice include wild strawberry, clover, yarrow, larkspur, lupine, and spirea. Shrubs include Douglas maple, mallow ninebark, huckleberry, ocean spray, and wild rose.

The trail passes a few elk-hunting camps (elk hunters are the primary users of the Wenaha-Tucannon Wilderness), but hikers who prefer a more pristine setting will find potential campsites along the entire route. The Tucannon River, nothing more than a mountain stream here in its headwaters, is never far from the trail, and anglers may be tempted to wet their lines

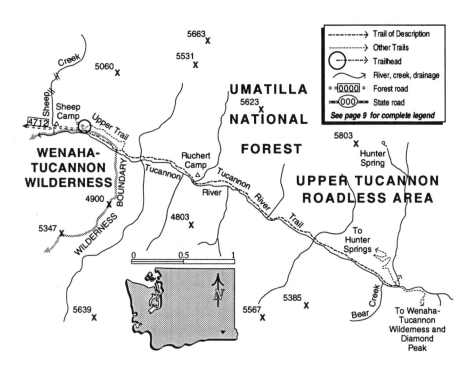

in the many fine, easily accessible pools along the way.

The forest opens up enough at times to allow glimpses of the heavily timbered, north-facing slopes across the creek. The waters of Bear Creek, which join the Tucannon from the south, signal your arrival at the end of the Tucannon River Trail. Here you reach a junction. The right fork crosses the Tucannon, briefly climbs above Bear Creek, then winds toward the Diamond Peak high country. The left fork climbs northward out of the canyon, leading to Hunter Spring and ultimately to Forest Road 40 coming from Pomeroy.

There are a few campsites at this junction. To obtain views of the surrounding country, hidden for the past four miles, take the left fork for about half a mile to an open hillside, where the lay of the land becomes apparent. From the junction, you must retrace your route back to the trailhead. □

HIKE 2 *PANJAB CREEK LOOP*

General description: A twelve-mile, weekend backpack loop at the northern tip of the Blue Mountains, with scenery ranging from windswept ridges to deep, forested canyons in the Wenaha-Tucannon Wilderness.
Elevation gain and loss: 2,720 feet.
Trailhead elevation: 3,300 feet.
High point: 5,600 feet.
Maps: Panjab Creek 7.5-minute USGS quad; Wenaha-Tucannon Wilderness map; Umatilla National Forest map.
Season: Late May through mid-October.
Water availability: Available at intervals all along the route.

Finding the trailhead: From U.S. 12, ten miles north of Dayton, turn east onto Tucannon Road; a sign here indicates Camp Wooten. Follow this paved road through the Tucannon River valley and ignore the left fork to Camp Wooten and Tucannon Campground after twenty-eight miles. The pavement ends here, but a good gravel road continues. Avoid a right fork after another 1.75 miles; proceed toward Panjab Campground. In another 2.6 miles the road forks once again. Hikers bound for the Tucannon River Trail will bear left, but you should go straight, almost immediately passing the Rattlesnake Trailhead, the terminus of this hike. After 2.4 miles you reach the Panjab Trailhead on the left (east) side of the road.

If you're approaching from the east, turn south off U.S. 12 onto the paved Tatman Mountain Road (a sign here indicates Camp Wooten) about 4.25 miles west of Pomeroy. After 1.2 miles continue straight ahead on pavement (Linnville Gulch Road), ignoring the Tatman Mountain Road, which forks to the left. Linnville Gulch Road climbs steadily for 5.4 miles, then the pavement ends at the juncture with Blind Grade Road, and it becomes a good dirt road. In two miles the road plummets into the canyon of the Tucannon River. There you join the Tucannon River Road, turn left, and follow the above directions to the trailhead. Since the trailheads are only 2.4 miles apart, you won't need a car shuttle.

The hike: An inland range whose vegetation and climate more closely resemble that of the Rocky Mountains than the coastal Cascade Range, the Blue Mountains stretch northeastward from central Oregon for nearly 200 miles to just south of the Snake River in southeastern Washington.

Over a mile high, the heavily forested plateaus of the northern Blue Mountains are deeply cut by numerous stream and river valleys, reminiscent of the canyon and mesa country of the Southwest. Heavy timber dominates the landscape, but open, wildflower-speckled meadows atop the table-like ridges offer expansive vistas to hikers. These meadows also provide summer grazing for the abundant Rocky Mountain elk of the Blue Mountain herd, transplanted from Yellowstone National Park in 1930. Surveying scenery ranging from shady canyon bottoms to prime elk habitat atop grassy ridges, this route offers an excellent introduction to the attractions of Washington's portion of the Wenaha-Tucannon Wilderness.

The trail begins by immediately crossing Panjab Creek. Although the ford

HIKE 2 *PANJAB CREEK LOOP*

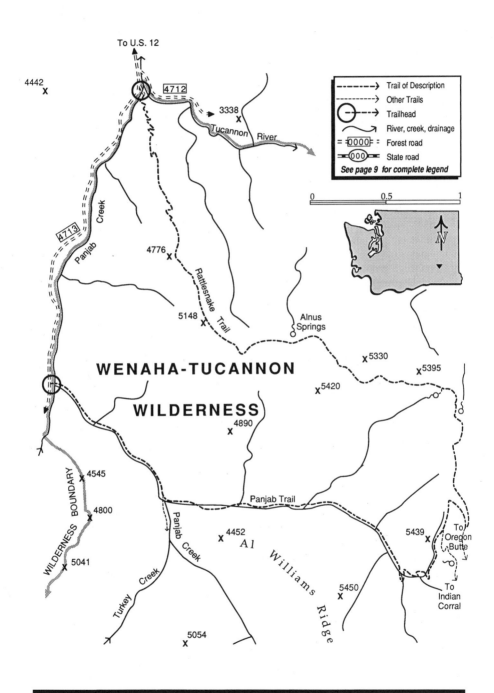

To U.S. 12

4442

4712

3338

Tucannon River

Trail of Description
Other Trails
Trailhead
River, creek, drainage
Forest road
State road
See page 9 for complete legend

0   0.5   1

N

4713

Panjab Creek

4776

Rattlesnake Trail

5148

Alnus Springs

5330

5395

WENAHA-TUCANNON

5420

WILDERNESS

4890

WILDERNESS BOUNDARY

4545

4800

Panjab Trail

5439

To Oregon Butte

5041

Panjab Creek

4452

Al

5450

To Indian Corral

Turkey Creek

Williams Ridge

5054

is easy, you may want to search up or downstream for a log crossing to avoid wetting your feet.

The first 1.5 miles of trail gently ascend along Panjab Creek, shaded by tall grand fir, Englemann spruce, and Douglas-fir. Avoid the unmaintained lower trail.

Turn left at the signed junction and follow the moderately climbing trail along a Panjab Creek tributary. You'll encounter shrubs such as currant, raspberry, Douglas maple, and wild rose.

You eventually hop across a small creek twice, then quickly climb up and away from the canyon. In spring a brilliant wildflower display greets you in the first sunny opening, including larkspur, lupine, red Indian paintbrush, fern-leaved desert parsley, and waterleaf.

Welcome vistas become more apparent as the trail gains elevation, from timbered Al Williams Ridge in the southwest to the depths of Panjab Creek canyon in the west. As you approach the ridgetop, ignore a well-worn, right-forking trail (leading toward the Oregon Butte high country) and enter a subalpine forest of Englemann spruce, western larch, lodgepole pine, and subalpine fir. Just below this junction is the last reliable water for the next 1.5 miles.

Upon reaching the ridgetop you'll leave the timber and head southeastward. Your brief stint along the margin of this fine subalpine spread ends at the junction with the Rattlesnake Trail, doubling back across the meadow on a higher contour. Some hikers will continue southward along the ridge trail, to Dunlap Spring, Oregon Butte, and the heart of the Wenaha-Tucannon Wilderness.

But your trail leads you north, traversing the open, grassy ridgeline, offering good views to the timbered tableland beyond the Tucannon River's abysmal depths. You'll pass above a spring 0.75 mile from the previous junction, and after another quarter mile, just beyond several elk hunting camps, the short trail to Fir Spring departs to your left (west).

This reliable spring, as well as Alnus Spring 1.25 miles ahead, allows backpackers to stay the night on this scenic ridge. Since these springs are the only available water for ridge-dwelling elk, it's best to camp away from them and haul your water to your campsite.

After more pleasant ridge walking, you'll pass above Alnus Spring, named after the alder, an *Alnus* species that crowds the spring. Vistas now include distant grain fields in the north beyond timbered Blue Mountain mesas.

As you approach the northern terminus of this mile-high ridge, the vegetation begins to reflect decreasing precipitation. Present are ponderosa pine, Douglas-fir, currant, and curl-leaf mountain mahogany.

Once the trail begins steadily descending, views down Panjab Creek canyon will accompany you for the remainder of the trip. Frequent sunny openings reveal springtime color, thanks to wildflowers such as arrowleaf balsamroot, lupine, wallflower, desert parsley, yarrow, and blue penstemon. Shrubs include serviceberry and the ubiquitous mallow ninebark—sometimes mistaken for currant but without the berries.

After a few minor switchbacks the trail emerges onto level ground at the confluence of Panjab Creek and Tucannon River.

You'll cross Panjab Creek on a large log, ending this fine hike at the Rattlesnake Trailhead. From here, it's 2.4 miles up the road to your car at the Panjab Trailhead. □

HIKE 3 TEEPEE SPRING TO OREGON BUTTE

General description: A moderate 5.8 mile day hike leading to a grand vista atop the highest point in Washington's Blue Mountains, in the Wenaha-Tucannon Wilderness.

Elevation gain and loss: +1,250 feet; -340 feet.

Trailhead elevation: 5,490 feet.

High point: Oregon Butte, 6,401 feet.

Maps: Oregon Butte 7.5-minute USGS quad; Wenaha-Tucannon Wilderness map; Umatilla National Forest map.

Season: July through mid-October.

Water availability: Available at Oregon Butte Spring, 2.25 miles from the trailhead.

Finding the trailhead: Hikers approaching from the east should follow directions given in Hike 2 to the junction of the Blind Grade and Tucannon River roads. Continue southward up the Tucannon River Road for another 11.1 miles—two miles beyond the end of pavement—to the junction with Forest Road 4620, signed for Godman Guard Station.

Turn right and follow this steep dirt road for 4.2 miles to Forest Road 46 at Mountain Top Junction. Bear left here. Follow this good dirt road as it ascends the ridge southward, ignoring several lesser-used spur roads enroute.

After another 12.1 miles, bear left on descending Forest Road 4608 at a junction; the right fork is signed for Tollgate. You'll pass the Godman Guard Station and several signed spur roads as you follow this narrow, winding dirt road for 3.5 miles to another junction. Bear right, following a rough road for another 2.8 miles to the spacious trailhead parking area.

If approaching from Dayton, follow South 4th Street south for one mile from U.S. Highway 12, then turn left (east) on East mustard Street (Skyline Drive) and drive 15.2 miles to Mountain Top Junction, where you follow the directions above to reach the trailhead.

The hike: Oregon Butte, the apex of the Blue Mountains in southeastern Washington, offers far-ranging views stretching into nearby Oregon and Idaho. This trip is a fine introduction to the remote backcountry of the Wenaha-Tucannon Wilderness. Numerous springs, abundant possible campsites, and a wide choice of cross-country side trips along the high ridges offer ample incentive for an extended backpack along the ridgetop trail south of Oregon Butte. Adventurous hikers can follow this nineteen-mile-long trail to the Wenaha River, just over the state line in Oregon, where they will find good fishing for rainbows (be sure to obtain an Oregon state fishing license).

From the trailhead, the Mount Misery Trail climbs steadily eastward on the shady north slope of the ridge beneath a canopy of Engelmann spruce, subalpine fir, and western larch. Trailside slopes are covered in a green carpet of arnica and vanilla leaf.

The grade moderates upon reaching West Butte Ridge after one mile where the trail forks. The left fork 0.8 mile long, contours through spruce-fir forest on the north slope of West Butte, while the right fork, 0.1 mile longer, climbs up and over the butte and offers good vistas. Both trails rejoin on the saddle

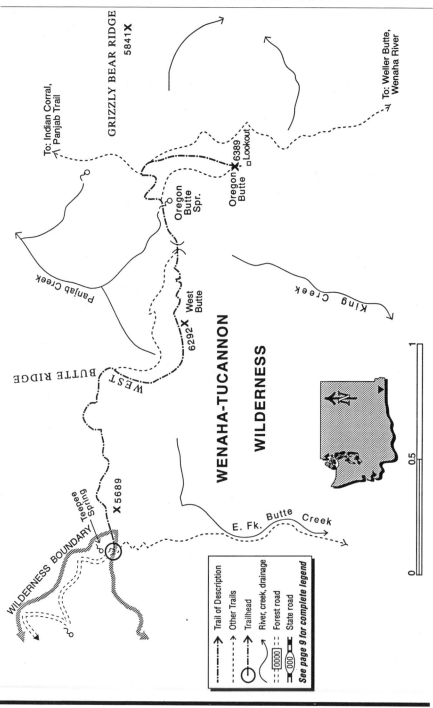

just east of West Butte, beyond which you contour easily for 0.25 mile to cold Oregon Butte Spring. This vigorous spring is piped into a long log water trough and is a logical resting place before climbing on to Oregon Butte. Between the spring and the ridge north of Oregon Butte, numerous unsigned trails can be confusing. The path that climbs steeply from the spring is the shortest but most strenuous way to the summit.

Follow the main trail north from the spring through a wildflower-speckled park and into a pine and fir forest. After curving around one switchback, ignore the steep, well-worn path shortcutting the next switchback, and after another 0.1 mile, bear right where a northbound trail continues straight ahead.

From that junction you'll quickly climb to a saddle in the ridge ahead just north of a campsite, 0.4 mile from the spring. Leave the trail here and proceed south past the campsite, beyond which you will find the ridgetop trail continuing nearly a half mile to the lookout atop Oregon Butte.

Views are far-ranging and panoramic, reaching as far as the peaks of the Seven Devils in Idaho and to the lofty, snow-streaked Wallawas in Oregon. The Blue Mountains, with their forested plateaus, grassy parks, and gaping, basalt-rimmed canyons, surround you to the east, south, and west. And far to the north and west sprawl the heat-hazy wheat fields of the Columbia Plateau.

When you tire of the fabulous vistas, simply retrace your route to the trailhead. □

HIKE 4 *JUNIPER DUNES WILDERNESS*

General description: An easy two-mile (or longer) round-trip day hike through one of eastern Washington's most unique landscapes.
Elevation gain and loss: +170 feet, -120 feet to the first juniper grove.
Trailhead elevation: 820 feet.
High point: 950 feet.
Maps: Levey NE 7.5-minute USGS quad.
Season: March through mid-June; mid-September through November.
Water availability: None; carry an adequate supply.

Finding the trailhead: From the Pasco-Kahlotus Road, twenty-two miles northeast of Pasco or 17.2 miles southeast of Kahlotus, turn west onto the Snake River Road, where a sign indicates Eltopia. Follow this blacktop through rolling wheatfields for 3.4 miles, then turn left onto gravel-surfaced East Blackman Ridge Road. After another 2.4 miles turn left onto Jay Road. Follow this dirt road for two miles to its dead end at the trailhead.

The hike: Sand dunes aren't unheard of in eastern Washington; they form along the banks of the Columbia and Snake rivers. But nowhere else are they as abundant as in the Juniper Dunes, where nearly ten square miles of sand dunes and groves of western juniper are protected under the jurisdiction of the Bureau of Land Management (BLM). This is the only wilderness area in the entire Columbia Basin.

The landscape here is fascinating. Miles and miles of sand dunes—some

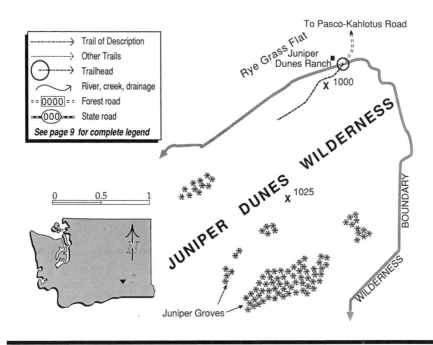

cloaked with shrubs, wildflowers, and junipers, and others nearly barren—rise in marked contrast to the surrounding fields of grain.

The area is characterized by hundreds of sand dunes with no prominent ridges or drainages. All drainages end in interdune depressions. There is no particular destination other than the dunes and the junipers. Most hikers only walk a mile or so from the trailhead. So if you're looking for solitude, you'll likely find it beyond that point.

The trailhead lies on the property of the Juniper Dunes Ranch, only 100 yards from the wilderness boundary on public land. The owner allows day hiking only. In other words, no overnight parking is permitted. Also prohibited is entry during the period of highest fire danger, June 15 through September 15.

Respect the property rights of the owner of Juniper Dunes Ranch to ensure future access to the area. Enter the area only if the time and conditions are appropriate, according to the sign at the trailhead. Never build fires, do not park overnight, and always be sure gates are closed.

From the trailhead you walk through a stock gate (be sure to close it behind you), follow jeep tracks south across Rye Grass Flat, pass through another stock gate, and enter the wilderness area. From here the trail, sometimes disappearing in the sand, leads southwest for about a mile to the first stand of western junipers. In the spring you'll enjoy a colorful display of wildflowers, including yarrow, common phacelia, blue penstemon, hawksbeard, winged dock, wallflower, desert parsley, flax, wyethia, and evening primrose. Shrubs

The Juniper Dunes Wilderness, created in 1984, is the only wilderness area administered by the Bureau of Land Management in Washington. Encompassing the largest area of sand dunes and western juniper in the state, this is one of the few places to hike in all of the Columbia Basin. Ron Adkison photo.

include sagebrush, bitterbrush, and rabbitbrush, which has bright yellow flowers in the fall.

Once you reach the first junipers, you can either backtrack to the trailhead or roam the dunes at will. □

HIKE 5 *YAKIMA CANYON RIM SCENIC TRAIL*

General description: A nine-mile, round-trip day hike or overnighter following a portion of the Yakima Canyon Rim Scenic Trail above the spectacular 2,000-foot-deep trench of the Yakima River in eastern Washington's L.T. Murray Wildlife Recreation Area.

Elevation gain and loss: +2,245 feet, -337 feet.

Trailhead elevation: 1,300 feet.

High point: Peak 3208.

Maps: Badger Pocket 15-minute, and Pomona 7.5-minute USGS quads; Washington Department of Game Yakima Canyon Rim Trail map.

Season: Mid-March through November.

Water availability: Water is scarce along the trail; carry an adequate supply.

Finding the trailhead: From Interstate 82 just north of Selah, take the Firing Center exit (Exit 26). Proceed west on Canyon Road for 0.7 mile, then turn

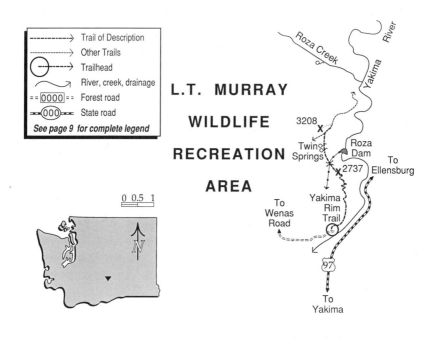

left onto Harrison Road. After two miles, turn right onto North Wenas Road, and where that road curves sharply to the left after 2.8 miles, continue straight ahead onto dirt-surfaced Gibson Road. Turn right (east) within a quarter mile onto Buffalo Road, passing scattered farms and driving through semi-arid grasslands for 2.75 miles to the parking area above the trailhead.

The hike: The Columbia Basin, that vast semi-arid, basalt-shrouded landscape between the Rocky Mountains and the Cascade Range, is not simply a large, featureless depression as the name might suggest. Along the western margin of the basin, for example, lies a region of great ridges (anticlines) separated by deep troughs (synclines). The Horse Heaven Hills, Saddle Mountains, Yakima Ridge, and Frenchman Hills, among others, are familiar features to eastern Washingtonians. Collectively, this region is known to geologists as the Yakima Folds.

The uplifting of the ridges was such a painstakingly slow process that rivers such as the Columbia and Yakima were not diverted by the rising landscape but were able to maintain their original courses, with the down-cutting of the rivers keeping pace with the uplifting land.

This fine grassland hike along the basalt-capped ridge (part of the Yakima Folds complex) that towers above Yakima Canyon follows the initial 4.5 miles of the eighteen-mile-long Yakima Canyon Rim Scenic Trail, constructed by the Department of Game in 1977. Water is scarce along the trail, and Twin

Springs and intermittent Roza Creek constitute the only available water. If you plan to hike the entire eighteen-mile route (a car shuttle is necessary), you must keep these limited water sources in mind. Always purify the water before drinking.

From the parking area, briefly follow the road north down to the trailhead. Even though firewood is nonexistent, a sign at the trailhead reminds you that no open fires are allowed. If you're camping, carry a stove. After following the trail east to the canyon rim, you'll begin ascending the rim northward, heading for numerous false summits along the ridgeline. The trail is nearly impossible to lose, but "Horse Trail" signs are placed at intervals to keep you on course.

A number of colorful wildflowers adorn these grassy slopes during April and May, including the ubiquitous yarrow, desert parsley, wild mustard, tarweed (or fiddleneck), Indian paintbrush, buckwheat, phacelia, golden-aster, wooly sunflower, and single-flowered false sunflower.

If you stop to rest during this two-mile ascent you'll enjoy expansive vistas, from Mount Adams in the southwest to Mount Rainier and the Cascade crest in the west to the parched ridges of the Yakima Folds in the east and southeast.

The rimrock trail finally reaches the first true summit along the initial segment of the hike, Peak 2737, at an abandoned fenceline. It then drops 237 feet to a saddle overlooking Roza Dam on the Yakima River and briefly passes under a power line, momentarily disrupting your "wilderness" jaunt.

To get an idea of how thick the layers of basalt are in this area, consider that, in 1981, the Shell Oil Company drilled a wildcat well near Roza Dam and didn't punch through the basalt until reaching a depth of approximately one mile. The supply of natural gas was so meager, however, that Shell abandoned the well.

Beyond the power line, you'll negotiate a short uphill stretch before steeply dropping to Twin Springs. Along this stretch in the springtime, you may notice the beautiful, ground-hugging pink flowers of a species of *Lewisia*, closely related to the famous bitterroot, once an important food source for Native Americans of the region.

Twin Springs is a welcome change of pace, a veritable oasis in this rimrock country. Numerous shrubs compete for moisture at this lush site, including serviceberry, chokecherry, and a few five-foot-tall specimens of tall mahonia, a species of Oregon grape. Poison ivy is also common.

There is a level spot here, but it's best to leave the water source undisturbed in consideration of local wildlife and camp on the ridge instead, enjoying the vistas and perhaps a glorious sunrise.

Beyond Twin Springs the trail climbs steeply back to the rim, soon traversing the east slopes of Peak 3208, 2,000 feet above the floor of the canyon. Where the trail begins its plunge into Roza Creek's broad canyon, leave the trail and head uphill to the summit of Peak 3208 for a commanding view.

From the peak, retrace your route to the trailhead. □

HIKE 6 GINKGO PETRIFIED FOREST STATE PARK

General description: An easy 1.5-mile loop through a desert region of central Washington, where the fossil remnants of an ancient forest offer glimpses into the distant past.

Elevation gain and loss: 330 feet.

Trailhead elevation: 1,050 feet.

High point: 1,380 feet.

Maps: Ginkgo 7.5-minute USGS quad.

Season: All year (but remember that temperatures can exceed 100 degrees during the summer).

Water availability: None; carry an adequate supply.

Finding the trailhead: From Interstate 90 on the west side of the Columbia River, about twenty-six miles east of Ellensburg and forty-two miles west of Moses Lake, take the Vantage exit and proceed north. After passing the Interpretive Center, the road bends west. Follow signs pointing to "Trails." You'll reach the trailhead parking area on the right (north) side of the road 2.75 miles from I-90.

The hike: This short hike through Ginkgo Petrified Forest, in addition to being a fine leg-stretcher for travelers along I-90, provides many insights into the past natural history of the region.

During the Miocene epoch (twenty-six million to twelve million years ago) the landscape of central Washington was the complete opposite of what it is today. Since there was no Cascade Range at that time to intercept incoming Pacific Ocean moisture, the Vantage area enjoyed a humid climate, supporting lush forests, lakes, swamps, and streams.

Periodically, basalt gushed from numerous fissures in the earth's crust throughout today's Columbia Basin, spreading over the landscape and burying everything in its path. The cliffs enclosing the Columbia River near Vantage are composed of this basalt. Each layer represents a successive lava flow.

The petrified logs you see today at the Ginkgo Forest were entombed by these outpourings of basalt. Many of the trees weren't incinerated by the molten rock, as you might expect, but were protected by the abundant moisture that rapidly cooled the lava.

Logs from distant places, including remnants of spruce and Douglas-fir, drifted into Lake Vantage from cooler climates and were preserved along with locally occurring species such as elm, ginkgo, sycamore, maple, and hickory. In fact, more than 200 species of trees representing more than fifty genera have been identified in the Ginkgo Petrified Forest.

Ginkgo trees were widespread 100 to 200 million years ago, when the world's climate was much different. The only surviving member of this class of tree is *Ginkgo biloba*, which occurs naturally in an isolated region in China and is planted as an ornamental in this country.

From the trailhead follow the paved path to the east, passing the display showing a map of the trail system constructed by the Civilian Conservation Corps during the 1930s.

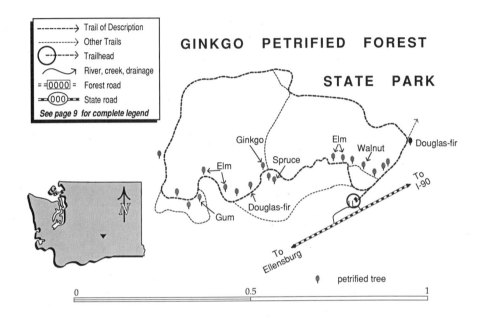

You'll start out on the hiking trail and loop back via any one of the interpretive trails.

Ignore two left-branching interpretive trails and a right-forking set of faint jeep tracks within the first quarter mile.

You'll soon leave the paved path, climbing westward along a low ridge. The alkaline ground is sparsely covered with sagebrush, greasewood, and bunchgrass. Keep an eye out for rattlesnakes; gopher snakes are also common. As you gain elevation the Columbia River comes into view.

Just before the trail bends eastward back toward the trailhead, take the upper left fork if you want to see many more petrified logs. But whichever trail you take back to your car, you'll surely have gained an appreciation of the dramatic changes that have altered the environment over the past few million years. □

HIKE 7 _OBSERVATION PEAK_

General description: A twelve-mile, round-trip day hike in the Trapper Creek Wilderness of Washington's southern Cascades, leading from virgin valley-bottom forest to a grassy summit and featuring panoramic vistas.
Elevation gain and loss: 3,077 feet.
Trailhead elevation: 1,130 feet.
High point: Observation Peak, 4,207 feet.
Maps: Wind River and Lookout Mtn. 7.5-minute USGS quads; Gifford Pinchot National Forest map.
Season: June through October.
Water availability: Small streams between 1 and 3.75 miles.

Finding the trailhead: From the Carson turnoff on State Route 14, about forty-seven miles east of Vancouver, follow paved Wind River Road northward through the forested Wind River Valley for about fifteen miles (passing the turnoff to the Wind River Ranger Station after 9.5 miles) to the Government Mineral Springs turnoff and bear left. Cross the Wind River, then turn right after 0.4 mile. A sign here points to Trapper Creek Wilderness Trailhead opposite left-forking Little Soda Springs Road. Follow dirt Forest Road 5401 for .4 mile to the parking area at the trailhead.

The hike: Washington's southern Cascades offer a different kind of wilderness experience for hikers used to the rugged, heavily glaciated country so common elsewhere in the state.

Volcanic rocks, lava flows, and cinder cones dominate the densely forested, gently rolling landscape. Glaciation was minor, excavating only small basins on the flanks of the highest peaks.

A hike in the southern Cascades, far from overbearing peaks and crowded hiking trails, allows you to contemplate nature, both in its simplicity and its complexity. A hike in these hushed forests also encourages introspection.

From the summit of Observation Peak, more than 100 separate clearcuts can be seen. To the logging industry, every tree in the forest represents a source of income. Loggers argue that wilderness "locks up" the timber resource forever, and that there is too much wilderness. After all, what good is timber if it can't be cut and sold for a profit? This argument is one of the central issues dividing environmentalists and participants in extractive industries such as mining and logging.

Fortunately, environmentalists won the battle in the heavily forested Trapper Creek Wilderness. But, more often than not, those powerful industries get their way when the Forest Service "releases" roadless areas for development. As U.S. citizens, it is our responsibility to voice our opinions about the management of our forests to district rangers, forest supervisors and congressional representatives.

Begin this hike on the Trapper Creek Trail, quickly avoiding right-forking Dry Creek Trail. Rise gently through a shady forest of western hemlock, Douglas-fir, silver fir, and western redcedar, some of which are impressively large.

You'll reach a four-way junction after a mile; turn right onto Observation

Trail. The route leads through a Douglas-fir-dominated forest on a moderate grade. Ahead, several small creeks and springs cross the trail. Views are quite limited.

You'll cross the last stream after 3.75 miles; tank up here. After another quarter mile, the Big Slide Trail forks left, descending into the depths of Trapper Creek. That trail, or the Sun Shine Trail which is intersected a half mile ahead on viewless Howe Ridge, can be used to loop back to the trailhead, adding very little extra mileage to the return trip.

From Howe Ridge, the trail traverses east slopes clothed in an open forest of Douglas-fir, white and lodgepole pine, and silver fir. Huckleberry dominates the understory, while bear grass and red Indian paintbrush brighten the slopes in early summer.

After a long mile from Howe Ridge, you'll reach a ridgetop junction. The right fork leads to Berry Camp and Ridge Trail in a quarter mile.

Turn left for Observation Peak, reaching its grassy, wildflower-speckled summit after hiking a half mile through fir forest.

A level spot just below the top offers a scenic campsite for water-toting backpackers.

Mount Adams, Mount Rainier, Mount St. Helens, and miles of eruption-flattened forest dominate the view from northeast to northwest. Mount Hood rises majestically beyond Columbia Gorge in the south. And in the east a few prominent Cascade Crest peaks rise out of the forest in Indian Heaven country. The remainder of the view overlooks clearcuts and more clearcuts. Keep an eye out for black-tailed deer and Roosevelt elk, both of which are common in the area.

From the peak, either retrace the route to the trailhead or try one of the above-mentioned trails to loop back via Trapper Creek. □

HIKE 8 *FALLS CREEK FALLS*

General description: A pleasant three-mile, round-trip day hike through low-elevation forest to one of the most impressive waterfalls accessible by trail in the Gifford Pinchot National Forest.

Elevation gain and loss: 680 feet.

Trailhead elevation: 1,320 feet.

High point: 2,000 feet.

Maps: Wind River 7.5-minute USGS quad, Gifford Pinchot National Forest map.

Season: Mid-May through September.

Water availability: Abundant along entire route.

Finding the trailhead: Follow Wind River Road north from Carson off State Route 14, passing the turnoff to Government Mineral Springs after fifteen miles. After another 0.7 mile turn right where a sign indicates Falls Creek Trail. Follow this gravel road, avoiding two signed turnoffs and left-branching Forest Road 610 after 1.6 miles. Two miles from Wind River Road turn right

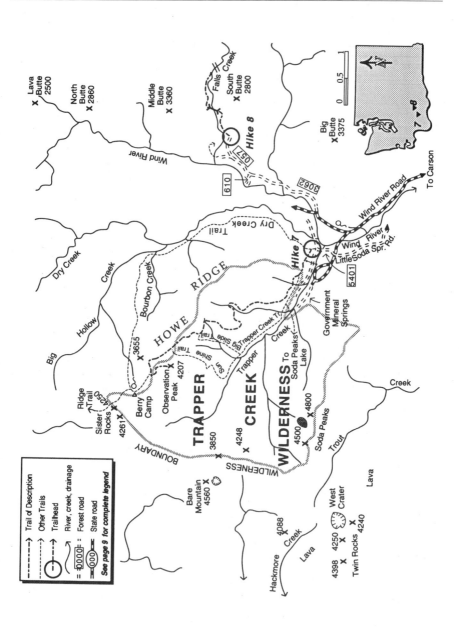

where a sign points to Trail No. 152A onto Forest Road 3062/057; you'll reach the turnaround at the trailhead within 0.4 mile.

The hike: To hikers familiar with the southern Cascades, waterfalls and the Columbia Gorge are synonymous. But the trails to those waterfalls, mostly on the Oregon side, are often crowded, owing to their proximity to Portland and easy access from I-84.

Falls Creek Falls, a three-tiered descent of about 200 feet, well off the beaten track, is the exciting destination of this pleasant, easy day hike above the Wind River.

The trail briefly follows an old road from the trailhead, passing through second-growth Douglas-fir.

Soon the route narrows and enters a virgin forest of Douglas-fir and western larch. The larch, the only deciduous conifer in the state of Washington, is found typically on the drier eastern slopes of the Cascades. But the western slopes of the southern Cascades are comparatively dry, and the valley of lower Falls Creek provides a suitable habitat for drought-tolerant trees such as the larch.

Tumultuous Falls Creek, always close at hand but often inaccessible, is interrupted at times by many deep, inviting pools.

The trail proceeds through giant western hemlocks and Douglas-fir to an excellent bridge across the creek after 0.6 mile. A small campsite is located on a bench above the bridge, beside the trail. Beyond this point, redcedar joins the forest, and the trail begins rising moderately across corrugated slopes. You'll cross a boulder-strewn gully, which may become impassable after heavy rains.

The terrain becomes increasingly rocky as an overpowering roar fills the air. Suddenly the falls appear, perhaps the most dramatic descent in Washington's southern Cascades.

The trail ends opposite the lower fall amid spray-dampened boulders—a cool spot on even the hottest summer days.

From the falls, retrace the route to the trailhead. ☐

HIKE 9 *CULTUS CREEK LOOP*

General description: A 6.6-mile loop, day hike or overnighter, featuring mountain lakes, subalpine forests and meadows, and huckleberry thickets in Washington's Indian Heaven Wilderness on the southern Cascade crest.
Elevation gain and loss: 1,450 feet.
Trailhead elevation: 3,988 feet.
High point: 5,237 feet.
Maps: Lone Butte 7.5-minute USGS quad; Gifford Pinchot National Forest map.
Season: July through October.
Water availability: Available along entire route.

Finding the trailhead: From Trout Lake (twenty miles north of White Salmon off State Highway 14), follow State Highway 141 east for about eight miles to the Peterson Prairie Campground. Then turn north onto dirt-surfaced Forest

Road 24, following signs indicating Sawtooth Berry Fields, and after about nine miles you'll reach Cultus Creek Campground. The hikers' parking area lies just west of Forest Road 24 at the north end of the campground.

The hike: The Indian Heaven Wilderness sits astride the crest of the Cascade Range south of Mount Adams. Several prominent, mile-high peaks rise above a densely forested, gently rolling landscape. Although far removed from population centers, this remote wilderness, encircled by logging roads and countless clearcuts, bears evidence of man.

Many lakes, some with good-sized trout, provide destinations for day hikers and backpackers alike. Be sure to purify the water. Weekend trips are probably the best way to enjoy this small 20,650-acre wilderness. Besides fishing, this area is renowned for its huckleberry thickets, and berry picking is a popular activity in August and September. Horse packing is common here. The area is also infamous for its mosquitoes, which reach their peak of intolerability during July.

From the parking area, walk southeastward along the campground loop road to the sign marking the beginning of Trail 33. This trail climbs steadily southwestward through a forest of hemlock, spruce, and fir.

The trail approaches Cultus Creek after 0.75 mile but quickly jogs north, climbing away from the creek. At a bend in the trail, you'll enjoy a fine vista north, including Sawtooth Mountain, Mount Adams, Goat Rocks, and Mount Rainier.

From here to Cultus Lake, the route traverses a subalpine basin which an ancient glacier carved into the slopes of Bird Mountain.

After hiking 2.25 miles from the trailhead, you'll reach a junction with a left-forking trail leading to Lake Wapiki, 1.5 miles from the outlet of 5,050-foot Cultus Lake.

Turning right, the trail soon climbs over a 5,100-foot saddle amid hemlocks and firs, then descends a quarter mile to the Lemei Lake Trail, branching left. Red heather, bear grass, and avalanche lilies are common here. Bear right, quickly descending to quarter-mile-long Clear Lake. Like most lakes in Indian Heaven, Clear Lake has no inflow or outflow. A good view of craggy Lemei Rock is available from the trail west of the lake.

Beyond Clear Lake, the trail descends to join the Pacific Crest Trail (PCT) above Deer Lake, immediately after crossing an early-season creek. Fair campsites are located on benches below the trail, but the best campsites in the area are located at Bear Lake, half a mile to the south along the PCT.

Turn right (north) on the PCT, gently traversing the west slopes of Bird Mountain through a subalpine forest. Numerous early-season creeks cross the trail, most of which offer possible camping. Ignore stretches of the abandoned Cascade Crest Trail that frequently cross the PCT. Avalanche lilies are common here in early summer.

The trail eventually leads northeast, passes above a shallow tarn (possible campsites), and continues through a jumble of volcanic boulders to the signed Wood Lake Trail, branching left.

You'll come to a junction 2.1 miles from Deer Lake. Turn right here, quickly reaching a saddle at 5,237 feet. Experienced hikers may want to leave the trail and follow the crest of the Cascades south for 0.75 mile to 5,706-foot Bird Mountain for an all-encompassing vista.

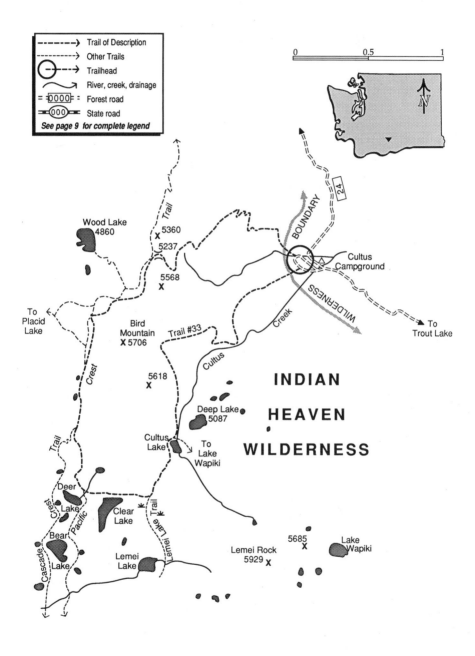

Trail of Description
Other Trails
Trailhead
River, creek, drainage
Forest road
State road
See page 9 for complete legend

0   0.5   1

N

Wood Lake
4860

X 5360
5237

5568
X

To ←
Placid
Lake

Bird
Mountain
X 5706

Trail #33

Cultus

BOUNDARY

24

Cultus
Campground

WILDERNESS

Creek

To
Trout Lake

INDIAN

5618
X

Deep Lake
5087

HEAVEN

Crest

WILDERNESS

Cultus
Lake

To
Lake
Wapiki

Trail

Deer
Lake

Clear
Lake

Crest

Pacific

Lemei Lake Trail

Bear
Lake

Cascade

Lemei
Lake

5685
X

Lake
Wapiki

Lemei Rock
5929 X

Back at the saddle, follow the trail as it descends steadily for 1.5 miles to the trailhead. Abundant huckleberries and views of Mount Adams are major distractions along the final segment of this fine hike. □

HIKE 10 *SPENCER BUTTE*

General description: A 3.2-mile, round-trip day hike to a former lookout site midway between Mount Adams and Mount St. Helens in the Gifford Pinchot National Forest.
Elevation gain and loss: 747 feet.
Trailhead elevation: 3,500 feet.
High point: Spencer Butte, 4,247 feet.
Maps: Spencer Butte 7.5-minute USGS quad; Gifford Pinchot National Forest map.
Season: Mid-June through October.
Water availability: None; carry an adequate supply.

Finding the trailhead: Follow Road 90 east from Cougar past Yale Lake and Swift Reservoir for 18.2 miles to northbound Forest Road 25, signed for Mount St. Helens, and turn north.

Follow this road for 5.3 miles to the junction with eastbound Forest Road 93 just beyond the Muddy River and bear right onto Forest Road 93. Follow this one-lane paved road with turnouts (beware of logging trucks) for 7.5 miles to the sign for the Spencer Butte Trailhead.

The hike: Considerable effort is normally required to reach mountain peaks and enjoy their panoramic vistas. But by following the short, easy trail to Spencer Butte, virtually anyone can gaze out upon hundreds of square miles of mountain country, from Mount Adams and Mount St. Helens to Oregon's Mount Jefferson.

From the trailhead, walk into a forest of western hemlock, silver fir, Douglas-fir, and white pine. Shrubs here consist of huckleberry and vine maple, while the ground-hugging understory contains bunchberry, bracken fern, and bear grass, the short-lived blooms of which are a favorite with grazing Roosevelt elk.

The trail, deep in crunchy pumice from the 1980 eruption of Mount St. Helens, soon begins ascending the western slopes of Breezy Point through young trees. You'll reach the ridge crest after 0.75 mile. Proceed northward.

The trail cuts a swath through a stand of small firs, passes a few cottonwoods (normally found along stream courses), and reaches the high point of the ridge at an elevation of 4,247 feet.

Looking to the west, you'll see the east side of squat Mount St. Helens, lined by the paths of numerous 1980 mudflows. The volcano seems a mere stone's throw away.

To the east, slopes fall steadily away into the deep canyon of the Lewis River.

Mount Adams, often cloud-capped in early summer, looms boldly on the eastern horizon.

To the south, beyond miles of patchy forests, Mounts Hood and Jefferson appear as distant, hazy mirages.

The trail continues northward from the summit for 1.5 miles to another trailhead, but most hikers return the way they came. □

HIKE 11   *LEWIS RIVER TO BOLT CAMP OR FOREST ROAD 90*

General description: A five-mile round-trip or 9.4-mile one-way day hike or backpack along the last remaining primitive section of the Lewis River in the Gifford Pinchot National Forest.

Elevation gain and loss: +100 feet to Bolt Camp; or +600 feet, -200 feet to Forest Road 90.

Trailhead elevation: 1,100 feet.

High point: 1,200 feet at Bolt Camp or 1,600 feet along upper river.

Maps: Burnt Peak 7.5-minute USGS quad (Spencer Butte 7.5-minute USGS quad required for upper portion of river); Gifford Pinchot National Forest map.

Season: March through mid-December

Water availability: Lewis River provides a continuous supply.

Finding the trailhead: Follow Road 90 east from Cougar for 23.1 miles (4.75 miles east of Lewis River bridge) to the hard-to-spot junction with left-forking (westbound) Forest Road 9039. Turn here, following gravel Forest Road 9039 for 0.7 mile to the bridge over the Lewis River. The trail begins on the north side of the river.

The hike: Born on the icy flanks of Mount Adams and draining a vast region of the southern Cascades, the Lewis River cuts a deep swath through the mountains on its journey to the lower Columbia.

Excessive logging has marred this densely forested region, and logging roads follow the Lewis for much of its length. However, a fine, easy trail follows the river for 9.5 miles along its middle reaches. The Forest Service, for the time being, has allowed it to remain in primitive condition.

Hikers can enjoy this leisurely hike along the wide river through a lush low-elevation forest of western redcedar, Douglas-fir, western hemlock, and big-leaf maple. All drinking water obtained from the river should be purified.

Anglers are attracted by the promise of landing rainbow and large Dolly Varden trout. Be sure to check current fishing regulations. The season generally runs from May 30 through October 31.

The trail heads northeast from the bridge, passing a spur trail leading to the river. After a third of a mile, another trail joins the river route on the left. Follow the riverside trail through shady virgin forest. The ground is carpeted by ferns, vanilla leaf, and oxalis, and thimbleberries and raspberries offer good summertime snacking en route. The lush understory makes camping almost impossible.

The river alternates between noisy rapids and calm, slow stretches where fishing is most productive. The trail also alternates between the river bank

HIKE 10 *SPENCER BUTTE*
HIKE 11 *LEWIS RIVER TO BOLT CAMP OR FOREST ROAD 90*

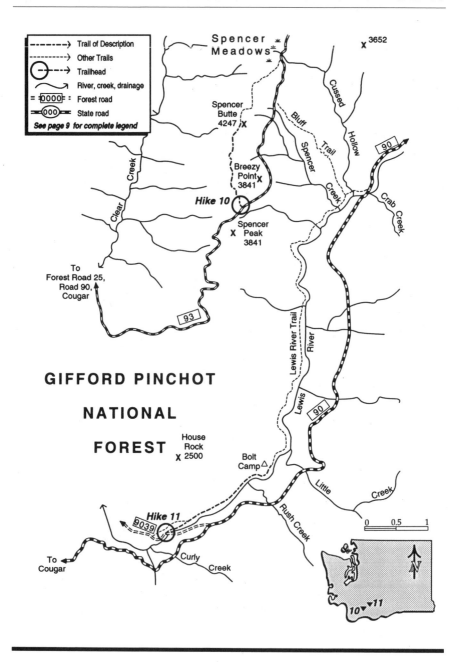

and the forest, which has all the characteristics of a temperate rain forest.

Since the forest floor is already densely covered with vegetation, it's difficult for new plants to establish themselves. The best chance a tree seedling has to get started is on a slightly decayed fallen log or stump, called a "nurse log." Plants also may establish footholds on decayed parts of living trees, such as on broken branches.

Large Rush Creek joins the river from the southeast at 2.1 miles, and after 2.7 miles hikers reach Bolt Camp shelter, a lean-to surrounded by good campsites. The trail continues along the north bank of the river, and hikers who've arranged for transportation can hike the entire 9.4 miles to Forest Road 90 below Lower Lewis River Falls. □

HIKE 12 *NORWAY PASS*

General description: A 4.6-mile, round-trip day hike, surveying the destruction and subsequent revegetation of an area in the Mount St. Helens National Volcanic Monument laid waste by the 1980 eruption.
Elevation gain and loss: 908 feet.
Trailhead elevation: 3,600 feet.
High point: Norway Pass, 4,508 feet.
Maps: Spirit Lake SE 7.5-minute USGS quad; Mount St. Helens and Vicinity USGS quad; National Monument visitors map.
Season: Late June through mid-October.
Water availability: None en route, but available at trailhead.

Finding the trailhead: Forest Road 99, branching west from Forest Road 25, twenty-two miles south of Randle and forty-four miles from Cougar, is the main thoroughfare into Mount St. Helens National Volcanic Monument. Follow Forest Raod 99 west from its junction with Forest Road 25 (both are paved) for nine miles to Forest Road 26 and turn right for 0.9 mile to the Norway Pass Trailhead parking area.

The Goat Mountain Trailhead (Hike 13) can be reached by continuing north on Road 26 for another 3.7 miles, then turn west just north of Ryan Lake and following Road 2612 westward for 0.4 mile to the trailhead parking area.

The hike: From the large parking area, Boundary Trail will lead you steadily upward among flattened trees and standing snags stripped of all bark and branches by the intense blast from the volcano. The trail passes many small trees, mostly hemlock and silver fir, that survived the blast because they were insulated by a deep blanket of snow.

After a series of switchbacks, the route levels off and heads northwest to 4,508-foot Norway Pass and a head-on view of the blown-away north side of Mount St. Helens. At times the lava dome building in the crater is visible, but it's frequently obscured by clouds of steam.

Log-jammed Spirit Lake lies below the pass. The slopes above the lake have been swept bare of logs and debris, perhaps by a giant wave created by the blast.

Plant pioneers are rapidly spreading throughout the devastated area, adding

The hike to Norway Pass near Mount St. Helens offers a close-up look at all the destructive force of a volcanic eruption considered relatively minor by geologists. Ron Adkison photo.

a green patina to the ash-gray landscape. Among them are fireweed, raspberry, huckleberry, wild strawberry, valerian, false Solomon's seal, alder, thimbleberry, ferns, grasses, penstemon, avalanche lily, pearly everlasting, and elderberry.

The trail has been reconstructed beyond Norway Pass and now connects with the Truman Trail, allowing hikers to return to Road 99 at Windy Ridge via the Spirit Lake basin. It offers hikers the opportunity of a unique backpack but not without the dangers inherent in an active volcanic area. □

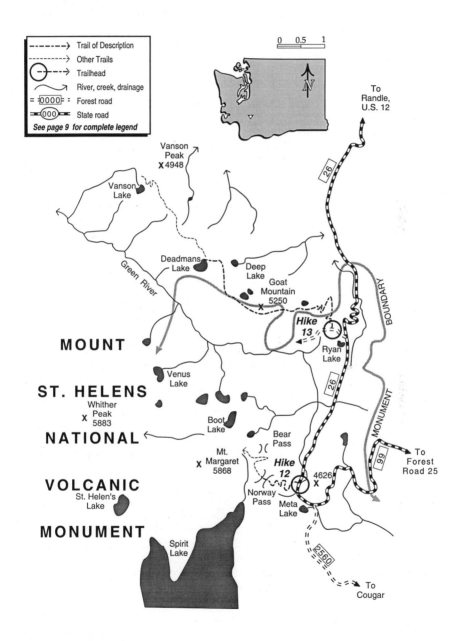

Trail of Description
Other Trails
Trailhead
River, creek, drainage
Forest road
State road
See page 9 for complete legend

0   0.5   1

To Randle, U.S. 12

26

Vanson Peak X 4948

Vanson Lake

BOUNDARY

Deadmans Lake

Deep Lake

Goat Mountain 5250 X

Hike 13

Ryan Lake

Green River

MOUNT

Venus Lake

ST. HELENS

Whither Peak X 5883

Boot Lake

Bear Pass

NATIONAL

Mt. Margaret X 5868

Hike 12

4626 X

26

MONUMENT

99

To Forest Road 25

VOLCANIC

St. Helen's Lake

Norway Pass

Meta Lake

MONUMENT

Spirit Lake

2560

To Cougar

HIKE 13 *GOAT MOUNTAIN AND DEADMAN'S LAKE*

General description: An eleven-mile, round-trip day hike or overnighter along the fringe of the 1980 blast zone north of Mount St. Helens in the Gifford Pinchot National Forest-Mount St. Helens National Volcanic Monument.
Elevation gain and loss: +2,000 feet, -1,000 feet.
Trailhead elevation: 3,300 feet.
High point: 5,300 feet.
Maps: Spirit Lake SW and Spirit Lake SE 7.5-minute USGS quads; Gifford Pinchot National Forest map.
Season: July through mid-October.
Water availability: None readily available until Deadman's Lake.

Finding the trailhead: Follow directions under Hike 12.

The hike: Goat Mountain, rising beside Green River just north of the blast zone, narrowly escaped the full force of the 1980 eruption of Mount St. Helens. Patches of timber on its flanks were killed by hot gases; they were not blown down as were forests closer to the mountain. The trail alternates between unscathed forest and heat-killed trees and offers startling views into the heart of the blast zone.

From the trailhead, climb quickly to a logging road and follow it along the lower edge of a salvage-logged clearcut. Numerous seedlings have been planted here, each protected from the intense sun by shingles. Following sun-drenched switchbacks, you'll get no relief from the heat until the trail leads into a Douglas-fir-dominated forest.

After a long, shady traverse, the switchbacks resume, passing by the abandoned pre-eruption trail that ascends the clearcut.

Enjoy a well-earned vista where the trail finally crests Goat Mountain: Mount Rainier rises to the north, Mount Adams rises above the partially devastated forests of Strawberry Mountain to the east, Mount Hood stands far to the south, seen across the barren landscape where the virgin timber once stood, and finally, the source of all the destruction, the truncated mass of Mount St. Helens, rises above the glacier-carved north slope of the Mount Venus-Mount Whittier ridge. Waterfalls, hidden before the 1980 eruption, tumble from the numerous lake basins below the ridge. The sight of the four volcanoes, viewed from a landscape swept clean by what geologists consider a relatively minor eruption, offers a stark reminder of the forces that shaped the Cascades in the past and will continue to reshape the range in the future.

The trail passes through occasional stunted trees—Douglas-fir, western white pine, mountain hemlock, silver fir, and some lodgepole pine—their branches pointing in the direction of the prevailing wind. Wildflowers include red Indian paintbrush, yarrow, wild strawberry, thimbleberry, lupine, larkspur, and bear grass. The abundant elk in the area prefer to graze upon the latter.

A possible campsite exists next to a small tarn on the north flank of the first summit on the ridge. You'll have to leave the trail to find the tarn.

The trail proceeds in and out of the blast zone, traverses below a peak dominated by granitic rock, and then reaches a saddle above two small tarns lying on a bench on the north side of the mountain and surrounded by heat-killed timber.

Beyond this point, a steady descent leads into virgin timber, passes above and west of invisible Deep Lake, and finally, after 5.5 miles, reaches good campsites at Deadman's Lake (named before the eruption) at an elevation of 4,300 feet.

Vanson Peak, a former lookout site featuring superb vistas, can be reached by following the trail 2.5 miles from the lake.

Retrace your footsteps to return to the trailhead. □

HIKE 14 *ELK PASS TO BADGER LAKE*

General description: A 8.2-mile, round-trip day hike or overnighter to a remote subalpine lake in the Gifford Pinchot National Forest.
Elevation gain and loss: +1,070 feet, -310 feet.
Trailhead elevation: 4,080 feet.
High point: 4,940 feet at Badger Lake.
Maps: French Butte 7.5-minute USGS quad; Gifford Pinchot National Forest map.
Season: July through October.
Water availability: None available until Badger Lake.

Finding the trailhead: Follow paved Forest Road 25 south from Randle (signed for Mount St. Helens and Cispus River) for 23.5 miles to Elk Pass and the Boundary Trail trailhead. Or follow Road 90 east from Cougar for 18.2 miles and turn north onto Forest Road 25, reaching Elk Pass after another 20.8 miles.

The hike: A series of north-south ridges about fifteen miles west of Mount Adams, capped by craggy summits more than a mile high, constitutes one of the last remaining roadless areas not formally designated as wilderness in the Gifford Pinchot National Forest.

The drainages dividing these ridges have been logged, and each hosts a network of roads. Unfortunately, the sounds of logging are sometimes close at hand. This highly scenic area deserves protection so that it may be enjoyed by future generations.

The trail leads generally east from Elk Pass along a silver-fir-clad ridge to Badger Lake. It's not unusual to see a large herd of elk en route.

After 2.5 miles, the trail coming up from Mosquito Meadows joins the Boundary Trail on the left (north). Continuing southeast, the trail parallels a recently constructed logging road—another threat to this trail and the forest.

You may enjoy glimpses north toward Mount Rainier, framed by trailside silver firs.

Continue slogging through pumice inches deep and, after 4.1 miles, you'll reach a junction.

If you take the left fork, you'll climb nearly 800 feet in 0.6 mile to the rocky summit of 5,664-foot Badger Peak, where you'll get far-ranging views of the South Cascades.

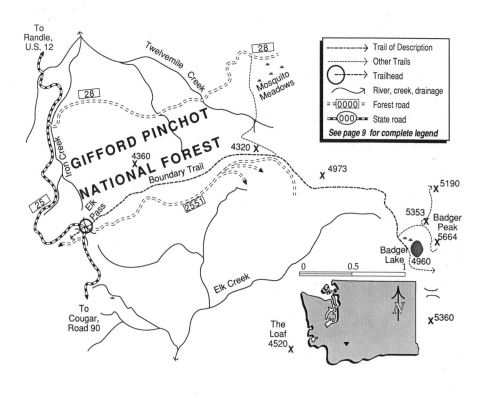

The right fork, the continuation of the Boundary Trail, reaches Badger Lake at 4,940 feet within 0.1 mile, then continues along the ridge through the Dark Divide Roadless Area to Kirk Rock and the Shark Rock Scenic Area.

Badger Lake, which may remain frozen until early July, makes a fine base camp from which to explore this seldom-visited area. The lake is too shallow to support fish, but it's quite attractive nonetheless.

After enjoying this beautiful but threatened area, return to Elk Pass along the same route. □

HIKE 15 *BOULDER CREEK TO SUMMIT PRAIRIE*

General description: A moderate nine-mile round trip day hike to a glorious viewpoint in the Dark Divide Roadless Area of the Gifford Pinchot National Forest.

Elevation gain and loss: +1,400 feet; -300 feet.

Trailhead elevation: 4,130 feet.

High point: Summit Prairie lookout site, 5,238 feet.

Maps: East Canyon Ridge 7.5-minute USGS quad; Gifford Pinchot National Forest map.

Season: Late June through October.

Water availability: Springs at 1.7, 2.1, and 2.4 miles.

Finding the trailhead: From Trout Lake, proceed 1.25 miles north toward Randle and the prominently signed Forest Road 23. Follow this road northwest (pavement ends after twenty two miles) for twenty five miles to Forest Road 2334—signed for Council Lake and Boundary Trail—and turn left.

That spur road can also be reached from Randle by following signed Forest Road 25 south for eight miles to Forest Road 23, which you follow for another twenty-five miles to the above-mentioned junction, 0.9 mile south of signed Baby Shoe Pass.

Follow wide gravel Road 2334 for 1.2 miles and bear left where the spur to Council Lake forks right. After another 2.3 miles, turn right into a much narrower dirt road, which is signed for Boulder Trail. This is an unmaintained dirt road that is often rutted and possibly blocked by blowdowns. Proceed about 0.1 mile to a junction with a right-forking spur road. Park at the small turnout on the north side of the road.

The hike: This scenic hike leads through hushed forests past small meadows beneath the volcanic cliffs of Table Mountain and finally to a former lookout site with grand views of four ice-clad volcanoes, vast forests, and the rugged peaks of the Dark Divide Roadless Area.

The initial 0.6 mile of the hike follows the jeep trail indicated on the map, carving a swath through a tall forest of large silver fir and western hemlock to the end of the road and the beginning of the Boulder Trail. Thereafter, the trail quickly crosses a Boulder Creek tributary fifty yards below a lovely waterfall, then climbs moderately up shady east-facing slopes for a half mile to the signed intersection with the Boundary Trail; then turn left (southwest).

The grade eases beyond this junction, and lupine and red columbine enliven trailside slopes. Trees frame views that extend eastward to the immense snowy cone of Mount Adams, while closer at hand, the dark basalt cliffs of Table Mountain loom skyward to the west.

Pass above a wet, willow-choked meadow and above a small cold spring; then dip into and out of several minor gullies and bear right at the junction with Table Mountain Trail after another 0.8 mile.

The nearly level trail ahead skirts the base of the cliffs of Table Mountain's southwest face, alternating between hemlock and fir forest and wildflower-speckled openings. Soon you'll cross three small creeks; gain the ridge west of Table Mountain and then follow the undulating trail through heavy forest

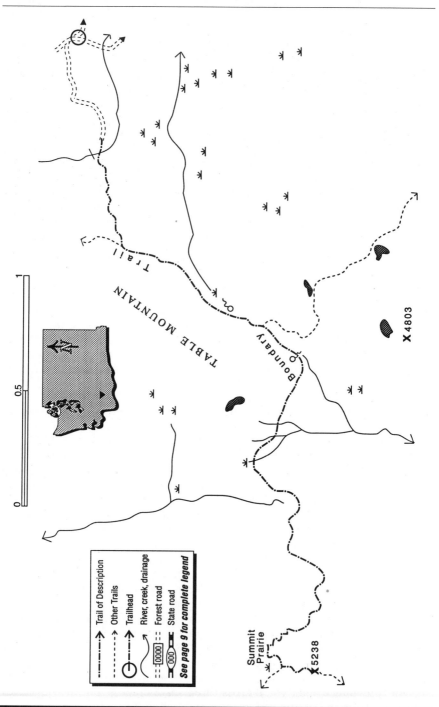

Views from Summit Prairie reveal mountains and forests for as far as the eye can see. Ron Adkison photo.

as it follows the ridge westward, sometimes steeply, to a signed junction 2.5 miles from the last.

Summit Prairie is a very small tree-rimmed meadow that lies just north-west or downhill from the junction. Turn right, ascending Quartz Creek Ridge for 0.1 mile to the former lookout site, where only the concrete footings remain.

Only a small opening exists on the summit amid the thick forest where the brilliant summer blossoms of mariposa, tiger lily, lupine, and red columbine may momentarily distract you from the tremendous vistas. Prominent features in the south include Lemei Rock and Bird Mountain in Indian Heaven Wilderness and beyond rises Mount Hood. The Dark Divide high country—a scenic concentration of craggy peaks, open ridges, and deep canyons—foregrounds the broad, truncated cone of Mount St. Helens.

Goat Rocks and Mount Rainier dominate the northward view, while Mount Adams, featuring the great icefalls of the Adams Glacier, rises grandly to the east and seems like its only a stone's throw away.

Retrace the route to the trailhead. □

HIKE 16 *HORSESHOE MEADOW*

General description: An 11.4-mile, round-trip backpack leading to a subalpine meadow at the foot of Mount Adams, an excellent base camp for days of alpine exploration.

Elevation gain and loss: 1,880 feet.

Trailhead elevation: 4,020 feet.

High point: 5,900 feet.

Maps: Mount Adams West 7.5-minute USGS quad or Mount Adams Wilderness map; Gifford Pinchot National Forest map.

Season: July through September.

Water availability: Abundant in the Horseshoe Meadow area early in the season but may be scarce later.

Finding the trailhead: From Trout Lake, head north toward Randle. After 1.25 miles, bear left onto Forest Road 23. The pavement ends twenty-two miles from Trout Lake, turning into a good gravel road. Turn right onto dirt Forest Road 521, 13.5 miles from Trout Lake, and reach the Pacific Crest Trail after 0.3 mile.

You can also reach the trailhead by following mostly paved Forest Road 90 up the Lewis River to Forest Road 23, about forty-nine miles from Cougar. Then follow Forest Road 23 south for six miles to Forest Road 521, and thence 0.3 mile to the trailhead.

The hike: Washington's five volcanoes dominate the western half of the state from the Columbia River to the Canadian border. Three of the volcanoes—Mount St. Helens, Mount Rainier, and Mount Baker—are major tourist attractions, with paved roads leading to each of their flanks. The other two—Mount Adams and Glacier Peak—remain unfamiliar to many Washingtonians, owing to their distance from population centers and the difficulty with which they are reached.

To know Mount Adams, you must first drive many miles of unpaved, busy logging roads, and then hike several miles to reach the mountain's base. Three superb trails, the Pacific Crest, the Highline, and Round-the-Mountain Trail, nearly encircle the mountain, traversing alpine meadows and timberline forests and offering access to a variety of climbing routes from difficult ice climbs to a non-technical class 2 climb (scramble).

Second in Washington only to Mount Rainier in sheer bulk, Mount Adams is the one volcano in the state to have formed astride the crest of the Cascades; all the others rise west of the main backbone of the range.

This second highest of Washington's peaks hosts a large glacier system emanating from a summit icecap more than 200 feet thick. In fact, the Klickitat Glacier, flowing down the east slope of the mountain, occupies the second-largest cirque in the state. Only Mount Rainier's Carbon Glacier has carved a larger one.

Mount Adams may take second place to Mount Rainier in many respects, but it offers solitude and a wilderness experience unavailable in the popular national park to the north.

Mount Adams itself is broad and asymmetrical, and geologists believe that

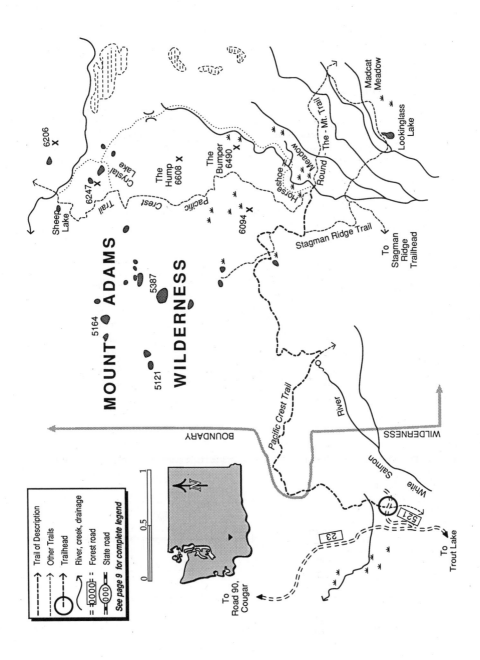

it is composed of a series of andesite cones overlying one another. Geologists also consider Mount Adams a dormant volcano, and what little activity that presently exists (steam and hydrogen sulfide gas emissions from the summit area) appears to be diminishing.

This hike offers access to the western base of the mountain and the Round-the-Mountain Trail. Using Horseshoe Meadow as a base camp, you'll find numerous possible cross-country routes that invite further exploration to many alpine meadows, glacial valleys, and parasitic cinder cones. Mosquitoes can be a nuisance during July. Keep an eye out for the black-tailed deer and Roosevelt elk that inhabit the area.

From the trailhead, the Pacific Crest Trail (PCT) leads northward into mixed conifer forest, soon crossing a small creek above a campsite. You'll enter the Mount Adams Wilderness after another quarter mile. After a steady ascent, the PCT levels off, then runs southeast through young timber past a spur trail that drops to a spring issuing from beneath a boulder—the source of the White Salmon River.

At the first switchback beyond the spur trail, a trail branches right from the PCT, quickly leading past a fair campsite.

The PCT climbs steadily toward the ever-enlarging mountain, entering the corrugated topography of a moraine dotted with boulders and stunted timber. Wildflowers include false hellebore, lupine, and phlox. Huckleberry is common all along the route.

You'll cross a small creek at the north end of a small meadow after 4.7 miles and reach a junction. The left fork leads half a mile northwest to a campsite, and the right fork climbs eastward to rejoin the PCT.

Proceed straight ahead on the PCT, passing right-forking Stagman Ridge Trail after 0.75 mile.

Another half mile of moraine climbing will lead you to the west end of Horseshoe Meadow and the junction with the Round-the-Mountain Trail.

The aptly named meadow is carpeted with red and white heather and is surrounded by moraines clad in subalpine fir, mountain hemlock, and whitebark pine. Beyond it rises massive, ice-clad Mount Adams.

Be sure to camp in the timber, well away from the meadow. For more solitude, follow the left fork of the stream past the meadow up into a timberline basin.

Experienced hikers can follow that creek upstream, crossing a ridge east of The Hump, then descend past Crystal Lake to Sheep Lake and the PCT. That rewarding loop totals about five miles.

From Horseshoe Meadow, return the same way to the trailhead. □

HIKE 17 *POTATO HILL TO FOGGY FLAT*

General description: A 12.2 mile round trip backpack in the Mount Adams Wilderness, leading from peaceful forests and lava flows to the fields of wildflowers and the ice-clad flanks of Washington's second tallest volcano.
Elevation gain and loss: +1,800 feet; -300 feet.
Trailhead elevation: 4.750 feet.
High point: Foggy Flat, 6,000 feet.

Maps: Green Mountain, Glaciate Butte, and Mount Adams East 7.5 minute USGS quads (Muddy Meadows Trail not shown on quads) or Mount Adams Wilderness map; Gifford Pinchot National Forest map.

Season: July through September.

Water availability: Lava Spring, 1.6 miles, Green Timber Camp, 5.5 miles, and Foggy Flat.

Permit: Required; obtain at Trout Lake Ranger Station, or self-register near the trailhead.

Finding the trailhead: From Trout Lake, follow mostly paved Forest Road 23 (see Hikes 15 & 16) for 24.4 miles to Forest Road 2329 (0.5 mile north of Baby Shoe Pass) and turn right. Ignoring several signed junctions, follow the one lane road which is paved for the first 1.5 miles and gravelled thereafter, for 10.2 miles to the junction with paved Forest Road 5603. Turn right and drive another 1.7 miles to the Pacific Crest Trail trailhead parking area. It is on the north side of the road, beneath the tall cinder cone of Potato Hill.

Or, from Randle, follow Forest Road 25 south for one mile, then turn onto Forest Road 23. Drive another 17.4 miles, then turn onto the one lane paved Forest Road 21. After 4.8 miles, turn right onto gravelled Forest Road 56. About three miles ahead, bear right onto Forest Road 5603, reaching the trailhead after another 6.8 miles or 32.9 miles from Randle.

The hike: This highly scenic and pleasant two-to three-day backpack surveys nearly the full range of scenery in the Mount Adams Wilderness, from open pine forests to fir thickets, from flower-filled meadows to broken lava flows, and from clear spring-fed streams to glacial torrents. A worthwhile side trip on the Highline Trail from Foggy Flat climbs above timberline to the very foot

Mount Adams dominates the skyline above the upper Muddy Fork Trail. Ron Adkison.

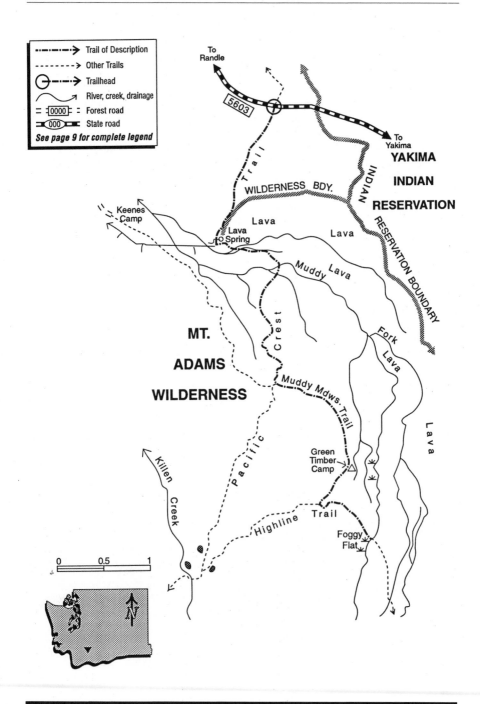

Legend:
- Trail of Description
- Other Trails
- Trailhead
- River, creek, drainage
- 0000 Forest road
- 000 State road

See page 9 for complete legend

To Randle

5603

To Yakima

YAKIMA INDIAN RESERVATION

WILDERNESS BDY.

INDIAN RESERVATION BOUNDARY

Trail

Keenes Camp

Lava

Lava Spring

Lava

Lava

Muddy

Lava

Crest

Fork

Lava

MT. ADAMS WILDERNESS

Muddy Mdws. Trail

Pacific

Lava

Killen Creek

Green Timber Camp

Highline Trail

Foggy Flat

0   0.5   1

of Mount Adams where broken glaciers, fresh moraines, and vast lava fields invite further exploration by experienced hikers and mountaineers.

The trail maintains a gentle to moderate grade, but the trail is sandy with Mount St. Helens fallout. Carry a good insect repellant—mosquitoes are troublesome from the Muddy Meadows Trail to timberline.

The southbound Pacific Crest Trail (PCT) begins opposite the trailhead. Obtain a backcountry permit at the Trout Lake Ranger Station or be sure to fill one out at the register box located a few yards down the trail. The initial 1.6 miles of the trail is a pleasant, gentle descent. Lupine and shoulder-high beargrass grow among the open forest of young lodgepole pines. Trees frame glimpses of massive Mount Adams. Descend along the western margin of a recent lava flow, soon thereafter reaching the cold, vigorous waters of Lava Spring and the wilderness boundary. A good campsite lies just above and east of the spring, and other sites could be established nearby.

Beyond the spring, the trail ascends at a gentle grade, skirting the southern edge of the lava flow and then fording a silty stream before curving southeast to bridge the torrent of Muddy Fork, which is laden with glacial silt. Then enter a peaceful forest of tall silver firs and hike moderately uphill for about three quarters of a mile before entering a burned forest of charred and sun-bleached snags.

The trail ahead enters a pine, fir, and hemlock forest, passing amid beautiful meadows speckled with wildflowers before it reaches a four-way junction 2.4 miles from Lava Spring. Turn left (east) at the junction onto Muddy Meadows Trail, climbing a gentle to moderate grade through forests and meadows for 1.25 miles to Green Timber Camp. There is a good campsite near a small stream.

The forest thins above the camp, and the trail winds upward over old glacial moraines to the Highline Trail, 1.7 miles from the Pacific Crest Trail.

Turning left (southeast), the Highline Trail descends briefly before climbing, sometimes steeply, past small meadows and timberline forest for 0.9 mile to the lovely green spread of Foggy Flat. Enlivened by a myriad of wildflowers, rimmed by subalpine forest and rubbly moraines, watered by a cold, clear creek, and backdropped by the north face of Mount Adams, Foggy Flat makes an immensely scenic basecamp. From there it is possible to make forays toward the ice-clad flanks of Mount Adams, only a short distance away via the Highline Trail. Look for campsites well back into the forest and avoid camping too close to the fragile meadow.

After enjoying this memorable trip, retrace the route to the trailhead. □

HIKE 18 *WALUPT CREEK LOOP*

General description: A 13.4-mile loop backpack making a grand tour of the southern Goat Rocks Wilderness.
Elevation gain and loss: 2,650 feet.
Trailhead elevation: 3,930 feet.
High point: 5,900 feet.
Maps: Walupt Lake 7.5-minute USGS quad; Goat Rocks Wilderness map; Gifford Pinchot National Forest map.
Season: July through mid-October.
Water availability: Plentiful.

Finding the trailhead: From Packwood follow U.S. Highway 12 west for 2.5 miles or go thirteen miles east from Randle to southeast-bound Johnson Creek Road No. 21. Drive this good dirt road, following signs for Walupt Lake at junctions, for 15.5 miles to eastbound Forest Road 2160. Enjoy an excellent view here of Mount Adams in the south and the Goat Rocks in the northeast. This gravel road with paved sections leads four miles to the trailhead at the campground on the north shore of Walupt Lake.

The hike: Lakes, broad vistas, rushing streams, and timberline forests combine to make this weekender a fine introduction to the scenic Goat Rocks Wilderness, one of Washington's oldest primitive areas. The Goat Rocks, which form a high, jagged crest, are the eroded remnants of an ancient volcano that's been extinct for nearly two million years.

On this hike, water is almost as plentiful as mosquitoes. From the trailhead, proceed eastward, quickly passing the return leg of the loop, the Nannie Ridge Trail, on the left (north).

Continue eastward along the north shore of Walupt Lake through shady mixed-conifer forest. After two miles, cross Walupt Creek, then switchback steadily through Douglas-fir, white pine, lodgepole pine, Englemann spruce, western larch, mountain hemlock, and silver fir to a small creek draining a broad bench. En route, enjoy tree-framed glimpses of the jagged Goat Rocks and subalpine Nannie Ridge. The small stream is easy to cross. Continue over it and follow along another small stream, soon passing by a broad, beautiful meadow. The Cascade crest rises eastward from this point, and conical Lakeview Mountain, elevation 6,660 feet, fills the sky to the south.

A spur trail to a scenic lakeside campsite leaves the main trail above the meadow after four miles of hiking. You'll come to another fork after 0.1 mile. The left fork leads to the same small lake and more campsites. Bear right and reach the Pacific Crest Trail (PCT) after a third of a mile.

Turn left onto the PCT, traversing mostly open slopes rich with the color and fragrance of a variety of wildflowers, including lupine, red Indian paintbrush, red columbine, purple aster, cinquefoil, bear grass, lousewort, and mariposa lily. The trail eventually enters a thick forest of subalpine fir beyond a small stream. From here to Walupt Creek, occasional views northward to the spectacular Goat Rocks help pass the time.

You'll reach Walupt Creek and numerous possible campsites eight miles from

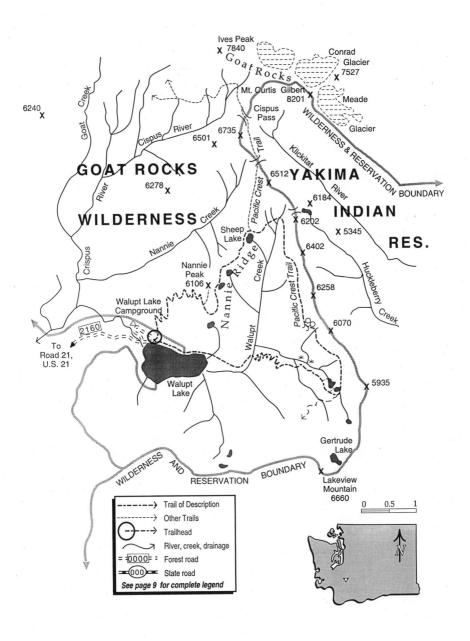

Ives Peak
X 7840

Goat Rocks

Conrad Glacier
X 7527

Mt. Curtis Gilbert
8201 X

Meade Glacier

Cispus Pass

6240 X

Goat Creek

Cispus River

6501 X 6735 X

Goat Rocks River

Pacific Crest Trail

GOAT ROCKS

6278 X

WILDERNESS & RESERVATION
BOUNDARY

6512 **YAKIMA**

Klickitat River

6184
X
6202

X 5345

INDIAN

WILDERNESS

Crispus Creek

Nannie Creek

Sheep Lake

6402

RES.

Crispus River

Nannie Peak
6106 X

Nannie Ridge

6258

Walupt Creek

Pacific Crest Trail

Huckleberry Creek

Walupt Lake
Campground

2160

6070

To
Road 21,
U.S. 21

Walupt Lake

5935

Gertrude Lake

WILDERNESS AND RESERVATION BOUNDARY

Lakeview Mountain
6660

	Trail of Description
	Other Trails
	Trailhead
	River, creek, drainage
= 0000 =	Forest road
= 000 =	State road

See page 9 for complete legend

0   0.5   1

N

the trailhead. Hop across the creek and jog west, crossing two more cascading creeks, and traverse the north wall of the basin.

The Nannie Ridge Trail starts on the north side of Sheep Lake, and you'll part company here with PCT travelers and turn left. Camp at 5,710-foot Sheep Lake to enjoy a superb view of Mount Adams across the water.

The ridgeline trail ascends a low hill beyond the lake, affording one last unforgettable view of the Goat Rocks. The undulating trail then passes 400 feet above a remote lakelet and descends to avoid the cliff-bound east side of 6,106-foot Nannie Peak to another pond with good, timbered campsites.

From the pond, you must climb 300 feet to regain Nannie Ridge. At the ridge, the faint trail to Nannie Peak beckons with the promise of more far-flung vistas.

The main trail, badly eroded in places, switchbacks steadily into increasing timber to complete the loop at Walupt Lake. □

HIKE 19 McCOY PASS TO DARK MEADOW

General description: A moderate 4.6 mile round trip day hike or overnighter to a beautiful hanging valley meadow in the Dark Divide Roadless Area of the Gifford Pinchot National Forest.
Elevation gain and loss: +880; -450 feet.
Trailhead elevation: 3,920 feet.
High point: 4,800 feet.
Maps: McCoy Peak 7.5-minute USGS quad; Gifford Pinchot National Forest map.
Season: July through October.
Water availability: Spring at 1.9 miles.

Finding the trailhead: From Randle, proceed south on signed Forest Road 25 for one mile, then turn left onto Forest Road 23 and drive another 7.9 miles to Forest Road 28 and turn right (south). After another mile, turn left onto unpaved Forest Road 29 at Yellowjacket Ponds Recreation Site: the sign points to Boundary Trail. Follow this good one lane gravel road, with turnouts, as it steadily ascends southward high above McCoy Creek. The final three miles are narrow and rocky. After fifteen miles you reach the Boundary Trail at McCoy Pass, where there is limited parking in roadside turnouts.

The hike: From the 5,000-foot-plus divide between the Lewis and Cispus rivers, three prominent ridges extend more than ten miles northward toward the lowland valley of the Cispus. These four major ridges are rugged and capped by craggy summits. They are some of the most outstanding peaks west of the Cascade crest in southern Washington. This scenic high country is traversed by more than a dozen trails, including the forty-three-mile long Boundary Trail. It is wonderful hiking country and often overlooked by Washington hikers.

The trip to Dark Meadow is a short but occasionally steep hike, crossing

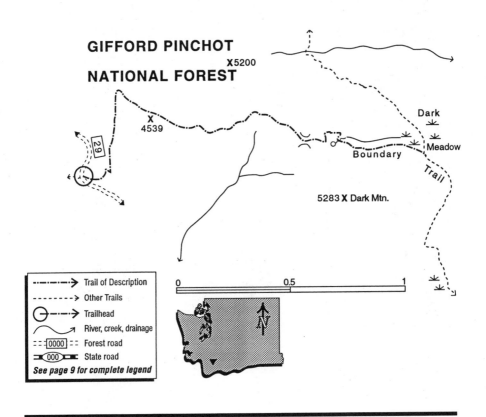

GIFFORD PINCHOT
X5200
NATIONAL FOREST

X
4539

29

Dark

Meadow

Boundary

Trail

5283 **X** Dark Mtn.

· — · · — · · —>	Trail of Description
- - - - - - - ->	Other Trails
⊖ — · · —>	Trailhead
⌒	River, creek, drainage
= = {0000} = =	Forest road
◼⟨000⟩◼	State road

See page 9 for complete legend

0   0.5   1

N

the eastermost north-south divide en route to a peaceful meadow and fabulous views of Mount Adams and Goat Rocks.

There are good possible campsites at Dark Meadow, and side trip opportunities along the Boundary and Juniper Ridge trails may entice some hikers, even families with children, to spend more than a day in this scenic basin.

The trail begins on the east side of McCoy Pass, initially winding among some very large Douglas-firs, western hemlocks, and silver firs before ascending a moderate grade into a younger fir forest.

Switchback up the sloping crest of a northwest-trending ridge, which is followed eastward to a sidehill ascent upon south-facing slopes. These open slopes are thick with shrubs such as tobacco brush (*ceanothus*) and evergreen huckleberry, and enlivened by the blooms of tiger lily, lupine, paintbrush, and beargrass.

Expansive views stretch southward across the vast, sloping plateau of the Cascades to the peaks of Indian Heaven and beyond to Mount Hood.

Approaching the ridge ahead, the trail cuts a swath through thickets of huckleberry and mountain ash and finally mounts the crest just north of the

A hiker takes a break before entering Dark Meadow. Ron Adkison photo.

black volcanic battlements of Dark Mountain. Below and to the east lies the verdant basin harboring Dark Meadow, and beyond rises Table Mountain and the perpetually white Mount Adams. The vast huckleberry thickets and scattered trees are unusual in the western Cascades. This region is still recovering from the devastating fires of 1902 and 1918.

From the ridge, the trail descends at a moderate grade amid huckleberry thickets, briefly levels off on a small bench and then curves into the lower level of the basin after it passes below a small spring. Fill water bottles here if staying overnight.

In the meadows on the basin floor, wind among willow thickets to meet northbound Trail 263 to Juniper Ridge, 2.6 miles from the trailhead. The Boundary Trail continues southeastward for 3.25 miles to Summit Prairie.

Good possible campsites lie in the forest east of the meadow. □

HIKE 20 McCOY PASS TO HOLDAWAY BUTTE

General description: A moderate 5.6-mile round trip day hike to a grand vista point in the Dark Divide Roadless Area of the Gifford Pinchot National Forest.

Elevation gain and loss: +1,000 feet; -50 feet.

Trailhead elevation: 3,920 feet.

High point: Holdaway Butte, 4,873 feet.

Maps: McCoy Peak 7.5-minute USGS quad; Gifford Pinchot National Forest map.

Season: Late June through October.

Water availability: None; carry an adequate supply.

Finding the trailhead: Follow directions given in Hike 19.

The hike: Holdaway Butte, only a minor bump on the lofty ridge dividing Yellowjacket and McCoy creeks, doesn't compare to the spectacular craggy summits that dominate the Dark Divide Roadless Area. What the butte offers is a short hike to expansive vistas of not only the Dark Divide country but also much of Washington's southern Cascades.

The trail heads west from McCoy Pass, traversing south-facing slopes in fir forest. Vine maple and evergreen huckleberry form the shrubby understory, while bracken fern, beargrass, and Oregon grape bedeck the trail.

After 0.7 mile, the trail crosses to the north slope of the ridge via a 4,000-foot saddle then descends gently into a small basin dotted with meadows where Alaska yellow cedars appear amidst the fir forest.

Views from Holdaway Butte. Ron Adkison photo.

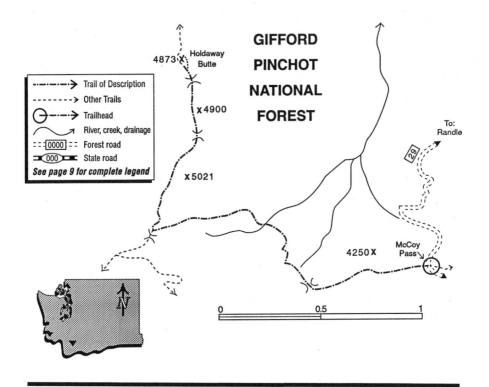

GIFFORD
PINCHOT
NATIONAL
FOREST

4873 X   Holdaway
Butte

X 4900

X 5021

To:
Randle

4250 X

McCoy
Pass

Legend:

- ·—·—·—> Trail of Description
- ------> Other Trails
- ⊖·—·—> Trailhead
- River, creek, drainage
- = = [0000] = = Forest road
- State road

See page 9 for complete legend

0   0.5   1

On the western skyline above are two prominent, brush-clad buttes and
the trail soon begin a moderately steep ascent to the saddle between them.

Topping out on the 4,525-foot saddle 1.7 miles from the trailhead, a junction appears; turn right, climbing steeply. The grade soon eases, and a pleasant
traverse ensues. The vegetation alternates from huckleberry thickets to stands
of fir and hemlock just west of the ridge's crest.

Surmount the crest just north of Point 5021, then traverse easy terrain to
another saddle immediately south of Holdaway Butte. Leave the main trail
here and follow the steep, pumice-covered path north up the ridge for 0.1 mile
to the open summit.

Rugged McCoy Peak ridge stretches away to the north, its steep slopes
plunging more than 3,000 feet into the canyons of Yellowjacket and McCoy
creeks. From the south to the northwest are several prominent Dark Divide
peaks: Hat Rock, Craggy Peak, Shark and Kirk rocks, Badger Peak, and the
curious splintered crag of Pinto Rock.

Mount St. Helens and the tall peaks of the Mount Margaret country rise
to the western skyline. The blocky crest of Juniper Ridge to the east
foregrounds a grand view of the immense ice dome of Mount Adams. ☐

HIKE 21 *BUTTER CREEK TO THE TATOOSH RANGE*

General description: A fine round-trip day hike or overnighter leading to the grassy crest of the Tatoosh Range south of Mount Rainier National Park in the Tatoosh Wilderness. Distances: three miles to first junction; 3.75 miles to Tatoosh Lakes; 4.75 miles to Tatoosh Lookout site.

Elevation gain and loss: 1,800 feet; +1,900 feet, -700 feet to Tatoosh Lakes; +2,518 feet to lookout site.

Trailhead elevation: 2,800 feet.

High point: 5,600 feet; 5,700 feet above lakes; 6,318 feet at lookout site.

Maps: Packwood 15-minute USGS quad or Mount Rainier National Park USGS quad (trail not shown), Gifford Pinchot National Forest map.

Season: July through early October.

Water availability: Seasonal spring at end of maintained trail; abundant water supply at Tatoosh Lakes.

Finding the trailhead: From U.S. Highway 12 in Packwood, turn northwest onto Skate Creek Road No. 52, opposite the ranger station, and drive four miles to eastbound Forest Road 5270, signed for Tatoosh Trail. Follow this dirt road six miles, bear right at a fork in the road and reach the trailhead after another mile. Parking is limited to turnouts alongside the road.

The hike: The Tatoosh Range is composed of a large body of granodiorite, an erosion-resistant granitic rock. Ancient glaciers, however, carved deep cirques and jagged peaks out of this rock. Geologists believe that the Tatoosh Range in pre-Mount Rainier times (more than one million years ago) bore a strong resemblance to the Tatoosh of today. The range is part of the ancient Cascade landscape upon which Mount Rainier was built. It lies partly within Mount Rainier National Park and is protected from development on its southern portion in the new Tatoosh Wilderness.

This scenic day hike or overnighter will lead you into the heart of the Tatoosh Wilderness. Broad, sloping alpine meadows, peaks, vista points, and two lakes constitute the major attractions of this strenuous ascent. Carry plenty of water, as little is available en route. As usual, mosquitoes and biting flies may annoy you in early to midsummer.

From the trailhead, the splendid view up the canyon to craggy Tatoosh summits and ice-bound Mount Rainier is just a sample of the scenery to come. The trail begins in a shady forest of western hemlock, silver fir, and Douglas-fir and soon switchbacks into a drier forest of Douglas-fir.

A traverse above a Butter Creek tributary follows, across wildflower-brightened slopes clad in silver fir and Alaska yellow-cedar. Ahead loom the grassy western slopes of the Tatoosh.

Finally, amid those flower-filled meadows, the trail switchbacks past a spring and reaches a junction. Trails lead north, south, and east, and all are faint in places and sometimes hard to follow.

For excellent vistas of Mount Rainier and the northern Tatoosh, follow the trail heading north for half a mile to a west-trending ridge. Take the southern trail for half a mile across meadowed slopes and through stands of Alaska yellow-cedar, mountain hemlock, and subalpine fir to another west-trending

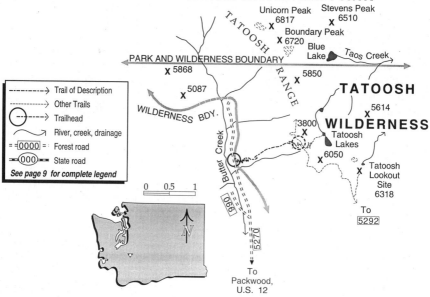

ridge offering fine vistas of Mount Adams, Mount St. Helens, and the tip of Mount Hood in the south. For even better views, continue following this faint trail southeastward, and then turn north for another 0.75 mile to Peak 6318, former site of the Tatoosh Lookout. If you head east from the junction, you can switchback upward on the well-worn path (watch for deer and elk) to the 5,700-foot saddle overlooking the remote Tatoosh Lakes, a timberline campsite for experienced cross-country travelers.

There's a fair campsite just south of the junction, where early-season trickles provide a source of water.

After enjoying this scenic and uncrowded range, retrace the route to the trailhead. ☐

The high meadows of the Tatoosh Range south of Mount Rainier are spectacular in their own right, but as elsewhere in the southern Cascades, the inescapable presence of the Mountain dominates the scenery. Ron Adkison photo.

One of three species of marmot in the state, the hoary marmot is a boisterous, well-known denizen of alpine heights, one of the few animals adapted to survive in that harsh climate. Bob Arrington photo.

Sighting a velvet-antlered buck is one of many rewards awaiting backcountry travelers. Bob Arrington photo.

HIKE 22 *CARLTON CREEK TO FISH AND CRAG LAKES*

General description: An eleven-mile round-trip backpack to three Cascade-crest lakes southeast of Mount Rainier National Park in the William O. Douglas Wilderness.

Elevation gain and loss: +1,900 feet, -50 feet.

Trailhead elevation: 3,150 feet.

High point: 5,000 feet.

Maps: White Pass, Bumping Lake 15-minute USGS quads; Gifford Pinchot or Wenatchee National Forest maps.

Season: Mid-July through mid-October.

Water availability: Abundant along entire route.

Finding the trailhead: Drive State Route 123 to its junction with eastbound Forest Road 44 (Carlton Creek Road), a quarter mile south of the Mount Rainier National Park boundary, about fifty-four miles southeast of Enumclaw and 9.5 miles northeast of Packwood. Follow gravel Forest Road 44 northeastward (there are some steep and narrow stretches) for 7.1 miles to the trailhead at a permanent roadblock. Park here, where a spur road descends to Carlton Creek.

The hike: North of the Bumping River, the Cascade crest sheds its blanket of timber and rises to craggy heights. Many timberline lakes rest in shady, east-facing cirques below the 6,000-foot-plus peaks.

This fine weekender visits three mountain lakes at the headwaters of the Bumping River in the William O. Douglas Wilderness. Douglas, an ardent conservationist and associate justice of the U.S. Supreme Court, was born and raised in the Yakima Valley in the shadow of this 167,000-acre wildland.

Finding water will be no problem, but abundant water usually means clouds of mosquitoes during early summer. Trout fishing in the lakes is fair.

From the trailhead, walk down the short spur road to Carlton Creek and cross it via a large yellow-cedar log. The trail skirts the edge of a replanted clearcut and enters the William O. Douglas Wilderness. It has muddy sections, fallen logs, and lots of exposed tree roots. During the final 1.5 miles to Carlton Pass, numerous small streams cross the trail, further hampering steady progress.

Midway to the pass, the trail crosses a boulder-strewn clearing below a talus slope. Surrounded by dense forest, this shady microclimate hosts plants such as red heather, phlox, and hellebore, which are typically found in colder high-elevation habitats.

The trail surmounts the Cascade crest at 4,160-foot Carlton Pass amid a forest of silver firs, then gently descends along the north shore of marshy Fish Lake to a juncture with the Pacific Crest Trail (PCT).

Fish Lake is in a state of transition from lake to meadow. There are campsites at the lake, but they're too close to the shore and should be avoided. Campsites are available a quarter mile south along the PCT.

Turn left at the junction and climb the south-facing slope via five switchbacks. The PCT contours above Buck Lake before crossing the outlet stream of Crag Lake. The trail then switchbacks once and heads for the lake basin, soon reaching a short spur leading down to the lake and good campsites.

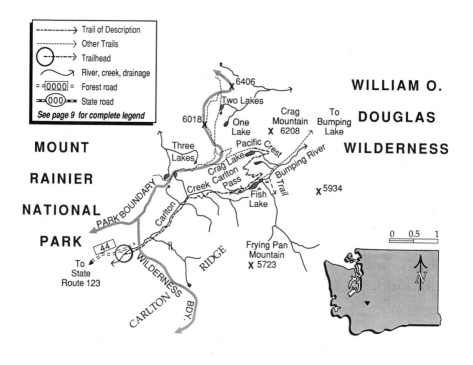

Crag Lake itself makes a good base camp for exploring the lakes to the north along the Cascade crest. Three Lakes, two of which lie within Mount Rainier National Park, are an easy two-mile jaunt west of Crag Lake.

Return the same way. ☐

HIKE 23 *BEAR CREEK MOUNTAIN*

General description: A moderate 7.2 mile round trip day hike to an alpine peak in the Goat Rocks Wilderness.
Elevation gain and loss: 1,320 feet.
Trailhead elevation: 6,010 feet.
High point: Bear Creek Mountain, 7,336 feet.
Maps: White Pass 15-minute USGS quad or Goat Rocks Wilderness map (topographic); Wenatchee National Forest map.
Season: Mid-July through September.
Water availability: Available sporadically along initial 2.8 miles.

Finding the trailhead: From U.S. Highway 12, eight miles east of White Pass and forty-seven miles west of Interstate 82 in Yakima, turn southwest onto paved Tieton Road (Forest Road 12) which is signed for Clear Lake. Follow the pavement around the west and south shores of Clear Lake (sometimes dry) for 5.3 miles, then turn right just beyond Cold Creek onto gravel Forest Road 1205. After 2.7 miles, bear right where Road 742 forks left, uphill.

Turn left after another 2.1 miles onto road 757, where a sign indicates Bear Creek Mountain Trail. Continue straight ahead after another 0.4 mile, ignoring a road that forks to the right. You'll reach a sign pointing to your trail after another 0.5 mile; bear right and, after 1.4 miles, turn right again onto an

A hiker enjoys the views from the summit of Bear Creek Mountain. Ron Adkison photo.

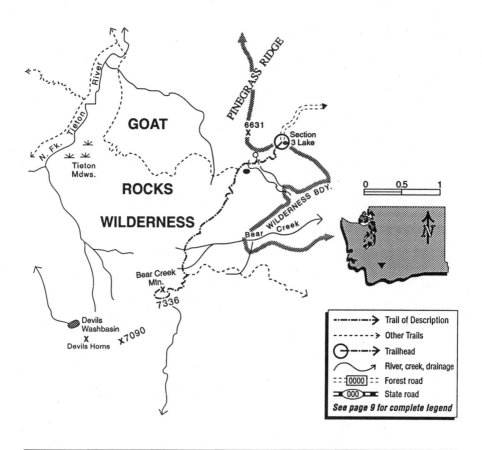

unsigned road that climbs a hill. This road is rough, narrow, and rutted, and must be driven with care. The road is passable to passenger cars with high clearance.

The trailhead parking area is at Section 3 Lake, after another 2.4 miles or 14.8 miles from U.S. Highway 12.

The hike: Beginning at one of the highest elevation trailheads in Washington's Cascades, this scenic dayhike leads through timberline forests, across meadows filled with flowers most of the summer and ascends a glacier-carved cirque, ending atop an alpine peak where glorious vistas unfold of the snowy Goat Rocks, Mount Rainier, and Mount Adams.

The scenic basins traversed en route and the small creeks that drain them may invite an overnight stay, which makes this area a particularly good choice for families introducing their children to high mountain backpacking.

For the adventurous and experienced backpacker, Devils Washbasin, a small

The trail to Bear Creek Mountain wends through beautiful meadows. Ron Adkison photo.

lake 1.5 difficult cross-country miles from Bear Creek Mountain, offers a dramatic destination and fishing for pan-sized cutthroats.

From the trailhead, the trail curves gently uphill past Section 3 Lake (not much more than a frog-filled pond) and into a timberline forest of subalpine fir and mountain hemlock. The dark volcanic spires of Pinegrass Ridge jut skyward west of the trail.

Quite soon the wilderness boundary is passed, beyond which the trail curves southwest onto sunny slopes where trailside trees thin enough to offer glimpses of Bear Creek Mountain to the south.

After 0.5 mile, cross the runoff of three springs watering a verdant, sloping meadow enlivened by the brilliant colors of paintbrush, lupine, bog orchid, and elephanthead. The trail ahead traverses above a small tarn, passes through another flower-speckled meadow and crosses a spring's runoff, then opens up into a more expansive, but dry meadow; soon thereafter it meets Tieton Meadow Trail, forking right 0.9 mile from the trailhead.

Bear left and cross more lovely meadows and proceed into increasingly smaller groves of subalpine fir, mountain hemlock, whitebark pine, and Alaska yellow-cedar. Upon entering the spacious cirque beneath Bear Creek Mountain, cross several small streams while winding among stunted trees and flower-filled meadows. Another junction will be encountered 1.9 miles from the last; bear right and go uphill.

Views expand with every step as you labor up the steep, rocky, and sandy trail. Snow patches may obscure the trail until late summer in some years. Eventually the trail crests the ridge just east of the rocky peak. Follow the ridgeline trail as it winds upward among ground-hugging trees to the summit.

The vast panorama that unfolds is breathtaking. The caldera formed by the peaks of Goat Rocks and the great icy cones of Mount Adams and Mount Rainier dominate the view from south to west. Northward beyond Fifes Peaks, Norse Peak, and the forested cinder cone landscape of the William O. Douglas Wilderness, peaks as far away as Mount Daniel near Snoqualmie Pass are visible.

Northeastward, the horizon is punctuated by the Stuart Range, and eastward the forested plateaus of the Cascades fade into the hazy distance of the Yakima Valley. □

HIKE 24 ROUND PASS TO GOBBLERS KNOB AND GOAT LAKE

General description: A moderate 15.3-mile, round-trip backpack or strenuous all-day hike on the boundary of Mount Rainier National Park and Glacier View Wilderness, featuring awe-inspiring vistas and a secluded mountain lake.
Elevation gain and loss: +2,625 feet, -800 feet.
Trailhead elevation: 2,875 feet.
High point: Gobblers Knob, 5,485 feet.
Maps: Mount Wow 7.5-minute USGS quad; Mount Rainier National Park USGS quad.
Season: July through mid-October.
Water availability: Carry water if you're going only as far as the lookout. If you plan to stay overnight, you'll find all the water you need at Goat Lake, but it should be purified before drinking.

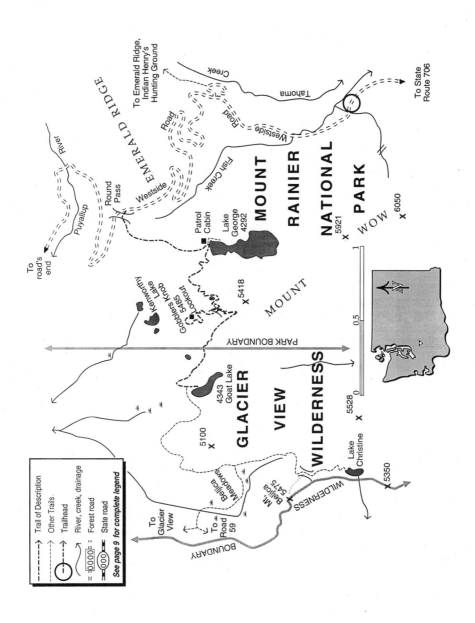

Permit: Required only for overnight camping in Mount Rainier National Park.

Finding the trailhead: Drive east from the Nisqually Entrance for 0.8 mile and turn northeast onto unpaved West Side Road. Due to a washout, the road is closed at the three-mile point, thus hikers must walk the final four miles of the road to reach the old Round Pass Trailhead. The Park Service is still in the planning process to decide the future of this road, so check with park headquarters on the status of this road before beginning the hike.

The hike: This overnighter offers a tremendous vista from the lookout atop 5,485-foot Gobblers Knob, an easy downhill stroll to Goat Lake within tiny (3,050 acres) Glacier View Wilderness, and solitude seldom enjoyed within the national park.

The hike begins at the road closure on the Westside Road. The closed road climbs gently at first, then moderately, gaining 1,000 feet of elevation in four miles as it switchbacks upon forested slopes to the beginning of the trail proper at Round Pass.

From Round Pass, the wide trail ascends an easy grade for 0.9 mile to Lake George, through a shady forest of western hemlock, Alaska yellow-cedar, silver fir and Douglas-fir. This scenic lake, elevation 4,292 feet, lies in a deep cirque gouged into the north flank of Mount Wow. It's a popular destination for day hikers and beginning backpackers. A patrol cabin lies at the north end of the lake, with numerous shady campsites nearby.

Turn right at Lake George and climb one mile through the forest to a junction just below the crest of Mount Wow.

To reach Gobblers Knob, turn right and climb through flower gardens below precipitous cliffs. The trail jogs around to the north ridge to reach the lookout. Subalpine fir, Alaska yellow-cedar, and hemlock cling to the summit rocks.

The view to the north and west is marred by clearcuts, but the remainder of the vista is simply magnificent. Perhaps no other vantage point offers such a commanding look at the immense hulk of Mount Rainier. Glaciers have reshaped this volcanic masterpiece by encircling it with a series of cirques and buttresses. In summer the muffled roar of glacial meltwater mingles with the soft sound of wind through the trees to calm city-weary hikers.

The view clockwise from Mount Rainier includes the Tatoosh Range, the distant Goat Rocks, craggy Mount Wow, the imposing cliff at High Rock, Mount St. Helens, and, closer at hand, the peaks of Mount Beljica and Glacier View, and the foothills of the Cascade Range disappearing into the often-hazy Puget Sound lowland. On clear days the outline of the Olympics is visible on the far western horizon.

After enjoying the vista, return to the junction, turn right, and, after one easy mile downhill, reach Goat Lake and campsites shaded by silver fir and hemlock.

You could easily spend an extra day exploring the Glacier View Wilderness, including hikes to Mount Beljica and the summit of Glacier View. □

HIKE 25 *VAN TRUMP PARK*

General description: A five-mile, round-trip day hike leading past a series of spectacular waterfalls to timberline flower gardens on the south flank of Mount Rainier in Mount Rainier National Park.

Elevation gain and loss: +2,000 feet, -250 feet.

Trailhead elevation: 3,600 feet.

High point: 5,600 feet.

Maps: Mount Rainier West 7.5 minute USGS quad or Mount Rainier National Park USGS quad.

Season: Mid-July through mid-October.

Water availability: Abundant.

Permit: Required for overnight camping (no camping allowed in Van Trump Park).

Finding the trailhead: Drive east from the Nisqually Entrance (at the southwestern corner of the park) and follow the road along the Nisqually River for ten miles. Park in the small parking area on the northwest side of the road just beyond milepost ten. Or drive 23.5 miles west from the Stevens Canyon Entrance to find the trailhead. There is an entrance fee.

The hike: Van Trump Park in Mount Rainier National Park is a hanging valley resplendent with summer wildflowers. The trail passes some of the park's most beautiful waterfalls and offers excellent views of Mount Rainier and its south-slope glaciers.

From the trailhead, the route climbs toward Van Trump Creek. You'll enjoy a good view southward across the canyon of the Nisqually River to jagged Tatoosh Range summits. After a quarter mile the trail bridges the creek above a spectacular, roaring cataract. Rarely out of sight and always within sound of the tumultuous creek, you'll climb steadily through a forest of Alaska yellow-cedar, silver fir, and hemlock.

After 1.25 miles, the trail crosses Van Trump Creek below another sheet of white water via a footlog and handrail. Round the bend and confront one of the most impressive descents in the park—thunderous Comet Falls plunging 320 feet from the hanging valley of Van Trump Park.

To reach the park, continue upward, gaining 700 feet of elevation in one mile to the ridge above the timberline meadows.

You can ascend this ridge northward toward Van Trump Glaciers, quickly trading flower meadows for rock and ice. Or you can head for 5,935-foot Mildred Point, the hill rising immediately northwest of Van Trump Park. To get there, descend to the creek bisecting the park and proceed southwest for half a mile. Then take a right-forking trail uphill for another half mile to the point, which offers a head-on view of the Kautz Glacier. Rainier looms directly above, and you'll certainly get a stiff neck if you gaze upward toward Point Success—the south summit—for too long.

After enjoying this scenic timberline locale, retrace the route through the forest and past roaring white water to the trailhead. ☐

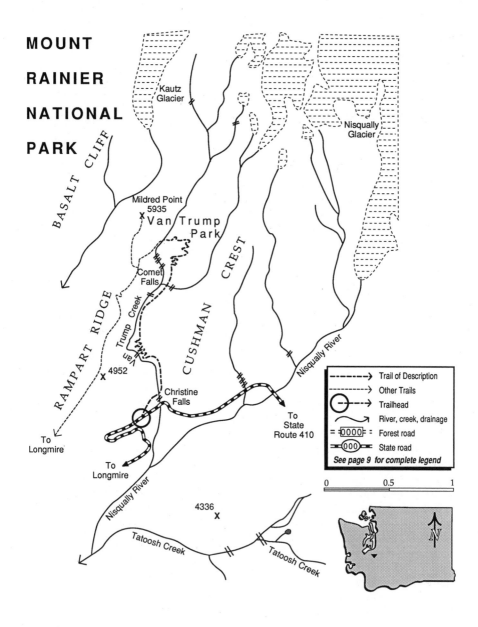

MOUNT

RAINIER

NATIONAL

PARK

BASALT CLIFF

Kautz Glacier

Nisqually Glacier

Mildred Point
5935
X Van Trump Park

Comet Falls

CUSHMAN CREST

Trump Creek

Van RAMPART RIDGE

X 4952

Christine Falls

To Longmire

To Longmire

Nisqually River

Nisqually River

To State Route 410

Trail of Description
Other Trails
Trailhead
River, creek, drainage
Forest road
State road
See page 9 for complete legend

0   0.5   1

4336
X

Tatoosh Creek

Tatoosh Creek

N

HIKE 26 STEVENS CANYON ROAD TO SNOW LAKE

General description: An easy 2.5-mile, round-trip day hike or overnighter to a timberline lake in the Tatoosh Range in Mount Rainier National Park.
Elevation gain and loss: +300 feet, -200 feet.
Trailhead elevation: 4,125 feet.
High point: Snow Lake, 4,750 feet.
Maps: Mount Rainier East 7.5-minute USGS quad or Mount Rainier National Park USGS quad.
Season: Mid-July through mid-October.
Water availability: Abundant.
Permit: For overnight camping, be sure to obtain a backcountry permit at the park entrance, the Hiker Center in Longmine, or any visitor center in the park.

Finding the trailhead: Proceed 15.5 miles west from the Stevens Canyon Entrance to the trailhead on the south side of the road, indicated by the usual small, metal destination-and-mileage sign. Or drive eighteen miles east from the Nisqually Entrance to the first trailhead east of Louise Lake. An entry fee is collected at all park entrances.

The hike: Resting in a deep cirque in the shadow of the highest Tatoosh Range summit, Snow Lake offers an easy and highly scenic destination for day hikers and beginning backpackers. This hike is an excellent choice for families with small children.

There is more to Mount Rainier National Park than The Mountain, and this hike is a good case in point. The granitic Tatoosh Range, glacier-carved and topped by jagged summits, is a worthy destination in its own right, and since Rainier isn't visible from Snow Lake, you may not even feel like you're in the park.

The trail climbs from the Stevens Canyon Road through alders and wildflowers to the ridge known as The Bench, amid the bleached snags of a defunct forest. In early summer, at least seven cascading creeks descend the northeastern slope of Peak 6524, directly above (southwest of) The Bench. Sections of the trail through fragile alpine meadows consist of wooden planks. Red heather, avalanche lily, pink spirea, bear grass, and lupine are among the colorful wildflowers here.

Views from this ridge are superb, including Mount Rainier and 11,138-foot Little Tahoma Peak, a spectacular crag in its own right but completely overshadowed by the bulk of Rainier. The grassy crest of Stevens Ridge, recovering from an old burn, forms the northeastern skyline. Far on the eastern horizon are the peaks of Nelson Ridge, east of the Cascade crest in the William O. Douglas Wilderness.

The trail descends through scrub timber—subalpine fir, mountain hemlock, Alaska yellow-cedar, whitebark pine, and silver fir—passing above Bench Lake after 0.7 mile. A brief stint across the floor of the basin leads to the stiff climb up to Snow Lake. A short, easy-to-find spur trail leads halfway around the lake to Snow Lake Camp (stoves only).

The trail continues along the western shore of emerald-green Snow Lake,

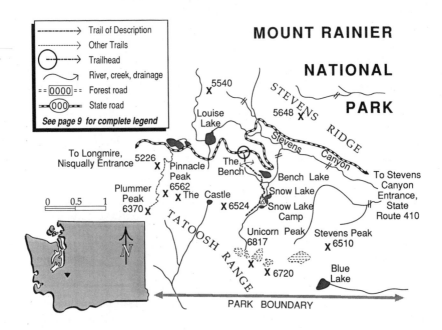

----------→	Trail of Description
----------→	Other Trails
◯─────→	Trailhead
↰	River, creek, drainage
== 0000 ==	Forest road
⊙000⊙	State road

See page 9 for complete legend

MOUNT RAINIER

NATIONAL

PARK

X 5540

Louise Lake

STEVENS RIDGE

5648 X

Stevens Canyon

To Longmire, Nisqually Entrance   5226 X

Pinnacle Peak

The Bench

Bench Lake

To Stevens Canyon Entrance, State Route 410

Plummer Peak 6370 X

6562 X X The Castle

X 6524

Snow Lake

Snow Lake Camp

0   0.5   1

TATOOSH RANGE

Unicorn Peak 6817

Stevens Peak X 6510

X 6720

Blue Lake

PARK BOUNDARY

elevation 4,700 feet, fed by the milky meltwater of Unicorn Glacier, to the headwall at the south end of the cirque. Lovely waterfalls enter the basin from three sides.

Snow Lake is a good introduction to timberline camping. Campsites are sheltered by stunted Alaska yellow-cedar, subalpine fir, and mountain hemlock. Trout fishing in Snow Lake is poor, but anglers may have better luck in nearby Bench Lake.

If you're an experienced hiker, you can continue upward toward the glacier and the 6,817-foot horn of Unicorn Peak, looming due south of Snow Lake, but the unstable talus slopes make that route hazardous. Return the way you came. □

HIKE 27 *YAKIMA PARK TO GRAND PARK*

General description: An eleven-mile, round-trip backpack leading to the largest timberline park in Mount Rainier National Park.

Elevation gain and loss: +800 feet, -1,640 feet.

Trailhead elevation: 6,400 feet.

High point: 6,800 feet.

Maps: Sunrise 7.5-minute USGS quad or Mount Rainier National Park USGS quad.

Season: Mid-July through early October.

Water availability: Water is readily available until the last 1.25 miles.

Permit: Obtain a backcountry permit at the White River Hiker Center at the park entrance for overnight camping.

Finding the trailhead: Follow directions given for Hike 28, then proceed another 2.5 miles to the huge parking area at Sunrise Lodge. An entry fee is collected at the park entrance.

The hike: In its youth, perhaps 700,000 years ago, the volcanic cone that was to become Mount Rainier issued voluminous flows of andesitic lava from vents along its flanks. This lava flowed into and buried many of the canyons surrounding the cone.

Grand Park is the site of such a lava flow. The canyon of the "Grand Park River" was buried under 2,000 feet of andesitic lava. Since this material resists erosion, Grand Park's present-day plateau stands alone above areas of less-resistant rock that were eroded away by water and ice. To reach this isolated plateau, you'll start at the highest trailhead in the park and travel through an alpine environment before descending through subalpine forests and flower fields to Grand Park. There you'll find a flower-filled meadow nearly two miles long and three quarters of a mile wide, as well as an interesting perspective of the north side of Mount Rainier.

From the huge parking area next to the Sunrise Visitor Center in Yakima Park, follow the signs for the Wonderland Trail. After hiking north for 0.3 mile, bear left at a junction and proceed west along the ridge of the Sourdough Mountains.

In another 0.3 mile you'll reach a second junction, where you should also bear left. A grand vista to the north includes Mount Stuart, Glacier Peak, and on a clear day, Mount Baker.

On the northeastern flank of Rainier, you'll see the massive Emmons Glacier, which flows into the White River Canyon. That glacier, as well as many other Cascade Range glaciers, has receded noticeably during this century.

The Wonderland Trail leaves the stunted subalpine firs, whitebark pines, and Alaska yellow-cedars just below fenced-in Frozen Lake. Shortly beyond the lake is a three-way junction. If you want a close-up look at Rainier and its north-side glaciers, turn left and ascend Burroughs Mountain for one mile. If you're looking for far-reaching vistas, turn right toward the Mount Fremont lookout, 1.25 miles away.

But to reach Grand Park, take the middle fork and descend through barren alpine fells into the bowl of Berkeley Park and another junction after 0.7 mile. Only alpine cushion plants survive here, including red Indian paintbrush, lupine, white heather, phlox, and western anemone. Turn right, parting company with hikers using the Wonderland Trail, and proceed northward down Lodi Creek. You'll leave most day hikers behind.

As the trail descends, timber cover increases. First you'll see scattered islands of trees; those will eventually give way to subalpine forest broken occasionally along the creek by lovely meadows. The trail leaves the stream above Affi Falls after 4.1 miles, then ascends 400 feet along a gentle ridge to Point 5763 at the southwestern end of Grand Park. Another half mile leads to a junction. The

HIKE 27 *YAKIMA PARK TO GRAND PARK*
HIKE 28 *SUNRISE POINT TO UPPER PALISADES LAKE*

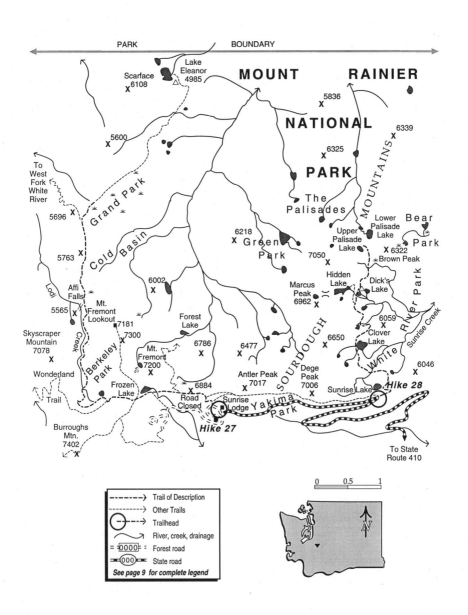

right fork skirts the northern edge of Grand Park, leading to Lake Eleanor in 3.5 miles. The left fork can be incorporated into a multiday loop trip in the northern portion of the park. Lake Eleanor has a backcountry campsite, or you can choose a "cross-country" campsite near Grand Park or in Cold Basin. Cross-country campsites must be located at least 0.25 mile from trails, 0.25 mile from designated campsites, and a minimum of 100 feet from lakes and streams. □

HIKE 28 *SUNRISE POINT TO UPPER PALISADES LAKE*

General description: A 7.4-mile, round-trip day hike or overnighter, offering access to seven subalpine lakes on the dry side of Mount Rainier in Mount Rainier National Park.
Elevation gain and loss: +640 feet; -900 feet.
Trailhead elevation: 6,100 feet.
Maps: White River Park 7.5-minute USGS quad or Mount Rainier National Park USGS quad.
Season: Mid-July through mid-October.
Water availability: Abundant.
Permit: A backcountry permit is required for overnight camping and can be obtained at the White River Hiker Center, the park entrance.

Finding the trailhead: From State Route 410 in Mount Rainier National Park, 3.4 miles north of Cayuse Pass and forty miles southeast of Enumclaw, turn west onto the road signed for White River and Sunrise. Follow this paved road 12.5 miles to the large parking area and Sunrise vista point, located where the road executes a horseshoe bend from east to west. An entry fee is collected at the park entrance.

The hike: This easy, scenic hike on the dry side of the park offers access to more than seven subalpine lakes on the eastern flank of the Sourdough Mountains. Campsites and water are abundant, as are mosquitoes during early summer. Equally attractive as a day hike or weekender, this hike has something for nearly everyone—peaks to climb, lakes to fish, flower gardens to enjoy, and solitude to relish amid subalpine grandeur.

From Sunrise Point, follow the trail along Sunrise Ridge northeastward for 0.3 mile through a hemlock-fir forest. Vistas are grand to the north, east, and south. The trail doubles back on a lower contour and after half a mile turns left to Sunrise Lake, first in a series of timberline lakes dotting the upper reaches of White River Park.

Bear right and proceed across the basin toward Clover Lake. En route you'll pass wildflowers such as buttercups, glacier lilies, and western mountain pasqueflowers. The trail skirts the western shore of the lake and passes a short, plainly visible spur trail to a camping area. Then the main trail gains a low ridge before descending steadily into the next basin, flanked by increasingly thick stands of mountain hemlock and subalpine fir.

Cross the floor of this basin, under the shadow of 6,962-foot Marcus Peak, to an unsigned junction about a mile north of Clover Lake. The left fork climbs quickly to the hanging valley in which Hidden Lake rests. (Hidden Lake is closed to camping) Green Park is an easy jaunt over the ridge from the lake.

Turn right at the junction, hop across Hidden Lake's outlet stream, and shortly reach a right-forking trail to Dick's Lake Camp (stoves only), located in the timber between two small lakes below the trail.

Bearing left, you'll make another brief ascent, but the trail soon levels off in a beautiful flower-decorated meadow next to a clear, meandering stream. Jagged summits loom above the rock glacier immediately to the west.

The trail then climbs to a saddle overlooking Upper Palisades Lake, nestled in a tiny cirque below the volcanic crags of The Palisades. This ridge of andesite, some geologists believe, was formed by molten magma associated with the Tatoosh Pluton that flowed on the surface, rather than cooling underground, as did the main body of the Tatoosh Range. The rocks of the Tatoosh Pluton predate Mount Rainier and comprise the foundation upon which the comparatively young volcano was built.

A faint trail branches right here toward 6,322-foot Brown Peak, the bump on the ridge 0.3 mile to the east.

Campsites are limited at the lake, but there is ample opportunity for cross-country camping. Return to the trailhead via the same route. □

HIKE 29 *CARBON GLACIER*

General description: A seven-mile, round-trip day hike, leading through rain forest to the snout of Washington's largest glacier in Mount Rainier National Park.
Elevation gain and loss: 1,275 feet.
Trailhead elevation: 2,325 feet.
High point: 3,600 feet.
Maps: Mowich Lake 7.5-minute USGS quad or Mount Rainier National Park USGS quad.
Season: June through October.
Water availability: Carbon River is silty, but clear water is available at 2.9 miles.
Permit: A permit for overnight camping can be obtained at the Carbon River Entrance Station.

Finding the trailhead: Follow State Route 165 first south then east from Buckley to the Carbon River Road and turn left; a sign here indicates Carbon River Ranger Station. The trailhead parking area, often packed on weekends, is twenty-three miles from Buckley at the Ipsut Creek campground. You'll have to pay an entry fee at the park entrance.

The hike: Ancient glaciers were largely responsible for creating the lakes and jagged peaks that attract thousands of backcountry enthusiasts to Washington each year. But those glaciers yielded to a warming trend that began about 10,000 years ago, and many present-day Washington glaciers are remnants of a recent cooling trend, known as the Little Ice Age, which

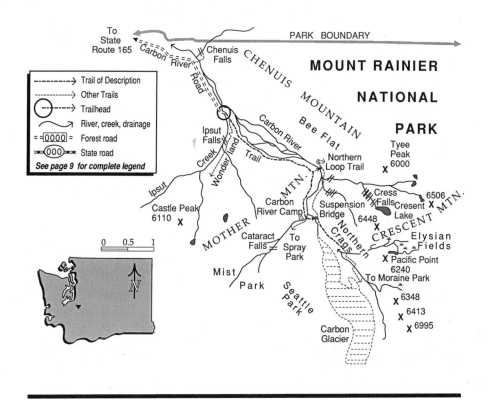

began around 1500 A.D. and ended in the early twentieth century.

Today, heavy precipitation in the Cascade Range nurtures the single largest system of glaciers in the contiguous United States, consisting of more than twenty-six glaciers, most of which emanate from the summit icecap of Mount Rainier.

The Carbon Glacier begins its journey below the largest rock face on Mount Rainier—the 3,000-foot-high Willis Wall just below 14,112-foot Liberty Cap, the mountain's northwest summit—and flows northwestward into the moist forests of the Carbon River (so named because of coal seams near the towns of Wilkeson and Carbonado in the Cascade foothills). Descending to an elevation of approximately 3,500 feet, this glacier reaches a lower elevation than any other in the United States, outside of Alaska.

This easy hike passes through rain forest en route to the snout of Carbon Glacier. Although glaciers and rain forests make for scenic contrast, they both originate from the same source—abundant moisture, caused, in this case, by storms blowing in from the Pacific Ocean.

From the trailhead at Ipsut Creek campground, take the left fork of the Wonderland Trail and proceed into a mossy forest of western hemlock, western redcedar, and Douglas-fir.

Flowing through a boulder-strewn bed, the milky, braided Carbon River—the milkiness is caused by fine particles of "glacial flour" ground from the bedrock by the movement of the ice—is always close at hand. Its flow fluctuates widely, depending upon temperature, time of year, and weather conditions.

The Northern Loop Trail, which can be used for the return trip, originates across the river after two miles. For now, bear right and follow above the river for 0.9 mile to the right-forking Spray Park Trail, reached just after crossing a clear, nonglacial stream. Carbon River Camp (no wood fires) lies nearby.

Stay on the main trail and you'll soon reach a large suspension bridge that spans the riverbed. The rock anchoring the bridge cables bears visible scratches from the abrasion of the ancient Carbon Glacier.

On the opposite side of the bridge is a junction. Take the left fork to loop back to the trailhead. To continue, turn right, climbing steadily to the snout of the glacier, buried under rock debris at the base of a precipitous wall of andesite known as the Northern Crags.

You can continue upward along the steep trail for a better look at the glacier and access to some of the most scenic alpine basins in the park: Moraine Park, Elysian Fields, and Vernal Park. □

HIKE 30 *RAVEN ROOST TO LITTLE CROW BASIN*

General description: A eighteen-mile, round-trip backpack along the scenic Cascade Crest northeast of Mount Rainier in the Norse Peak Wilderness.
Elevation gain and loss: +1,660 feet, -1,620 feet.
Trailhead elevation: 6,198 feet.
High point: Trailhead, 6,198 feet.
Maps: Lester and Bumping Lake 15-minute USGS quads; Wenatchee National Forest map.
Season: July through mid-October.
Water availability: Cougar Valley, 2.2 miles from trailhead, and at Little Crow Basin.

Finding the trailhead: Drive east from Chinook Pass on State Route 410 for 22.5 miles, or west 40.5 miles from Yakima to Little Naches River Road (Forest Road 19) and turn northwest, following the course of the Little Naches. Turn left onto Forest Road 1902 after 2.6 miles, quickly crossing the river via a bridge. At this and subsequent junctions, follow signs indicating Raven Roost. Follow this good dirt road for twelve miles to an excellent viewpoint, from which you can see Mount Rainier in the southwest and Fifes Peaks in the south, just beyond the short spur road to Raven Roost (an even better vista point). Dispersed camping is available at this junction. Trailhead parking is available at Raven Roost.

The hike: North of Chinook Pass and northeast of Mount Rainier, the Cascade crest loses elevation, and its contours become more rounded and heavily forested. Elk and deer inhabit the region, and quiet hikers often

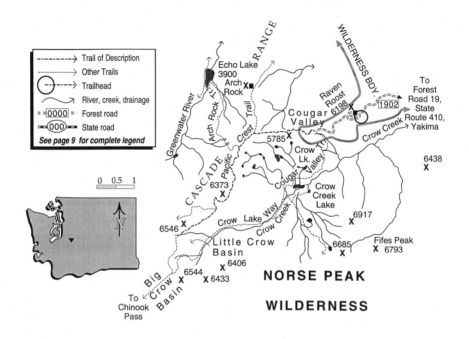

observe them feeding in the meadows in early morning and evening.

This is a ridgeline hike much of the way, and little water is available (only at Cougar Valley's Creek) until Little Crow Basin, nine miles from the trailhead. But the lack of appreciable elevation gain, broad vistas, and colorful wildflowers combine to make this a very attractive weekend trip.

From the trailhead at Raven Roost, follow the closed road generally southwest as it descends open, wildflower-speckled slopes, losing 900 feet of elevation in 2.25 miles to the meadows of Cougar Valley.

From the meadows of Cougar Valley, follow the right fork steeply uphill amid subalpine fir and Englemann spruce. After gaining the first ridge, you'll descend volcanic slopes above a shallow ravine, rich with the color of summer wildflowers. The undulating trail proceeds along this spur ridge for 2.3 miles to the Cascade crest and a junction with the Pacific Crest Trail (PCT).

Turning left onto the PCT, a pleasant 0.6-mile stroll around subalpine fir leads to the junction with the northwestbound Arch Rock Trail, which runs downhill to Saddle Springs and possible campsites three-quarters of a mile in and to Echo Lake, in the canyon of the Greenwater River, in 3.5 miles.

Bear left, continuing the ridgetop journey. Vistas both east and west from the crest are frequent, often dominated by the gleaming white bulk of Mount Rainier. Northward beyond Snoqualmie Pass and the Yakima River, two recognizable peaks in the Alpine Lakes region include the isolated crag of Mount Stuart and snowy Mount Daniel.

Much of the crest route passes through the site of an old burn. Wildflowers are common in sunny openings, including lupine, phlox, yarrow, wild strawberry, waterleaf, glacier lily, buttercup, yellow violet, and senecio.

Avoid numerous well-worn game trails that cross the PCT.

The trail begins descending along the east slope of Peak 6373 to a 5,760-foot saddle and a juncture with westbound Castle Mountain Trail, 5.6 miles from the trailhead.

Stay left; an easy traverse leads to the timberline bowl of Little Crow Basin, gouged into the east slope of the Cascades by an ancient glacier.

Camping is good in this basin. There's even a year-round source of water. Plenty of opportunity for off-trail wandering exists for those so inclined.

The possibility of a fine loop is almost irresistible to many hikers. You can return to the trailhead by following the PCT south over the ridge into the alpine bowl of Big Crow Basin. Head northeast in the basin and descend Crow Creek via the Crow Lake Way Trail. This forested valley walk is a fitting complement to the scenic hike along the crest. Total distance from Little Crow Basin to the trailhead is about twelve miles, mostly downhill. ☐

HIKE 31 *DEEP CREEK TO TUMAC MOUNTAIN*

General description: A ten-mile, round-trip day hike or weekender leading to a volcanic viewpoint in the southern William O. Douglas Wilderness.
Elevation gain and loss: 1,890 feet.
Trailhead elevation: 4,350 feet.
High point: Tumac Mountain, 6,340 feet.
Maps: Bumping Lake, White Pass 15-minute USGS quads; Wenatchee National Forest map.
Season: July through October.
Water availability: Water is abundant but must be purified before drinking.

Finding the trailhead: Proceed to the juncture of Bumping River Road and State Route 410, nineteen miles east of Chinook Pass and forty-four miles west of the I-84/U.S. Highway 12 junction north of Yakima. Follow Bumping River Road for 10.7 miles to the end of the pavement and turn left onto Forest Road 2008, indicated by a Deep Creek campground sign. There's a parking area for hikers at the entrance to Deep Creek Campground, twenty miles from State Route 410. The trail begins on the northwest side of the road at the Twin Sisters Trail sign.

HIKE 31 *DEEP CREEK TO TUMAC MOUNTAIN*

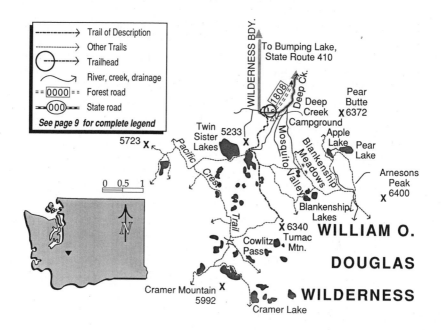

The hike: The volcanic Tumac Plateau, littered with dozens of lakes and ponds, stands in stark contrast to the jagged peaks and glaciers of Mount Rainier to the west, the alpine range of Nelson Ridge to the east, and the craggy head-waters of Bumping River to the north.

The glacier that overrode this lava plateau left behind many lakes as evidence of its passing, ranging from deep lakes of many acres to tiny, shallow ponds, making a superb breeding ground for mosquitoes well into the month of August.

Taken either as a day hike or an overnighter—with a layover at Twin Sisters Lakes, Mosquito Valley, or Pear and Apple lakes—this interesting trip is an excellent introduction to the southern half of the William O. Douglas Wilderness.

The trail heads west to circumnavigate Deep Creek campground before climbing south through a forest of silver fir, mountain hemlock, and Alaska yellow-cedar for 1.5 miles to the edge of the plateau at Little Twin Sister Lake. Fishing for pan-sized trout can be productive here and at other deep lakes on the plateau.

To reach the young volcanic cone of Tumac Mountain, turn left at the lake. You'll reach another junction after 0.4 mile. The left fork leads past true-to-its-name Mosquito Valley and beyond to beautiful Blankenship Meadows in 1.5 miles. A glance at your topographic map will reveal a network of trails on the plateau that can be arranged into a variety of loop trips.

Bear right at the junction toward your goal, visible on the nearby horizon to the southeast. The nearly level trail crosses subalpine meadows, discontinuous timber and abundant wildflowers. Many small subalpine fir trees are invading the flat, wet meadows, growing in sites where snow lingers and the growing season is short. Botanists believe there are a number of reasons for the regeneration of typically treeless sites such as these meadows. A series of dry winters, light frost conditions, an adequate seed crop, and abundant summer moisture may have created the right conditions for these trees to establish themselves. It's likely that many of the meadows on the Tumac Plateau and other sites throughout the Cascades eventually will be overtaken by forest.

The grade increases on the northwest ridge of the cone. The trail joins the westbound Cowlitz Trail just below the summit, leading to the PCT in two miles. Stay left and negotiate one final switchback across volcanic slopes carpeted with heather to reach the 6,340-foot summit of Tumac Mountain, a former lookout site fringed with stunted subalpine fir.

From the top, the entire Tumac Plateau and dozens of lakes will be spread out before your gaze. The alpine ridge on the eastern edge of the plateau hosts the highest peaks in the wilderness. To the south across miles of heavily forested mountains are the summits of the Goat Rocks, Mount Adams, and Mount St. Helens. To the west is inescapable Mount Rainier and the Tatoosh Range, and to the north, American Ridge rises above the Bumping River Canyon, with the startling jumble of volcanic crags—Fifes Peaks—pointing stark volcanic pinnacles into the sky. □

HIKE 32 *PETE'S CREEK TO COLONEL BOB*

General description: A moderate, 8.5-mile day hike or overnighter to a rocky vista point in the Colonel Bob Wilderness of the southwestern Olympic Mountains.
Elevation gain and loss: +3,592 feet, -100 feet.
Trailhead elevation: 1,000 feet.
High point: Colonel Bob, 4,492 feet.
Maps: Quinault Lake, Mt. Christie 15-minute USGS quad; Olympic National Forest map.
Season: July through mid-October.
Water availability: Scarce until year-round stream at 3.25 miles.

Finding the trailhead: Follow U.S. Highway 101 north from Hoquiam for 24.5 miles, and then turn right onto paved Donkey Creek Road (Forest Road 22), as indicated by a Humptulips Ranger Station sign. After seven miles, turn left (north) onto Forest Road 2302, signed for Campbell Tree Grove campground. Right away, pass the Humptulips Work Center (U.S. Forest Service), and come to the end of pavement in four miles. Following signs for Campbell Tree Grove at subsequent junctions, proceed northeastward on Forest Road 2302, a good gravel road, to the Pete's Creek Trailhead, 7.7 miles from pavement and 18.7 miles from the highway.

HIKE 32 *PETE'S CREEK TO COLONEL BOB*

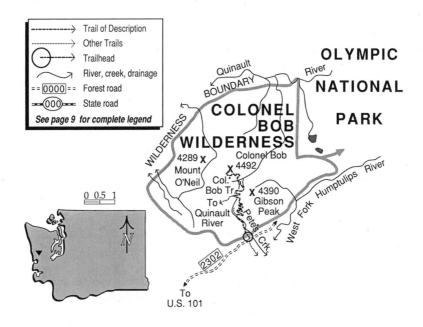

The hike: The entire western half of the Olympic Mountains consists of densely forested mountains dissected by a series of deep river valleys. Peaks become progressively higher toward the eastern half of this mass of mountains.

Rising abruptly from the coastal lowland, the mountains receive the brunt of Pacific Ocean storms and are drenched with enough precipitation to give this region the distinction of being the wettest in the contiguous United States.

Copious moisture in the form of deep, wet winter snowfall shortens the growing season at comparatively low elevations. Thus, the timberline of the west side of the Olympics is quite low, averaging about 5,000 feet in elevation.

These are the youngest of Washington's mountains. Their contours have yet to be rounded and subdued by erosion. Jagged peaks (horns), knife-edged ridges (aretes), glacial cirques (some empty, some brimming with ancient ice), and river valleys whose walls rise thousands of near-vertical feet from their floors all combine to give the range a youthful appearance.

From the Pete's Creek Trailhead, proceed northward at a moderate grade through a lush lowland forest of western hemlock and Douglas-fir. After .9 mile, cross the often-dry streambed of Pete's Creek (many small streams in the Olympics don't flow on the surface during the drier summer months). Avoid a short, left-forking spur trail and bear right.

The trail climbs steadily and, after two miles, passes a small campsite next to the now-flowing creek.

Presently the trail crosses a scree slope emanating from 4,390-foot Gibson

Peak and, after 2.5 miles, joins the Colonel Bob Trail, a longer route climbing up from the Quinault River.

Turn right, climbing steeply through raspberry thickets to a saddle at 3,400 feet elevation. To the north will be your first glimpses into the rugged interior of the Olympics.

Descend to a subalpine bench with running water and campsites sheltered by scattered Alaska yellow-cedars, mountain hemlocks, and silver firs. Mosquitoes are ever present in early summer. This bowl, carpeted by red and white heather, bear grass, pink spirea, and huckleberry, appears to have been excavated by a small glacier. From here, it's one mile and 1,000 feet up the timbered bowl to the 4,492-foot summit of Colonel Bob, a former lookout site.

Views reach deep into the Olympics, punctuated by myriad jagged summits. The deep trench of the Quinault River lies 4,000 feet below the peak to the north.

To the southwest, the blue Pacific stretches toward the horizon. Even the Satsop Towers, one of Washington's nuclear power plants, are visible to the southeast in the Chehalis River Valley. □

HIKE 33 QUINAULT LOOP TRAIL

General description: An easy, four-mile loop hike through the rain forest of the lower Quinault River Valley in Olympic National Forest.
Elevation gain and loss: 120 feet.
Trailhead elevation: 250 feet.
High point: 370 feet.
Maps: Olympic National Forest map and the Quinault Loop Trail map available at the ranger station in the village of Quinault.
Season: March through November.
Water availability: Available at intervals along first three miles.

Finding the trailhead: Follow directions given for Hike 34.

The hike: Conditions along the western slopes of the Olympics are ideal for the development of a temperate rain forest. The two primary environmental influences creating these conditions—abundant precipitation distributed throughout the year and moderate temperatures with little annual variation—exist from southeastern Alaska to northern California, but the western river valleys of the Olympics contain the best examples of temperate rain forest.

As moisture-laden storm clouds drift inland from the Pacific, they strike the western slopes of the Olympics and are forced to rise. As they rise they cool, and since cool air is unable to hold as much moisture as warm air, this moisture is released in quantity. But as the storm clouds descend the eastern side of the range toward Hood Canal and Puget Sound, the air warms again and the clouds retain much of what moisture is left, creating a dramatic rain shadow on the eastern and northern sides of the Olympics. This rain-shadow effect is visible throughout the mountains of the west but seems to be more pronounced in Washington, where very wet western slopes and very dry

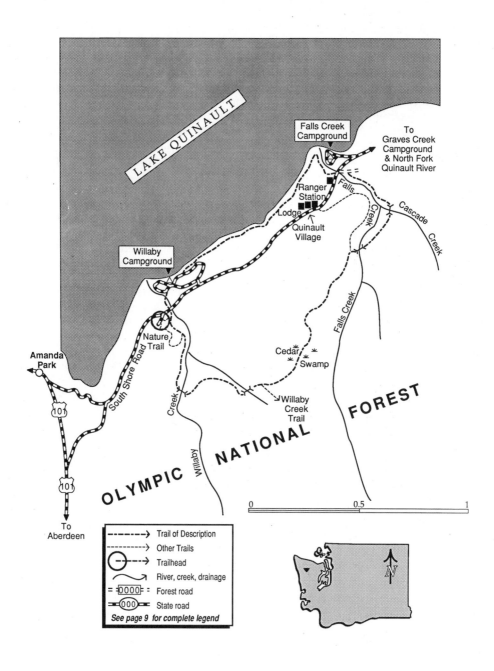

eastern slopes vividly illustrate the phenomenon. For example, approximately 145 inches of moisture fall annually in the lower Quinault River Valley, but a scant seventeen inches fall on the town of Sequim, on the dry northeastern side of the peninsula. Moderate temperatures and all the moisture on the western slopes help to create a fairyland forest where everything is some shade of green.

This easy and scenic loop trail through the Quinault Rain Forest is little used compared with the well-known and popular nature trails of the Hoh Rain Forest. Thus, visitors can enjoy and contemplate the forest in comparative solitude. The optimum season to visit is summer. July, August, and September tend to be the driest months of the year.

From the trailhead, follow the trail eastward toward Willaby Creek to a fork. If you negotiate the entire four-mile loop, you'll return via the left fork.

To start, bear right at the fork. After 0.3 mile you'll come to a junction with the Rain Forest Nature Trail. Keep left here and, at subsequent junctions, follow signs indicating the Loop Trail.

The route proceeds through a classic rain forest, and you'll be dwarfed by giant western redcedars, western hemlocks, Douglas-firs, and Sitka spruces, remnants of a once-vast forest. Vegetation here achieves atypical proportions. Notice the huge ferns and raspberries and devil's club that grows ten feet tall. The shady forest floor is carpeted by mosses, ferns, the tiny white flowers and clover-like leaves of oxalis, and beadruby—typical components of the rain-forest plant community.

The foliage of all trees is draped with clubmoss. Plants grow thick on the acidic forest floor. Fallen, rotting logs form the only suitable substrate on which new plants and trees can establish themselves, and these nurse logs are abundant along the trail.

Tree roots eventually spread around nurse logs to reach the ground, and after the nurse log decays and becomes part of the soil, a row or colonnade of trees is left, standing above the ground on stilts of roots.

Bear left after 1.2 miles where the Willaby Creek Trail forks right, and proceed through a cedar swamp. Many picturesque half-dead redcedars and snags stand throughout this marshy area.

Bearing right at a junction 0.7 mile from Willaby Creek Trail, cross Falls Creek and then Cascade Creek, reaching a dirt road after 1.1 miles.

Turn left onto this road, and you'll soon reach the main, paved road. Turn left again, crossing a bridge and resuming the trail walk along Falls Creek, opposite the campground.

This less-than-wild segment of the hike skirts the south shore of beautiful Lake Quinault before climbing through Willaby Campground and back to the trailhead. □

HIKE 34 *ENCHANTED VALLEY*

General description: A 26.2-mile, round-trip backpack in the southwestern Olympics, leading from rain forest to a classic peak-rimmed basin in Olympic National Park.

Elevation gain and loss: +1,493 feet, -400 feet.

Trailhead elevation: 907 feet.

High point: 2,000 feet.

Maps: Mount Christie and Mount Steel 15-minute USGS quads; Olympic National Park USGS quad; Olympic National Park map.

Season: March through mid-December.

Water availability: Abundant along entire route.

Permit: Obtaining a wilderness permit is an informal procedure in Olympic National Park. Simply fill out a permit at the trailhead register and attach it to your pack.

Finding the trailhead: From U.S. Highway 101, forty-six miles north of Hoquiam and sixty-five miles south of Forks, turn east onto Lake Quinault's South Shore Road. After 1.3 miles, pass the signed trailhead for the Rain Forest Trail on the south side of the road. Hike 33 begins here.

Continue past the village of Quinault and the Quinault ranger station after 2.1 miles. Pavement ends east of Lake Quinault after 7.7 miles. This often-narrow dirt road follows the south bank of Quinault River for another eleven miles to a parking area at the end of the road, 0.3 mile beyond Graves Creek campground.

The hike: Near the head of the Quinault River lies a narrow valley covered with grassy meadows and shaded by alders and bigleaf maples. White ribbons of water tumble down cliffs that rise nearly a mile above the well-named Enchanted Valley—truly one of the gems of Washington's backcountry.

A three-story log chalet, built in the 1930s, currently shelters the wilderness ranger at the west end of the valley. No overnight camping is allowed in the chalet, except in an emergency.

The undulating trail leading to the Enchanted Valley follows the course of one of the Olympic Peninsula's major drainages, the Quinault River, through a majestic lowland forest of hemlock, fir, and cedar, alternating with open groves of red alder and bigleaf maple. Numerous excellent campsites are available all along the route, often next to the tumultuous, milky-green glacial river. Black-tailed deer are especially common in the valley, and you may also see elk. Plan to spend at least three days to get the most out of this scenic hike—one of the classic valley-bottom hikes in the Olympics.

From the trailhead, you'll proceed steadily uphill for two miles through the upper limits of the rain-forest zone amid towering Douglas-firs, Sitka spruces, western hemlocks and western redcedars. (Ignore southeastbound Graves Creek Trail at the trail register near the trailhead.)

The route then descends to the Pony Creek Bridge, spanning a spectacular mini-gorge on the Quinault River. There are good campsites across the bridge on the north side of the river.

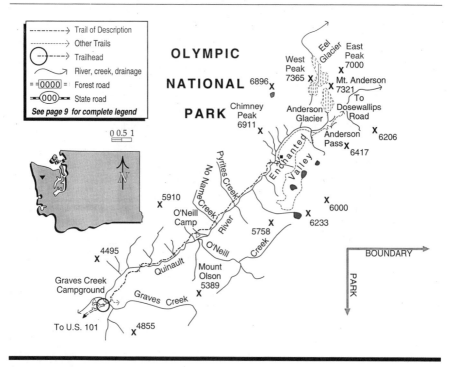

Silver fir begins to appear after the bridge, an indicator that you have passed above the rain-forest zone and into the lowland forest.

After seven miles, hiking either through grass-floored groves of big-leaf maple and red alder or stands of giant conifers, you reach a spur trail leading quickly down to O'Neill Camp. You may want to consider staying the night and hiking into the valley on the second day.

You'll catch fleeting glimpses of high peaks between No-Name and Pyrites creeks, between eight and 9.5 miles. At about 12.8 miles, the trail descends to another bridge over the Quinault, by which you'll cross back to the south bank, quickly reaching the chalet at the west end of the valley.

Rocky slopes rise on the northwest nearly 5,000 vertical feet to 6,911-foot Chimney Peak, decorated by numerous long, cascading creeks. At the head of the valley are some of the higher peaks in the Olympics: 7,365-foot West Peak and 7,321-foot Mount Anderson, separated by a small but active glacier (explaining the milky appearance of the river) at the head of Anderson Creek.

Campsites are numerous throughout the valley, and drinking water is piped in from a small creek near the chalet.

The trail continues beyond the valley. At a fork, you can ascend to Anderson Pass—access to the Anderson Glacier—and drop to the Dosewallips River. Or you can turn right at a fork below the pass to reach a series of alpine lakes high above Enchanted Valley.

After enjoying the scenic southwestern corner of Olympic National Park, retrace the route to the trailhead. □

The southern beaches of Olympic National Park, near Kalaloch, contrast with the dramatic rocky shoreline farther north. Steve Morehouse photo.

A wave-cut sea stack looms out of the mist on the wilderness coast of the Olympic Peninsula. Steve Morehouse photo.

After a storm, ocean-polished driftwood litters this pebbly beach at Olympic National Park. Jan Mack photo.

HIKE 35 *HOH RIVER TO MOSQUITO CREEK*

General description: A moderate, eleven-mile round-trip backpack along the southern wilderness coast of the Olympic Peninsula in Olympic National Park.
Elevation gain and loss: +800 feet, -700 feet.
Trailhead elevation: 20 feet.
High point: 400 feet.
Maps: Destruction Island and Forks 15-minute USGS quad; Olympic National Park USGS quad; Olympic National Park map.
Season: All year.
Water availability: Mosquito Creek is the only reliable source.
Permit: For overnight camping, obtain a backcountry permit either at Kalaloch Information Station south of the Hoh River or at the trailhead. You can also obtain a tide table (also available at the beach trailheads) and weather forecast at any coastal ranger station.

Finding the trailhead: From U.S. Highway 101, fourteen miles south of Forks and 50.5 miles north of Lake Quinault, turn southwest where a sign indicates the Cottonwood Recreation Area, just north of Oxbow Campground. Ignore the left turn to Cottonwood Campground after 2.3 miles. The pavement ends after five miles, and a good dirt road leads to the Oil City trailhead parking area along the Hoh River, ten miles from the highway.

The hike: Plan your hike according to the tide table. There are points along the beach route between the mouth of the Hoh River and Jefferson Cove that can only be negotiated at low to medium tide. Don't get cut off by an incoming tide! Tides can rise quickly, especially during stormy weather, and often there's no escape. Beach routes are quite often very narrow strips of sand or cobbles between the water and precipitous cliffs.

Be prepared for cold, windy, and wet weather even during summer. The ocean water is cold, and swimmers should be aware of the possibility of strong riptides and undertows. Check at a ranger station for information on clam digging, red-tide closures, and bag limits.

The park service advises hikers to carry all the water they'll need for hikes along the coast. Most creeks encountered along the coast are discolored by tree tannins upstream. This discoloration doesn't make these waters unsafe to drink, but giardia and other bacteria may. Purify any creek water obtained along the coast.

From the Oil City trailhead, the first half mile of the trail follows the north bank of the Hoh River (where Hoh Indians catch steelhead and salmon) through a forest of western hemlock, Sitka spruce, and red alder to the ocean.

The trail ends on the beach. Numerous sea stacks, used by nesting shore birds, lie offshore. Northwest along the beach, Hoh Head juts into the ocean.

At low to medium tide, proceed northwest toward Hoh Head along the narrow beach to Jefferson Cove, a short two miles from the trailhead. Since Hoh Head can't be rounded at even the lowest tide, you'll be forced to take an inland route to proceed north.

Most inland trails along the coast are steep, no-nonsense routes, and this

OLYMPIC
NATIONAL
PARK

565
X 661
X

------→	Trail of Description
------→	Other Trails
◯------→	Trailhead
⌒↗	River, creek, drainage
=[0000]=	Forest road
◉(000)◉	State road
See page 9 for complete legend	

Mosquito Creek

Extreme
Low Tide
Beach
Route

PACIFIC

OCEAN

BOUNDARY

0   0.5   1

N

Rope
Ladder

HOH
HEAD

X175

PARK

JEFFERSON
COVE

Beach

Route

Oil City
Trailhead

To
U.S.
101

Hoh
River

one is no exception. You must climb a short rope ladder up the cliffs, and the trail then climbs 400 vertical feet into the hemlock-spruce forest above Hoh Head.

One mile from the beach, you have two options. Take the left fork back down to the beach and proceed north, possible only at the lowest tide. Or to be safe, continue the remaining up-and-down two miles to Mosquito Creek through the forest. With a reliable water supply and good campsites, Mosquito Creek, 5.5 miles from the trailhead, makes a fine destination for a weekend hike.

A long stretch of beach, inviting exploration, lies north of the creek. Tide pools, habitat for sea urchins, sea lettuce, various crabs, small fish, and much more, reward hikers who take the time to look. Harbor seals, gulls, and cormorants are all fairly common along the coast. You may also see gray whales offshore.

Keep in mind that Mosquito Creek runs high after heavy rains and during winter. Don't attempt to cross this creek during high water, but be content confining your exploration to the south side of the creek. □

The Hoh River helps drain the Olympic Peninsula, the wettest region in the conterminous United States, receiving nearly twelve feet of precipitation annually. Steve Morehouse photo.

A carpet for ferns and moss covers the forest floor in Olympic National Park. Steve Morehouse photo.

Low tide at Olympic National Park's Hole in the Wall puts intertidal marine life, such as sea stars and sea anemones, on display. Steve Morehouse photo.

HIKE 36 RIALTO BEACH TO THE CHILEAN MEMORIAL

General description: A 7.2-mile, round-trip backpack along the central wilderness coast of the Olympic Peninsula in Olympic National Park.
Elevation gain and loss: Negligible.
Trailhead elevation: fourteen feet.
High point: Trailhead, fourteen feet.
Maps: La Push 15-minute USGS quad; Olympic National Park USGS quad; Olympic National Park map.
Season: All year.
Water availability: There's no water available, so carry what you'll need.
Permit: Obtain a backcountry permit at Mora Ranger Station, two miles east of the trailhead.

Finding the trailhead: Follow U.S. Highway 101 north from Forks for about one mile, then turn west, as indicated by a sign pointing to Mora and La Push.

Turn right after 7.6 miles at the Quillayute Prairie Fire Station and follow Mora Road for five miles to the large parking area at Rialto Beach.

The hike: This scenic weekend hike samples the southernmost portion of the Ozette Lake to Rialto Beach hike, a twenty-mile trip lasting several days.

Rialto Beach is quite popular, and you'll probably have plenty of company during the first mile or so.

Proceed north from the large parking area along the narrow, sloping, sandy beach. A forest of Sitka spruce, battered by salt spray and strong winds, lies above the beach beyond a wall of driftwood. Swept to sea by high storm tides or rivers, logs are quickly stripped of bark and branches. Their polished remains are then deposited along the beach during storms, when waves and high tides are especially brutal.

South beyond the mouth of the Quillayute River is a group of often-photographed islands, dominated by forested James Island. These islands and other rocks and sea stacks were, at one time, part of the mainland, but the relentless erosive surf has since isolated them offshore. Shore birds take advantage of the safety of these stacks and islands, using them for predator-free nesting sites.

You'll pass Ellen Creek after about half a mile. Camping is allowed on the beach from here north. After 1.4 miles you'll reach Hole in the Wall, a wave-cut arch in a rocky point. If the tide is high, a short but steep overland trail allows passage. The section of beach beyond Hole in the Wall has many excellent tide pools at low tide, and you'll pass more possible campsites in the driftwood. Just back in the Sitka spruce forest, mosquitoes and biting flies are abundant, but they're almost nonexistent along the beach.

Ahead lies a rocky headland that can be rounded at low tide only. Sea level varies approximately seven feet each twelve hours, and you must use a tide table to plan your passage around these headlands.

The campsites at the Chilean Memorial, in a sheltered cove east of Cape Johnson, are 3.6 miles from the trailhead. This rugged coastline has claimed the lives of many seamen, and the Chilean Memorial recognizes just one of many ships lost to the sea.

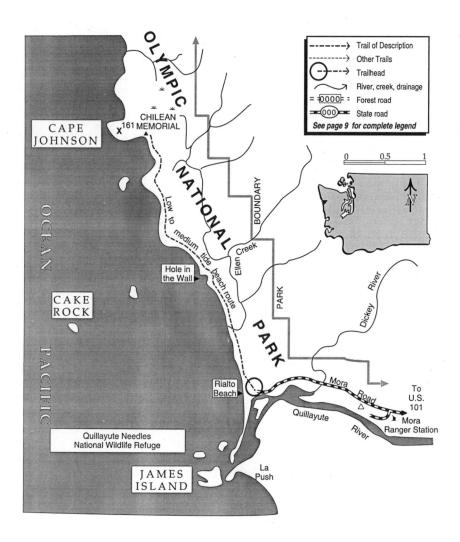

OLYMPIC

NATIONAL

PARK

CHILEAN MEMORIAL
x 161

CAPE JOHNSON

BOUNDARY

Ellen Creek

Low to medium tide beach route

Hole in the Wall

OCEAN

CAKE ROCK

PACIFIC

PARK

Dickey River

Rialto Beach

Mora Road

To U.S. 101

Quillayute

Quillayute River

Mora Ranger Station

Quillayute Needles National Wildlife Refuge

JAMES ISLAND

La Push

Legend

– – – –>	Trail of Description
– – – –>	Other Trails
◯– – –>	Trailhead
	River, creek, drainage
=▭0000▭=	Forest road
=◯000◯=	State road

See page 9 for complete legend

0   0.5   1

N

Forays north along the coast from a base camp at the Chilean Memorial will add to your enjoyment of a weekend hike along a wilderness beach. □

HIKE 37 *CAPE ALAVA LOOP*

General description: A superb, 9.3-mile loop day hike or backpack leading through the coastal forests of Olympic National Park to the beach.
Elevation gain and loss: 220 feet.
Trailhead elevation: thirty-six feet.
High point: 175 feet.
Maps: Ozette Lake 15-minute USGS quad; Olympic National Park USGS quad; Olympic National Park map.
Season: All year.
Water availability: There is no fresh water en route. Carry what you'll need.
Permit: Obtain a backcountry permit for overnight camping from the ranger station at the trailhead.

Finding the trailhead: From U.S. Highway 101, twelve miles north of Forks and forty-four miles west of Port Angeles, turn north where a sign indicates Ozette Lake and Neah Bay. This county road winds through forested hills for ten miles to State Route 112, where you turn left. After eleven miles turn left onto Ozette Road where a sign indicates Ozette Lake. Follow this winding road for twenty-one miles to the trailhead parking area at the north end of Ozette Lake. The last 2.8 miles are intermittently paved.

The hike: Ozette Lake, Washington's third-largest natural freshwater lake, lies less than two miles from the ocean in the northern segment of Washington's wilderness coast. Two trails depart from the north end of the lake and lead through coastal forest to the beach. These trails—one to Sand Point, the other to Cape Alava—form a superb 9.3-mile loop when connected by a three-mile walk along the beach. The loop is suitable as a day hike but even more enjoyable as an overnighter. (Campsites at Sand Point and Cape Alava are often crowded on summer weekends.) Only one point midway along the beach requires a low-tide passage, and an overland trail makes it possible to pass there during a higher tide.

You can take this hike in either direction, but the following description will lead you first to Sand Point, then north along the beach to Cape Alava, and back to the parking area.

From the trailhead, the route bridges the sluggish Ozette River and heads into a western hemlock forest. Turn left at the junction after 0.1 mile.

The trail is a cedar boardwalk all the way to the beach and can be quite slippery when wet. Soft-soled shoes are recommended.

The next 2.8 miles pass through a typical coastal forest of western hemlock and western redcedar. The trail is quite swampy in places. Understory plants include salal and pachystima, ferns and bunchberry. Trees are small; the area is recovering from an old burn.

By the time you're within sound of the pounding surf, Sitka spruce, the domi-

HIKE 37 *CAPE ALAVA LOOP*

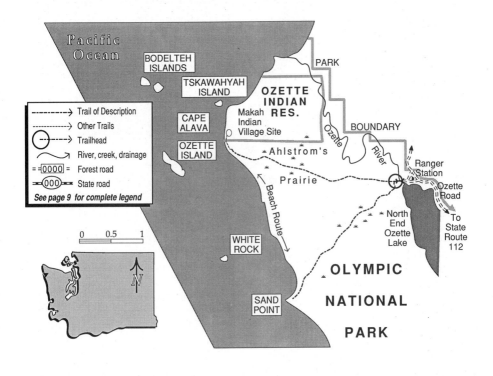

nant coastal tree, will have replaced western redcedar. Some of these spruces are quite large.

The boardwalk ends shortly before reaching Sand Point. Some hikers will continue south to Rialto Beach, a classic twenty-mile beach walk. But you'll turn north and proceed along the wide beach. Cobbles and soft sand make for slow going along this stretch. The sheer variety of detritus washed upon the shore is amazing. Lucky hikers may, at certain times of the year, find Japanese glass fishing-net floats, a prize among beachcombers.

Midway along the beach are Indian petroglyphs, located at the Wedding Rocks. One of these petroglyphs depicts a three-masted schooner, indicating they're of fairly recent origin. A short overland trail offers high-tide passage around the rocks.

To the northwest, forested Ozette Island and other members of the Flattery Rocks group stand just offshore from Cape Alava.

Secluded campsites lie just back of the beach in the spruce forest all along here. Black-tailed deer are quite common.

This pleasant walk terminates at a sign pointing to Ozette Ranger Station. This junction is located at Cape Alava, the westernmost point of land in the

The Cape Alava loop, a boardwalk trail, penetrates a thick forest of Sitka spruce, western hemlock, and western redcedar and crosses over swampy meadows in Olympic National Park. Steve Morehouse photo.

A mossy tree trunk in the rain forest of Olympic National Park hosts a shelflike fungus.
Cliff Leight photo.

forty-eight contiguous states. The view to the north includes mountainous Vancouver Island.

Half a mile north, on the tiny Ozette Indian Reservation, is the site of an ancient Makah Indian village. Washington State University conducted an archaeological dig here during the 1970s. Various artifacts that were recovered are currently on display at the Makah Cultural Center in Neah Bay.

From the junction the trail quickly climbs away from the beach into a spruce forest thick with ground-covering ferns that soon becomes a hemlock-cedar forest. The cedar boardwalk resumes once again and cuts through a narrow tree-rimmed meadow—a dying lake in the advanced stages of transformation. As the new meadow dries out, the forest will complete the cycle by reclaiming the site.

The route then cuts through a larger meadow, covered with ferns and grasses but steadily being invaded by forest trees. This is Ahlstrom's Prairie, the site of an old homestead. Many people of Scandinavian descent settled in this area in the 1890s.

From here back to the trailhead the boardwalk leads through the coastal forest for two more miles, completing a diverse and rewarding Olympic coast hike. □

HIKE 38 *HURRICANE RIDGE TO KLAHHANE RIDGE*

General description: A nine-mile, round-trip day hike in the northern mountains of Olympic National Park, featuring wildflowers, abundant wildlife, interesting geology, and far-flung panoramas of mountains and ocean.
Elevation gain and loss: +1,450 feet, -700 feet.
Trailhead elevation: 5,230 feet.
High point: 6,050 feet.
Maps: Mount Angeles 15-minute USGS quad; Olympic National Park USGS quad; Olympic National Park map.
Season: Mid-July through early October.
Water availability: Carry plenty of water.

Finding the trailhead: Follow directions given in Hike 39.

The hike: The Olympic Peninsula boasts amazing diversity. From the wilderness coast, the rain forests, deep river valleys, and ice-encrusted crags on the west to the dry rain-shadow forests on the east, the area has something for every outdoor enthusiast. Roads lead to many outstanding features, but to know the Olympic Peninsula, you must walk its trails, smell its smells, feel the wind and the rain, experience the contrast between ocean shores and mountain peaks.

Protected from hunting within the park, large mammals are easy to observe. But keep your distance from deer, elk, mountain goats, and bears. Despite their tame appearance, these animals are quite wild.

In their quest for salt, mountain goats have become nuisances in portions of the park. They chew on hiking boots or lick the ground where hikers have urinated; they're attracted to anything that smells or tastes of salt. Take necessary precautions to protect your gear, and keep in mind that

HIKE 38 *HURRICANE RIDGE TO KLAHHANE RIDGE*

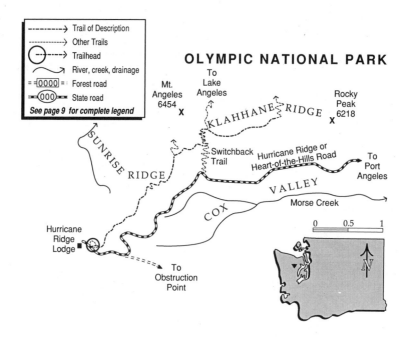

these creatures with their sharp horns can be dangerous.

Mountain goats are not native to the Olympics. They were transplanted here in the 1920s and have found their new environment ideal. Their numbers have increased to the point that overgrazing and trampling have become major concerns to park officials. As a result, park rangers have been capturing and removing goats from the park in an attempt to eliminate impacts caused by that non-native mammal. This controversial program should be in full swing by the 1990s.

The short hike to Klahhane Ridge offers a prime example of the impacts of by mountain goats. Most hikers will probably agree that this nonnative animal should go.

From the parking lot, take the paved path leading north, the High Ridge Trail, quickly turning right along the ridgetop. The pavement ends as the trail climbs through subalpine fir forest carpeted with wildflowers, including blue harebell, pearly everlasting, lousewort, red and magenta Indian paintbrush (endemic to the Olympics), phlox, red heather, avalanche lily, meadow rue, bistort, and wild pink.

Soon you'll come to a north-trending ridge. Take the right fork, cross the ridge, and proceed northeastward along east-facing slopes.

Many subalpine firs on this weather-tortured ridge wear skirts around their bases. Some of these ground-hugging branches actually take root. The remainder of the foliage on these stunted trees, which are exposed above snow line in winter, is trimmed by blowing ice and snow.

Dwarf juniper also grows along the trail as a ground-hugging mat on exposed sites. This shrub enjoys a range encompassing the entire northern hemisphere.

The undulating trail, which alternates between the ridgetop and the east slopes, forks about two miles from the trailhead. The faint left forking path climbs toward Mount Angeles, a peak composed of intensely folded volcanic and sedimentary rocks. The right fork heads east for half a mile to join the more direct Switchback Trail climbing from Hurricane Ridge Road.

Turn left and begin climbing steadily via switchbacks for 750 feet to a ridgetop junction at 6,000 feet elevation. Along the way you'll see timberline trees familiar throughout western Washington. Here, exposed to extreme weather conditions, the Alaska yellow-cedar forms a spreading mat. Growing between 3,000 and 7,000 feet elevation, this tree reaches great proportions in certain areas near the lower limit of its range. Easily distinguished from the redcedar, its foliage has a shaggy, droopy appearance, and its bark is whitish and stringy on mature trees. In fact, the Olympics boast the largest known yellow-cedar tree (in addition to the largest known subalpine fir, Douglas-fir, and western hemlock).

From this junction, craggy Mount Angeles tilts its distinctly layered sedimentary and volcanic breccia (broken and recemented volcanic rock) cliffs skyward.

Turn right and follow the trail eastward along Klahhane Ridge, passing trailside trees in krummholz form. Weather conditions are severe enough at this elevation that "trees" grow only as shrubs at ground level, protected during winter by an insulating blanket of snow.

The broken ridge is quite interesting. It's composed of volcanic breccia and pillow basalt—lava that erupted underwater and cooled rapidly.

But the most outstanding features of Klahhane Ridge are the vistas. To the north, the mountains plunge into the Strait of Juan de Fuca. Beyond rises Vancouver Island. On the mainland are the coast ranges of British Columbia, Mount Baker, and Glacier Peak.

Visualize the great Cordilleran Ice Sheet that traveled south from Canada more than 10,000 years ago. This ice sheet carved out the Strait of Juan de Fuca, isolated the San Juan Islands and Vancouver Island from the mainland, and abutted the north side of the Olympics—the northern slopes of Klahhane Ridge itself.

From here you can gaze into the heart of the Olympics, a high, horseshoe-shaped ridge of alpine peaks encircling the Elwha River drainage—a typical Olympic river valley, very deep and heavily timbered with precipitous slopes rising abruptly from the valley bottom.

Mount Olympus, crown of the Olympics, rises beyond the alpine Bailey Range, thrusting three rock pinnacles above a sea of ice, which is believed to be 1,000 feet thick in places.

This excellent hike with its dramatic vistas—enjoyed by only a small percentage of park visitors, most of whom are satisfied with the views from Hurricane Ridge or from their cars—lets you get a feel for the Olympics and a sense of the lay of the land—an up-and-down world of steep mountains, lush forests, rock and ice, meadows, flowers, and water, everywhere water. □

The largest members of the squirrel family, marmots accumulate layers of fat before hibernating for the winter. This one appears to be looking for a handout, but visitors are strongly discouraged against feeding wildlife. Michael S. Sample photo.

HIKE 39 *GRAND VALLEY*

General description: An eight- to ten-mile, round-trip backpack to a lake basin on the north side of the Olympics in Olympic National Park.
Elevation gain and loss: +950 feet, -1,650 feet.
Trailhead elevation: 6,150 feet.
High point: 6,500 feet.
Maps: Mount Angeles 15-minute USGS quad; Olympic National Park USGS quad; Olympic National Park map.
Season: July through early October.
Water availability: Abundant in Grand Valley.
Permit: Required for overnight camping; obtain at Hurricane Ridge visitor center.

Finding the trailhead: From Port Angeles, follow Hurricane Ridge Road south, past the national park visitor center, paying the entry fee at the entrance station. Then continue to the large parking area on Hurricane Ridge for a total of seventeen miles. (Hike 38 begins here.) Turn left at the eastern edge of the parking area and follow the narrow, winding dirt road for 7.4 miles to the Obstruction Point Trailhead, which can be crowded on weekends with motorists unfamiliar with mountain driving.

Black-tailed deer, a subspecies of mule deer, frequent dense forests of fir, hemlock, and cedar and lush grassy areas on the Olympic peninsula. Steve Morehouse photo.

The hike: The rewarding trail from Obstruction Point to Grand Valley will allow you to experience the wild high country of the Olympics with a minimum of effort, since the trail is downhill most of the way and starts at the highest trailhead in the Olympics.

Black-tailed deer are common, and the echoes of Olympic marmots (a species endemic to the Olympics) may accompany you on your descent into lake-filled Grand Valley.

No wood fires are allowed above 4,000 feet in this area, so be sure to bring a stove. All three lakes—Grand, Moose, and Gladys—host populations of brook trout, but fishing is generally best in Gladys Lake.

From the trailhead, trails lead in two directions: northeast along an alpine ridge for eight miles to the Deer Park trailhead and southeast along the divide above Badger Valley.

Take the right fork, the divide route, and traverse the undulating ridge, crossing alpine fells and passing isolated clumps of stunted subalpine fir. This gentle ridge represents an ancient, gentle upland, one of the few locations in the Olympics where erosion has not removed the broad plateau.

Views are superb for the first two miles; they include the Lillian and Elwha river drainages and the Bailey Range. Dominated by the icy dome of Mount Olympus, whose West Peak is the highest in the Olympics (a modest 7,965 feet), the Bailey Range forms the western arm of a horseshoe-shaped ridge of high peaks. The divide from Hurricane Ridge southward to Mount Anderson forms the eastern arm of the horseshoe.

Where the trail reaches its high point of 6,500 feet and begins descending, you'll be presented with two options. Most hikers will descend 1,500 feet in 2.25 miles into Grand Valley, but experienced cross-country hikers might consider following the faint trail south along the alpine ridge for three miles to Grand Pass, gateway to a land of jagged peaks and alpine parks.

If you follow the trail down to the valley, you'll first pass scattered krummholz subalpine fir, shrub-like trees stunted by the harsh environment above timberline. The route switchbacks down to a bench laced with tiny creeks, passes a tarn, and descends amid increasing timber to a junction four miles from the trailhead.

Emerald-green Grand Lake lies a quarter of a mile below and can be reached via a spur trail that branches off to the left. You can make a fine loop by taking that trail, first descending northward along Grand Creek and then climbing back to the trailhead via Badger Valley, about 4.5 miles from this junction. This option is especially inviting during inclement weather, but it adds 900 feet to the total elevation gain.

To reach Moose and Gladys lakes, turn right and ascend the beautiful, peak-rimmed valley. Moose Lake lies half a mile up the trail at an elevation of 5,050 feet, and Gladys Lake, at 5,400 feet, lies just east of the trail, half a mile beyond. Be a minimum-impact camper and camp at least 100 feet from lakes and streams in subalpine areas such as Grand Valley.

A day hike from camp to 6,450-foot Grand Pass is a rewarding excursion. □

HIKE 39 *GRAND VALLEY*

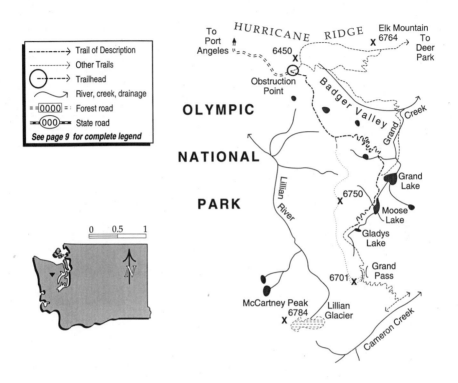

Legend:
- ---------→ Trail of Description
- ---------→ Other Trails
- ◯----→ Trailhead
- ↴ River, creek, drainage
- =‒0000‒= Forest road
- =(000)= State road
- **See page 9 for complete legend**

To Port Angeles
HURRICANE RIDGE
Elk Mountain X 6764
To Deer Park
6450 X
Obstruction Point
Badger Valley
Grand Creek
OLYMPIC
NATIONAL
PARK
Lillian River
6750 X
Grand Lake
Moose Lake
Gladys Lake
Grand Pass
6701 X
McCartney Peak 6784 X
Lillian Glacier
Cameron Creek

0   0.5   1

N

HIKE 40 *ROYAL BASIN*

General description: A fourteen-mile, round-trip backpack in the northeastern Olympics in Olympic National Park, featuring a large alpine cirque encircled by the greatest concentration of 7,000-foot peaks in the range, as well as a trout-filled mountain lake.
Elevation gain and loss: 2,500 feet.
Trailhead elevation: 2,600 feet.
High point: 5,100 feet.
Maps: Tyler Peak 15-minute USGS map; Olympic National Park USGS quad; Olympic National Park map.
Season: Mid-July through early October.
Water availability: Abundant.
Permit: For an overnight stay in Royal Basin, obtain a backcountry permit, usually available at the park boundary a few miles up the trail.

Finding the trailhead: Follow directions given for Hike 41.

The hike: The east side of the Olympics offers a prime example of the rain-shadow effect. Forests here are thick but not overgrown and mossy, as they are on the very wet west side, and the underbrush is much less dense. Only residual snow clings to the highest peaks, not the vast fields of ice present in the west.

This "dry side" hike will lead you through forested Royal Creek canyon to glacier-carved Royal Basin in the shadow of the Needles, a spectacular group of jagged peaks composed of erosion-resistant basalt. Mount Deception, the second-highest summit in the Olympics, rises to an elevation of 7,788 feet at the head of the basin. This peak helps to illustrate the rain shadow: while Mount Olympus, only 177 feet higher, lays buried under the thickest ice cap in Washington, only a few small patches of snow and ice cling to the shadiest flanks of Mount Deception.

Expect mosquitoes and biting flies until late summer. Fishing for pan-sized trout in Royal Lake is a favorite pastime, but bring extra food in case the fish aren't biting.

The trail begins on the west side of the road, just north of the bridge across the Dungeness River. An easy mile through a lovely forest of tall Douglas-fir and western hemlock leads to a junction at a crossing of Royal Creek. Good campsites are located here.

Take the right fork, entering Olympic National Park after less than a mile. Another 0.75 mile beyond is the register where you can obtain a permit.

The trail continues through the viewless forest, passing scattered stream-side campsites, giving you occasional views of smooth Gray Wolf Ridge, 3,000 feet above to the west, and an unnamed ridge of 7,000-foot-plus peaks rising east of the canyon.

As you gain elevation following the drainage south, you'll pass a series of flower-filled meadows lying in avalanche chutes between the timber. The grade steepens noticeably around 4.75 miles, ending at the lower (northern) end of Royal Basin, surrounded on three sides by high, sky-piercing crags.

Head through willow-clad meadows and soon you will pass the only camp-site where wood fires are allowed.

Subalpine fir is the dominant tree here, but you'll also see some lodgepole pine in the meadows. The grade soon steepens once again as you climb through forest for 0.75 mile to 5,100-foot Royal Lake, a tiny heart-shaped lake surrounded by spire-like subalpine firs. The basin above demands further exploration of its meadows, rock, and ice.

After exploring what many would consider the most scenic basin in all of the Olympics, simply backtrack to the trailhead. □

HIKE 41 TUBAL CAIN TRAIL TO BUCKHORN LAKE

General description: A twelve-mile, round-trip backpack into a scenic glacial valley on the east side of the Olympics in the Buckhorn Wilderness.
Elevation gain and loss: +2,000 feet, -100 feet.
Trailhead elevation: 3,250 feet.
High point: 5,250 feet.
Maps: Tyler Peak 15-minute USGS quad; Olympic National Forest map.
Season: July through mid-October.
Water availability: Abundant at 3.25 miles and at Buckhorn Lake.

Finding the trailhead: From Port Angeles, follow U.S. Highway 101 east for eighteen miles to Palo Alto Road, forking right (southwest) from the highway along the west side of Sequim Bay. This paved county road leads past farms for 5.6 miles to the end of pavement. Bear left onto Forest Road 28 after two more miles. Follow signs at subsequent junctions that indicate Tubal Cain Trail and Dungeness Trail. Leave Forest Road 28 after 8.5 miles, turning right onto Forest Road 2860 and following it deep into the Olympics. This road eventually descends toward the Dungeness River. It bridges the river 18.9 miles from U.S. 101, at the trailhead for Royal Basin (Hike 40) after another 1.7 miles. Continue along this road to the parking area and trailhead on the right (south) side of the road, 3.5 miles from the Dungeness River, and 23.1 miles from U.S. 101.

Northbound drivers can reach Palo Alto Road by turning left onto Louella Road and following it 0.9 mile. The turnoff onto Palo Alto Road lies a mile north of Sequim Recreation Area.

The hike: Five wilderness areas were created adjacent to Olympic National Park under the Washington Wilderness Act of 1984. The 45,601-acre Buckhorn Wilderness on the northeast side of the range is larger than the other four—Mount Skokomish, Colonel Bob, The Brothers, and Wonder Mountain.

This scenic hike rises through a "dry" east-side drainage to numerous timberline campsites above tiny but fish-filled Buckhorn Lake. Trails lead past the lake to Buckhorn and Marmot passes, offering scenic and rewarding side trips from a Buckhorn Lake base camp. Fishermen, photographers, and just plain mountain-lovers will find this a rewarding introduction to the Buckhorn Wilderness and an excellent way to spend an uncrowded weekend.

There are no fires allowed above 3,500 feet in all Olympic National Forest wilderness areas.

The trail quickly leads past a shelter and crosses Silver Creek; then it heads west across north-facing slopes shaded by Douglas-fir and western hemlock. Understory plants consist of salal, Oregon grape, bracken fern, thimbleberry, and rhododendron.

The trail jogs south above the Copper Creek drainage after half a mile. Ocean spray blooms among the rhododendron on these sunny slopes; its clusters of white flowers make it easy to identify during July.

A long traverse upon west-facing slopes follows, but the sight of majestic crags at the head of the canyon may put some bounce into your stride. You'll be in the midst of those crags quite soon.

HIKE 40   ROYAL BASIN
HIKE 41   TUBAL CAIN TRAIL TO BUCKHORN LAKE

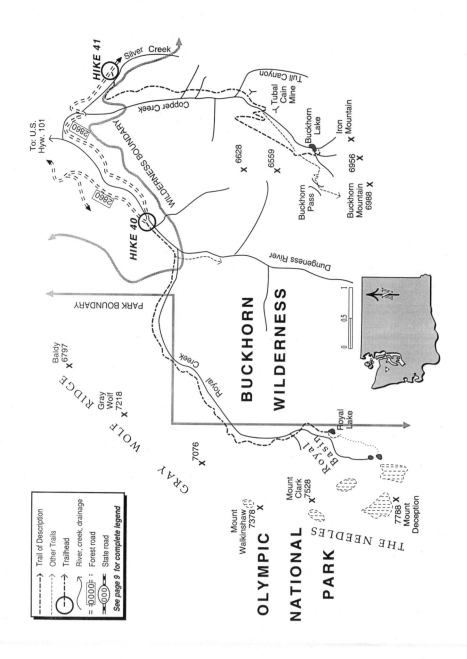

In the first 2.75 miles, you'll cross three small creeks; so there's plenty of drinking water for thirsty hikers.

After 2.75 miles, a left-branching trail leads to an old mine shaft near the mouth of Tull Canyon.

Another half a mile through a shady forest brings you to a crossing of Copper Creek and numerous streamside campsites. (Tubal Cain Mine lies up-slope to the east via a short trail.) The main trail presently switchbacks three times up the west slope of the Copper Creek canyon, passing widely scattered subalpine firs, Douglas-firs, Alaska yellow-cedars, white pines, and some lodgepole pines.

These grassy slopes were opened up by an old fire, as evidenced by the many sun-bleached snags, and they're ablaze with colorful wildflowers in midsummer.

As you near the end of the final northbound switchback, the San Juan Islands will become visible to the north, a dramatic contrast to the impressive peaks that dominate the scenery as you traverse to the south.

When the trail reaches a point opposite the tailings pile of Tubal Cain Mine, keep a close eye out in late July and August for a small, cushion-like plant with a five-petaled, bell-shaped blue flower with petals pointing upward. This is Piper's bellflower, a species found only in the Olympics. Don't confuse this interesting flower with the blue harebell, which bears blue flowers that droop downward.

Ahead is an impressive triad of prominent peaks, all of which approach 7,000 feet in elevation.

A steeper, abandoned trail joins your route on the left, just before you reach a junction 5.5 miles from the trailhead. From the junction, the right fork climbs one mile to broad Buckhorn Pass. The left fork leads to a bench laced with small creeks and shaded by subalpine fir. Campsites are good here.

Buckhorn Lake, downhill from the campsites at the end of the trail at 5,275 feet elevation, is brimming with hungry trout. ☐

HIKE 42 *MILDRED LAKES*

General description: A strenuous eight-mile, round-trip backpack to a lake basin on the "dry side" of the Olympics in the Mount Skokomish Wilderness.
Elevation gain and loss: +2,300 feet, -300 feet.
Trailhead elevation: 2,000 feet.
High point: 4,000 feet.
Maps: Mount Steel 15-minute USGS quad (trail and road to trailhead not on quad); Olympic National Forest map.
Season: Mid-July through early October.
Water availability: Available at two miles and at Mildred Lakes.

Finding the trailhead: From U.S. Highway 101, 13.5 miles north of Hoodsport, turn west onto Hamma Hamma Road (Road 25) where a sign indicates the Hamma Hamma Recreation Area. The two-lane pavement of Road 25 changes to one-lane pavement with occasional turnouts (watch for logging trucks) after 0.9 mile. This in turn changes to dirt after another 5.5 miles.

You'll pass the popular Lena Lakes Trailhead one mile from the end of pavement and the seldom-used Putvin Trailhead after another 4.2 miles. (A trail starts here and leads to a remote lake at the head of Whitehorse Creek.) The road becomes fairly rough during the last mile or so. The trailhead is just beyond a concrete bridge over the Hamma Hamma River, 13.1 miles from the highway.

The hike: The way to Mildred Lakes basin follows a very strenuous, unofficial use-trail for four up-and-down miles through thick brush and over and around fallen trees, gaining 2,300 feet of elevation en route. Despite the rigors of this hike, Mildred Lakes is a popular weekend destination. It's not uncommon for twenty to thirty or more people to be camped throughout the basin on a given summer weekend. Hikers who make it to the lakes enjoy a well-earned feeling of accomplishment, having penetrated the depths of the 15,686-acre Mount Skokomish Wilderness via one of its few trails. As an added attraction, the lower and upper lakes are filled with hungry cutthroat trout, some reaching ten to fourteen inches in length. Unfortunately, the air is similarly filled with hungry mosquitoes and clouds of biting flies. Campfires are not allowed above 3,500 feet.

The unsigned trail begins steeply but soon levels out somewhat as it proceeds over rocks and roots. Some logs have been cut from this section—the easiest portion of the route—and you'll pass many large stumps at first. Along with the young second-growth forest of Douglas-fir and western hemlock, they suggest that the slope was logged years ago.

After about a mile, you'll dip into a shallow draw and enjoy a fine view northwest across the Hamma Hamma drainage to 6,434-foot Mount Skokomish.

The trail climbs steeply again, leveling off along a 3,100-foot ridgetop. Enjoy good views from here to numerous peaks, including 6,000-foot Mount Henderson to the northwest. A short stint along the timbered ridge leads to a steep descent to a lovely creek. Weary hikers will find campsites here.

Follow the creek upstream along its east bank for a few hundred feet; then find a log crossing and proceed into a silver-fir forest.

Now the work begins. Climb steeply to a log crossing twenty-five feet above a narrow gully and resume the grueling ascent, constantly climbing over tree roots and fallen logs, sometimes on all fours. As if that weren't enough, mosquitoes and biting flies will constantly harass you.

The welcome end to this 1,000-foot climb will be found on a bouldery subalpine ridge, clothed in red heather, huckleberry, and scattered mountain hemlock. Enjoy the best vistas yet from this 4,000-foot ridge.

Mildred Lakes basin lies below to the west, but you can't see the lakes themselves because of heavy timber cover. The ridge beyond the basin hosts a series of broken basalt peaks, including 5,868-foot Mount Lincoln and Sawtooth Ridge, both within Olympic National Park, and 6,104-foot Mount Cruiser, just outside the park boundary.

The route drops to a bench, then 100 feet to the lower lake. Follow the small creek upstream to the upper and largest lake at 3,900 feet elevation.

You'll find the most isolated camps by following a path from the outlet of

HIKE 42 *MILDRED LAKES*

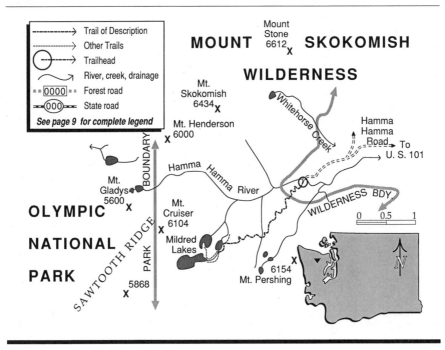

the upper lake to the middle lake, but fishing is best in the other lakes. Ignore an old abandoned trail descending from the lower lake along the Hamma Hamma River.

Cross-country jaunts are restricted due to heavy timber and brush, but persistent hikers climbing the basin to a 5,000-foot saddle east of Mount Lincoln will be rewarded with a fine view across the basin to the north and a glimpse southward deep into the Skokomish River valley. □

HIKE 43 *LAKE INGALLS*

General description: A moderate, ten-mile, round-trip backpack to an alpine lake in the Stuart Range in the Alpine Lakes Wilderness, a land of impressively high granite peaks.
Elevation gain and loss: +2,400 feet, -100 feet.
Trailhead elevation: 4,200 feet.
High point: 6,500 feet.
Maps: Mount Stuart 15-minute USGS quad; Wenatchee National Forest map.
Season: Mid-July through mid-October.
Water availability: Water is available at the trailhead and from several springs in the first four miles of the hike, and at Lake Ingalls.

Finding the trailhead: Follow State Route 970 about nine miles east from Cle Elum or 3.3 miles west from U.S. Highway 97 (fifteen miles north of Ellensburg) to northbound Teanaway Road, and turn north. Pavement on this county road ends after 12.75 miles. Bear right here onto Forest Road 9737, signed for Beverly Campground and Trail 1394. Follow this often rough dirt road, avoiding numerous signed spur roads, to its end at the trailhead and picnic area, 22.2 miles from State Route 970.

The hike: Sometimes termed the "High Sierra of Washington," the glacier-carved, lake-dotted terrain of the Stuart Range is a mecca for hikers and climbers. Part of the Wenatchee Mountains, a major spur ridge trending southeast from the Cascade crest in the center of the range, the Stuart Range is a large batholith of quartz diorite (loosely referred to as granite) sculpted and scoured by ancient glaciers into a land of jagged summits, U-shaped drainages, and lake basins by the dozen. Rising far above surrounding peaks and ridges is the apex of the range, 9,415-foot Mount Stuart, the goal of countless mountaineers because of its hard, stable rock, many challenging climbing routes, and rewarding vistas.

The hike to treeless Lake Ingalls traverses the edge of the Stuart Range batholith for five spectacular miles through an alpine world of impressive peaks and rocky basins. The lake makes a good base camp for alpine wanderings. Fishing can be productive, and as usual, mosquitoes are ever-present until August.

Beneath giant crags, the trail proceeds into a Douglas-fir forest, following the course of the North Fork Teanaway River, simply a cascading mountain stream here in its headwaters.

Turn right after 0.2 miles onto Trail 1390, closed to pack stock, and begin gently climbing corrugated slopes dotted with pine and fir and brightened by a variety of wildflowers. Views are superb up and down the Teanaway.

The Longs Pass Trail departs for a notch visible on the skyline above at 1.5 miles from the trailhead. Experienced hikers who enjoy loop trips will want to consider this route for the return trip. The route is self-explanatory on the Mount Stuart quad. However, a faint trail exists from Longs Pass to Ingalls Creek that isn't shown on the quad.

For now, bear left through rocky terrain dotted by increasingly stunted timber to the boundary of the Alpine Lakes Wilderness on a ridge at 6,500 feet elevation. A ribbon of stunted trees, including subalpine fir, Lyall larch, and whitebark pine, lines this exposed ridge. Views are excellent, from the fluted walls of Mount Stuart to the snowy cone of Mount Rainier.

Lake Ingalls lies less than one mile (as the crow flies) north across the bowl below the ridge. There are two ways to get there. From the ridge a trail signed "camping" descends into the basin, crossing numerous rivulets and campsites. It soon begins climbing glacier-smoothed rock and is easily lost. The second route contours around the basin through stands of Lyall larch, passing a broad bench with possible campsites en route. Wildflowers are numerous, including red and white heather, shooting star, buttercup, valerian, phlox, and Indian paintbrush.

The two trails join just south of Lake Ingalls, and you'll climb steeply through a notch in a low, rocky, glacier-smoothed ridge above the lake. Camping here is limited, and there are no trees in this austere landscape to shelter hikers

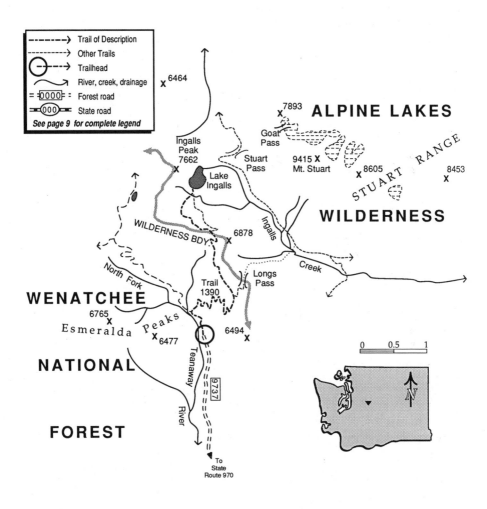

from battering winds. But a more scenic setting is hard to imagine. Surrounded by sawtooth summits, with a superb view across Ingalls Creek to Mount Stuart, and often affording good fishing, this lake is a deservedly popular destination.

An easy jaunt northeast from the lake along a low ridge leads to Stuart Pass in less than one mile. Experienced hikers who want to get a closer look at Mount Stuart can ascend from Stuart Pass for 1,200 feet via easy slopes to 7,600-foot Goat Pass, overlooking Stuart Lake.

If the Lake Ingalls area is too crowded, consider dropping into the scenic timberline basin north of Stuart Pass for excellent secluded base camps.

This fine weekender should whet your appetite for further exploration in the awe-inspiring Stuart Range, protected within the boundaries of the Alpine Lakes Wilderness. □

HIKE 44 *SNOW CREEK TO SHIELD LAKE VIA PRUSIK PASS*

General description: A rigorous twenty-four-mile, round-trip backpack into the heart of the Enchantment Lakes Basin, one of the most scenic lake basins in the Alpine Lakes Wilderness, if not the state.
Elevation gain and loss: +6,150 feet, -755 feet.
Trailhead elevation: 1,300 feet.
High point: Prusik Pass, 7,450 feet.
Maps: Leavenworth, Liberty, Mount Stuart, and Chiwaukum Mts. 15-minute USGS quads; Wenatchee National Forest map.
Season: Mid-July through early October.
Water availability: Abundant.
Permit: Permit required. See below.

Finding the trailhead: From U.S. Highway 2 at the west end of Leavenworth (33.4 miles east of Stevens Pass) turn south onto the signed Icicle Creek Road. Follow this paved road past several rural residences and then west up Icicle Creek. You'll reach the large parking area on the south side of the road after 4.2 miles.

The hike: The Enchantment Lakes Basin is, perhaps, the most scenic hiking area in the state. Numerous lakes—some forested, some alpine, some with fair fishing—lie on benches that proceed in stair-step fashion down the U-shaped drainage of Snow Creek. Jagged, broken alpine peaks surround the basin, attracting climbers from throughout the state to challenge the stable granitic rock. And for a few days to a week each October, the abundant Lyall larch in the upper basin put on an unforgettable display of orange and gold.

Since the Enchantments area has been heavily used, the Wenatchee National Forest has implemented a wilderness permit system. From June 15 through October 1 each year, permits are required for day as well as overnight use. Seventy-five percent of the daily quota of permits can be reserved by mail after March 1. A reservation fee of one dollar per person per day is required. You must drive to the Leavenworth Ranger Station to pick up your reserved

Beautiful views await hikers in the Enchantments. Cliff Leight photo.

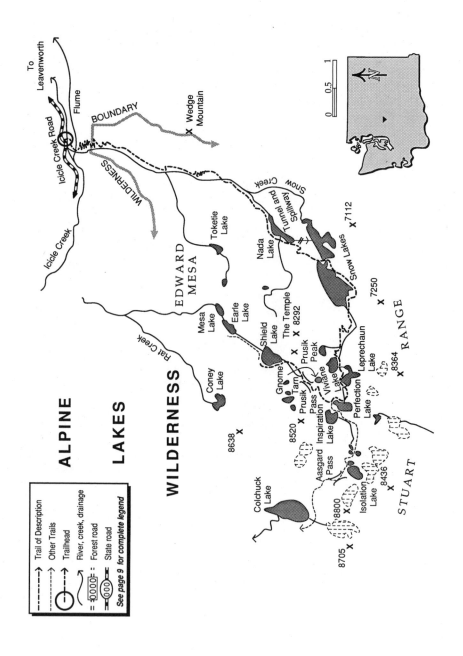

permits. The other twenty-five percent of the overnight permits are available on the day of the hike. Anytime after Labor Day is the best time to hike in the Enchantments if solitude is desirable. Although the permit system may seem like a hassle, daily entry quotas have decreased the number of visitors to the area.

High peaks loom thousands of feet above the parking lot, giving a hint of what lies ahead. No dogs are allowed on the trail, and no campfires are allowed in the basin. Mosquitoes are abundant.

Beginning amid glacier-smoothed rock along Icicle Creek, the trail climbs through bigleaf maple and Douglas fir, briefly parallels a canal and then begins climbing rocky slopes clothed in Douglas fir and ponderosa pine via numerous switchbacks.

Leveling off in lower Snow Creek canyon, the route passes two widely spaced redcedar-shaded campsites along Snow Creek within the first 2.5 miles. It crosses Snow Creek and ascends a tributary to the first of many lakes, 4,950-foot Nada Lake. Midway around the lake are a small creek and campsites amid a jumble of boulders, 5.8 miles from the trailhead.

The trail then climbs open, brushy slopes above the lake. A tunnel diverting water from Lower Snow Lake, just over the ridge to the south, sends a roaring spray of pressurized water down the slope next to the trail to feed Nada Lake, thus increasing the flow of Snow Creek for a local fish hatchery.

The trail levels off before crossing between the two Snow Lakes (just a narrow point in the lake—it's actually just one lake), after seven miles. You'll pass signed trails that lead to various campsites around the lakes. The trail skirts the shady south shore of the upper end of Snow Lakes and then begins a strenuous rocky climb up to the next bench in the basin.

The climb ends at nine miles in a rocky landscape next to 6,785-foot Viviane Lake. The basin above becomes increasingly alpine in character, with timber becoming sparse and stunted.

Continue past Leprechaun and Perfection lakes. At the north end of Perfection Lake, take the righthand trail at a junction, and hike through a timberline meadow to the notch to the left (west) of the pinnacle of 8,000-foot Prusik Peak. The route becomes faint amid sand and rocks, but the notch, 7,500-foot Prusik Pass, is close at hand and easy to attain after eleven miles.

The views from this high pass include the timberline basin of the Rat Lakes to the north, including round Shield Lake, narrow Earle Lake, and Mesa Lake. The large plateau of Edward Mesa, isolated from its surroundings by ancient glaciers, attracts the eye at the north end of the basin. To the south is an excellent view of the Enchantments, scoured by glaciers and dominated by the white granite of the Stuart Range pluton.

You can easily follow the trail down to 6,695-foot Shield Lake, but it splits into various paths near the lake. A trail leads around the west shore to the other lakes at the head of the Rat Creek drainage within 1.5 miles. You'll find fair campsites amid Lyall larch near the upper end of the lake, one mile below the pass. A side trip to Edward Mesa will reward you with far-ranging views and the possibility of seeing mountain goats. □

The Stuart Range forms the centerpiece of the eastern half of the Alpine Lakes Wilderness. Climbers come from all over the state to challenge the area's mighty granite crags. Ron Adkison photo.

HIKE 45 *RACHEL LAKE AND RAMPART LAKES*

General description: A moderate 9.5-mile, round-trip backpack in the southern Alpine Lakes Wilderness, featuring fishable timberline lakes and dramatic vistas of the unspoiled headwaters of the Yakima River.

Elevation gain and loss: +2,450 feet, -200 feet.

Trailhead elevation: 2,800 feet.

High point: 5,150 feet.

Maps: Snoqualmie Pass 15-minute USGS quad; Wenatchee National Forest map.

Season: Mid-July through mid-October.

Water availability: Abundant along the trail and at lakes.

Finding the trailhead: Proceed to Exit 62 on Interstate 90, forty-eight miles west of Ellensburg and thirty miles east of North Bend. Drive northeast toward Kachess Lake via paved Forest Road 49.

Turn left onto Forest Road 4930 after about five miles. A sign here and at subsequent junctions indicates Rachel Lake Trail. This good dirt road leads to a brief section of pavement which in turn leads to the trailhead parking area on the south side of the road, opposite the trailhead proper, 8.8 miles from I-90.

The hike: Proximity to urban areas of the Puget Lowland and easy access from I-90 combine to make the southern Alpine Lakes Wilderness one of the most popular, and sometimes overcrowded, hiking areas in the state. Hundreds of lakes and scenic basins, surrounded by rugged rocky ridges and peaks, many a short distance from road ends, attract hordes of hikers each weekend. Much of this spectacularly rugged country between I-90 and U.S. Highway 2 is protected from development within the Alpine Lakes Wilderness, which was designated by an act of Congress in 1976 and which encompasses more than 300,000 acres.

The route to Rachel and Rampart lakes follows a rugged, unmaintained trail, but despite its rigors this is a popular weekend hike. Solitude seekers should consider taking this hike on a weekday. This is a hiker-only trail, and no fires are allowed within a quarter mile of Rachel, Rampart, and Lila lakes. Fishing is fair, and water, mosquitoes, and biting flies are abundant.

From the trailhead, the route rises into a forest of hemlock and fir. Plentiful tree roots and several small streams will hamper your progress. The trail is overgrown where it passes through densely vegetated openings. Views are limited, with infrequent glimpses of Box Ridge and the head of aptly named Box Canyon.

After 2.5 miles of canyon walking, you'll cross two small creeks and begin a steep climb of 1,300 feet in one long mile. Part way along this strenuous, rock-and-root obstructed trail, you'll pass an interesting "weeping wall," where seepage drips down the rock like teardrops. You'll enjoy a good view of jagged Box Ridge near the top of the ascent.

Rachel Lake, elevation 4,650, is about 3.75 miles from the trailhead. Numerous fine campsites, shaded by hemlocks and firs, dot the eastern shore of this half-mile-long lake. Fishing for pan-sized trout can be productive.

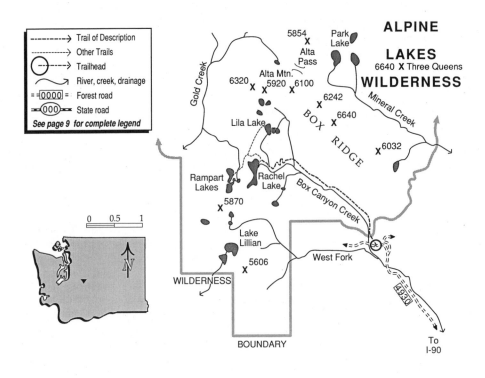

You'll reach Rampart Lakes, set on a bench just west of Rampart Ridge, by way of a one-mile trail from Rachel Lake, gaining about 600 feet of elevation en route. Views of jagged summits and the timberline setting make camping amid these lakes scenic and memorable.

Another trail branches right (north) on Rampart Ridge, leading to 5,200-foot Lila Lake, lying on a bench below Alta Mountain. Several nearby alpine tarns are easy to reach from Lila.

The three summits of Alta Mountain are an easy scramble from here, offering dramatic views of the glacially sculpted granite peaks of the Cascade crest. □

HIKE 46 FOREST ROAD 9030 TO ISLAND LAKE

General description: A moderate 10.5-mile, round-trip backpack offering access to eleven lakes in the southwest corner of the Alpine Lakes Wilderness.
Elevation gain and loss: +1,940 feet, -250 feet.
Trailhead elevation: 2,600 feet.
High point: 4,560 feet.
Maps: Bandera 7.5-minute USGS quad; Mount Baker-Snoqualmie National Forest map.
Season: July through October.
Water availability: Abundant at 1.5 and 2.5 miles and at Island Lake.

Finding the trailhead: Follow Interstate 90 to Exit 45, where a sign indicates Lookout Point Road. This exit lies about sixty-five miles west of Ellensburg and 14.5 miles east of North Bend. Upon exiting the interstate, turn northwest onto Forest Road 9030. The pavement ends after 0.4 mile. Proceed another 0.4 mile to a junction and turn right. Drive this often rough and narrow dirt road 2.3 miles to its end at the trailhead.

The hike: In the southwestern corner of the Alpine Lakes Wilderness, the land is cloaked in heavy forest, and few peaks rise above timberline. Elevations are generally lower than in much of the rest of the wilderness. Thus, this lake-dotted corner opens up for hiking earlier than many areas. The destination of this hike is the lake basin on the north side of Bandera Mountain.

The Talapus Lake Trailhead is only an hour's drive from Seattle, and the area hosts more than its share of hikers on some weekends. But this trail offers access to more than eleven lakes, so solitude-seekers can usually find an isolated spot to while away a weekend. Of course, weekdays are the optimum time to visit any hiking area.

This is a hiker-only trail, and wood fires are prohibited at Talapus, Olallie, and Melakwa lakes, all of which are accessed from this well-maintained and easy-to-follow trail.

The trail begins as an old logging road and proceeds into second-growth timber and, after a quarter of a mile, into a virgin forest of western hemlock, western redcedar, and Douglas-fir.

You'll enter the Alpine Lakes Wilderness and very soon cross the outlet just below Talapus Lake. Notice the huge green leaves of the skunk cabbage growing in a marshy area near the wilderness boundary. You aren't likely to see its yellow and green flowering head during summer, since it blooms quite early in spring.

Talapus Lake, two miles from the trailhead, offers a fine destination for a short day hike, especially for families with small children. Fishing is fair, and a few campsites, shaded by hemlock, fir, and cedar, dot the lower east shore. Bandera Mountain rises nearly 2,000 feet above the west side of the lake.

The trail leads upward under a canopy of silver fir and western hemlock for a long mile to the Olallie Lake Trail, which forks left. The 3,800-foot lake lies half a mile up that spur trail.

Bear right at that junction, ford the stream, stroll 0.2 mile to another junction, and this time, turn left. The right fork leads to another trailhead.

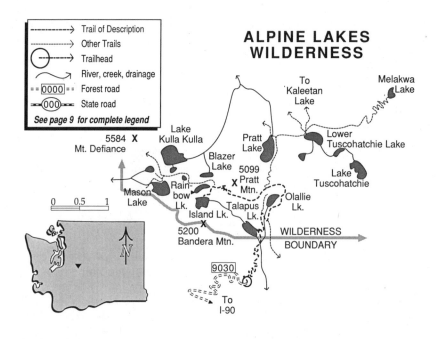

Legend:
- Trail of Description
- Other Trails
- Trailhead
- River, creek, drainage
- =0000= Forest road
- =(000)= State road

See page 9 for complete legend

ALPINE LAKES WILDERNESS

To Kaleetan Lake

Melakwa Lake

5584 X Mt. Defiance

Lake Kulla Kulla

Pratt Lake

Lower Tuscohatchie Lake

Blazer Lake

5099 X Pratt Mtn.

Lake Tuscohatchie

Mason Lake

Rainbow Lk.

Talapus Lk.

Olallie Lk.

Island Lk. X

0   0.5   1

5200 Bandera Mtn.

WILDERNESS BOUNDARY

9030

To I-90

N

Climb through the forest above invisible Olallie Lake, catching only a brief glimpse of the egg-shaped lake before reaching a ridgetop junction after 1.2 miles. You can descend northward toward Pratt Lake, 1.5 miles, and continue east to Lower Tuscohatchie Lake, 0.5 mile. Trails lead north four miles from that lake to Kaleetan Lake, nestled under the impressive spire of 6,259-foot Kaleetan Peak, and east 2.5 miles to 4,500-foot Melakwa Lake, surrounded by precipitous peaks.

If you bear left on the ridge you'll soon begin a westward traverse along the flower-decked trail on the south slopes of Pratt Mountain. Wildflowers along this sunny stretch include Indian paintbrush, lupine, tiger lily, and bear grass as well as much bracken fern. Views to the south include Talapus Lake, South Fork Snoqualmie River Canyon, and extensively clearcut slopes beyond.

The trail climbs a bit before dropping to a junction with the trail to Island Lake, 1.2 miles from the last junction. The left fork leads to sheltered campsites at Island Lake in less than half a mile. This lake lies at 4,250 feet in a cirque carved into the north flank of Bandera Mountain. It would make a good base camp for further exploration. Bandera Mountain or Pratt Mountain are easy scrambles for experienced hikers, both featuring far-reaching vistas. Closer at hand are Rainbow Lake, just over a timbered rise north of Island Lake, and a small tarn 0.75 mile west along the trail, both an easy stroll from an Island Lake camp. □

HIKE 47 *EAST FORK MILLER RIVER TO LAKE DOROTHY*

General description: An easy three-to-six-mile, round-trip day hike or backpack to Lake Dorothy, one of Washington's largest backcountry lakes in the Alpine Lakes Wilderness.

Elevation gain and loss: +1,000 feet to +1,160 feet.

Trailhead elevation: 2,150 feet.

High point: 3,100 to 3,200 feet.

Maps: Snoqualmie Lake and Big Snow Mtn. 7.5-minute USGS quads; Mount Baker-Snoqualmie National Forest map.

Season: Late June through October.

Water availability: Plentiful.

Finding the trailhead: From U.S. Highway 2, about four miles west of Skykomish ranger station and 18.3 miles west of Stevens Pass, or 49.3 miles east of Interstate 5 in Everett, turn south onto the Old Cascade Highway (just west of a tunnel on U.S. Highway 2) signed for Money Creek Campground. The road immediately crosses South Fork Skykomish River, passes the campground, and then the Burlington Northern railroad tracks at 0.4 mile. Bear left at the tracks, go another 0.6 mile and turn right (south) onto Miller River Road NE-Forest Road 6410. Avoid a right fork (6420) at once and follow Forest Road 6410, a good gravel road, for nine miles to its end at the trailhead. Portions of the final two miles are subject to washouts.

The hike: The largest of all Washington's backcountry lakes—Lake Dorothy—lies near the head of the East Fork Miller River. At 3,058 feet elevation and accessible by a rough trail only 1.5 miles from the trailhead, Dorothy is also one of the most popular backcountry lakes in the state. Dozens of campsites lie near the trail along the east side of the deep, 1.5-mile-long lake. Fishing from the shore is best after the fall turnover, an annual phenomenon which occurs when the water temperature cools. The colder water near the bottom and the warmer water near the surface circulate until the lake attains a uniform temperature. At that point, fish begin feeding in earnest. Fishing here is also productive after the ice breaks up in early summer. During the warm summer months, some hikers pack in a rubber raft to fish the deeper waters.

Lake Dorothy is a great spot to introduce children to the backcountry, as numerous families on any summer weekend will attest. The trail is rocky, muddy, and obstructed by tree roots in many places, but it's easy to follow.

Beginning in a montane forest of silver fir, mountain hemlock, and western redcedar, the trail climbs past several springs to the boundary of the Alpine Lakes Wilderness. The way stays above the east bank of the East Fork Miller River, simply a large creek at this point but full of slickrock cascades and waterfalls.

After 0.6 mile, you'll cross Camp Robber Creek via a steel bridge, just above its confluence with the East Fork Miller River in a beautiful area of slickrock cascades. A deep, inviting pool lies downstream below the bridge. On a hot summer day, you may find it hard to resist a swim.

Beyond the bridge, the trail, rocky and full of tree roots, crosses rotting plank

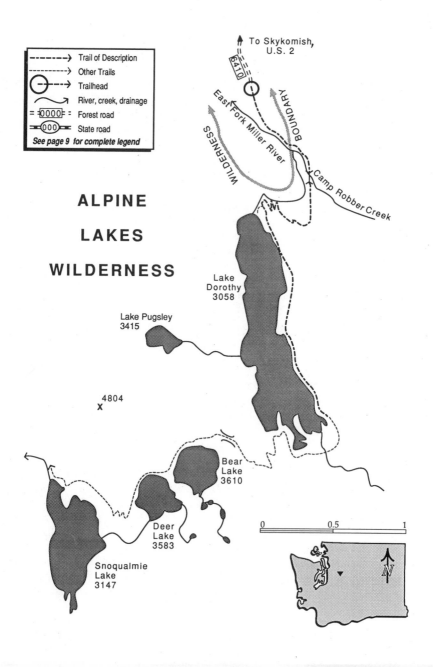

Trail of Description
Other Trails
Trailhead
River, creek, drainage
Forest road
State road
See page 9 for complete legend

To Skykomish, U.S. 2

6410

East Fork Miller River

BOUNDARY

WILDERNESS

Camp Robber Creek

ALPINE

LAKES

WILDERNESS

Lake Dorothy 3058

Lake Pugsley 3415

4804 X

Bear Lake 3610

Deer Lake 3583

Snoqualmie Lake 3147

0   0.5   1

N

bridges and winds upward through a typical moist forest plant community. Plants common along this shady stretch are huckleberry, whortleberry, bunchberry or Canada dogwood, black raspberry, queen's cup, devils club, vine maple, and ferns. The ground is carpeted with soft, green moss.

Rocky switchbacks soon lead to the lake's outlet stream, and a spur trail leads to the lower end of the lake. The Forest Service is revegetating various locations around Lake Dorothy to mitigate the impact of too many hikers' boots. Keep clear of these closed areas so that native vegetation can become re-established.

The main trail continues south above the east shore, passing many fine campsites. The massive granite bulk of 6,680-foot Big Snow Mountain looms four miles to the south.

The shores of the lake are cloaked in mountain hemlock, silver fir, Alaska yellow-cedar, and the five-needled white pine, many of which are dying from blister rust, a disease accidentally introduced into this country around the turn of the century by a shipment of white pine seedlings from Europe.

The trail continues from the three-mile point at the upper end of the lake over the low, forested ridge to the west, leading to Bear and Deer lakes after two more miles. ☐

HIKE 48 *LAKE CREEK TO HEATHER LAKE*

General description: A moderate six-mile, round-trip day hike or backpack to a large lake near Stevens Pass in the Henry M. Jackson Wilderness.
Elevation gain and loss: +1,260 feet, minus twenty-seven feet.
Trailhead elevation: 2,720 feet.
High point: 3,980 feet.
Maps: Labyrinth Mtn. and Captain Point 7.5-minute USGS quads; Wenatchee National Forest map.
Season: July through October.
Water availability: Abundant during first 1.25 miles and at the lake.

Finding the trailhead: Follow directions given under Hike 49 to the junction of Forest Roads 65 and 6700. Turn left on dirt Road 6700 (a sign points to U.S. Highway 2), cross the Little Wenatchee, and after 0.4 mile turn right onto Road 6701. (This junction can be reached by driving 12.2 miles north from U.S. Highway 2 at a junction signed "Smithbrook" four miles east of Stevens Pass.) Follow this good dirt road for 4.7 miles, and then turn left onto Forest Road 400, signed for Heather Lake Trail. This good dirt road leads through a patchwork of clearcuts and virgin timber for 2.2 miles to the small parking area at the end of the road.

The hike: North of Stevens Pass, the crest of the Cascade Range stays fairly low in elevation for nearly twenty miles to the Glacier Peak Wilderness boundary, allowing substantial moisture from Pacific storms to fall east of the crest. Thus, forests here maintain a moist, "west-side" character.

This scenic overnighter travels through such forests to Heather Lake, the

HIKE 48 *LAKE CREEK TO HEATHER LAKE*

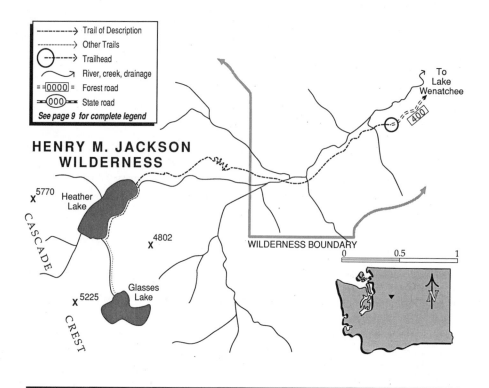

Trail of Description
Other Trails
Trailhead
River, creek, drainage
Forest road
State road

See page 9 for complete legend

HENRY M. JACKSON WILDERNESS

To
Lake
Wenatchee

400

x 5770 Heather Lake

CASCADE

x 4802

WILDERNESS BOUNDARY

0   0.5   1

Glasses Lake

x 5225

CREST

N

second-largest lake in the 103,591-acre Henry M. Jackson Wilderness. The hiker-only route is shady all the way but has a long, steep stretch near the end. The lake receives moderate to heavy use on some weekends, and mosquitoes and biting flies are a problem during midsummer.

The trail begins winding through a moist forest of western hemlock and silver fir—the dominant forest trees on the west slope of the Cascades at mid to upper elevations. After a pleasant one-mile stroll along the valley bottom, hop across a northbound tributary of Lake Creek (difficult to cross in early summer) and proceed a quarter mile to a bridge across Lake Creek. Notice the many potholes below the bridge worn into the bedrock by the tumultuous creek.

You'll enter the wilderness within another 0.3 mile and begin a steep climb up well-drained slopes dominated by drought-tolerant Douglas-fir, the most widespread tree in Washington.

Growing from sea level to montane forests and occasionally reaching up to timberline in isolated, dry locations, Douglas-fir is the most important commercial forest tree in the Pacific Northwest. Few large specimens exist today; however, it's not uncommon to see occasional 200-foot-tall individuals in the western Cascade foothills. The tree's bark is gray or reddish brown and deeply fissured. The needles are arranged in a spiral around the branches, like those of a hemlock or spruce. Unlike those of true firs, the two- to four-inch cones hang down as spruce or hemlock cones do.

Midway along the steep climb, you can enjoy a good view down Lake Creek canyon to 6,900-foot Labyrinth Mountain. You may notice a layer of volcanic ash under a thin covering of topsoil in trail cuts. This ash may have been deposited by the last major eruption of nearby Glacier Peak more than 12,000 years ago.

The trail levels off 0.75 mile east of the lake. A quick stroll through the forest will bring you to the eastern shore of peaceful Heather Lake, elevation 3,953 feet. The Cascade crest forms a timbered backdrop for many hemlock-sheltered campsites near the lake's outlet. Parallel grooves in the bedrock near the outlet testify to the ancient glacier that scooped out the bowl in which the lake now rests.

Red heather and huckleberry are common here, and fishing for pan-sized cutthroats is fair. If you're feeling adventurous, you might consider a strenuous jaunt to Glasses Lake, lying in the obvious hanging cirque southwest of Heather. Take the trail around the south shore of Heather Lake and scramble 600 feet upstream to the remote 4,626-foot Glasses Lake. □

HIKE 49 *MEANDER MEADOW—CADY RIDGE LOOP*

General description: A moderate sixteen-mile, loop backpack through virgin forests and along flower-decorated ridges north of Stevens Pass in the Henry M. Jackson Wilderness.
Elevation gain and loss: 3,220 feet.
Trailhead elevation: 3,040 feet.
High point: 5,760 feet.
Maps: Bench Mark Mtn. and Poe Mtn. 7.5-minute USGS quads; Wenatchee National Forest map.
Season: July through early October.
Water availability: Available along first 8.5 miles only.

Finding the trailhead: Drive eastward from Stevens Pass on U.S. Highway 2 for 19.5 miles to the Lake Wenatchee turnoff—State Route 207.

Follow this paved road, ignoring the left fork to Nason Creek Campground and the two right forks to Plain (State Route 209) and the Chiwawa Loop road. State Route 207 follows the north shore of Lake Wenatchee, passing a ranger station and reaching a junction two miles beyond. Bear left onto Forest Road 65 where the White River Road forks right. Bear right after six miles; a sign here points to Little Wenatchee Ford Campground. Road 6700 to U.S. Highway 2 forks left here. The road narrows to one-lane pavement after 1.1 miles. Bear left after another 0.1 mile.

Pavement ends 6.1 miles from the junction with Road 6700; stay left here and follow the rocky, narrow dirt road to its end at the trailhead, another 3.8 miles.

Or drive four miles east from Stevens Pass on U.S. Highway 2 and turn left

Common on drier mountain slopes east of the Cascade crest, arrowleaf balsamroot is one of the most conspicuous wildflowers springtime hikers will encounter. Bob Arrington photo.

(north) where a sign indicates "Smithbrook." Follow this rough dirt road (Forest Road 6700) for 12.6 miles to Forest Road 65 and turn left, traveling about ten miles to the trailhead.

The hike: A favorite with hikers who enjoy loop trips, this backpack of two or more days traces the route of an old Indian trail up the Little Wenatchee River to the Cascade crest and returns via scenic Cady Ridge, named for a nineteenth-century explorer. The meadows, hushed forests, and broad vistas you'll encounter will prove that there's more to a wilderness experience than jagged peaks and alpine lakes.

North of Stevens Pass the low elevation of the Cascade crest allows ample moisture to fall on the east side. Thus, vegetation on this well-watered east-side hike is more typical of the western slope. The typical rain shadow occurs farther east, where a series of high, southeast-trending ridges intercept the bulk of Pacific moisture.

From the trailhead, follow the Little Wenatchee Trail north into a dense, shady forest. The first four miles follows the canyon bottom, alternating between silver-fir forest and open avalanche swaths overgrown with Sitka alder, Douglas maple, and bracken fern. Up-canyon, the parklands of Poet Ridge, bright green in summer but flaming red after the first frosts of autumn, come into view.

Near the head of the canyon the river forks. The trail passes through a large grassy meadow and ascends slopes above the right (north) fork. The trail, rocky

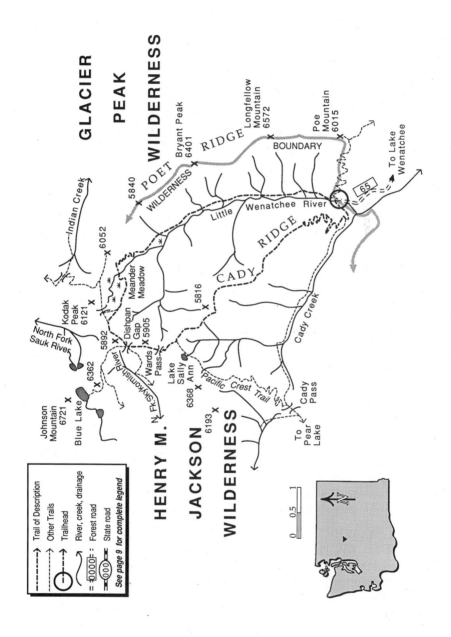

and brushy in places, rises steeply to timberline near the top of this 1,200-foot ascent, passing scattered patches of stunted fir and hemlock. The open slopes are thick with bracken fern, Sitka alder, grasses, and huckleberry.

The trail levels off then, and you'll get a good view down to subalpine Meander Meadow. Make a brief descent to it through huckleberry thickets, which usually offer the best berry-picking in late September.

Several good campsites lie above a tributary to the Little Wenatchee near the east end of the flat meadow, sheltered by stunted mountain hemlocks. It's possible to visualize a shallow lake here, which is probably what Meander Meadow once was. Many mountain lakes become meadows as they steadily fill up with silt from the slowly eroding mountains above.

The trail briefly fades out midway across the meadow, but simply head for a "Trail" sign at the meadow's southern edge, about six miles from the trailhead.

You'll leave the beautiful grassland behind as you ascend a moderate, open, north-facing slope clothed in heather and huckleberry for 0.75 mile to an unsigned junction. The right fork leads to the northbound Pacific Crest Trail (PCT) in 0.3 mile, seen traversing the south slopes of Kodak Peak, beyond which rises the alpine bulk of Indian Head Peak. To the east the view includes Poet (or Wenatchee) Ridge, capped by notable versemen Poe, Longfellow, Bryant and Irving. Beyond are the higher peaks of Whittier and Mount Jonathan.

Take the left fork, traversing south slopes above a scenic basin for 0.3 mile to the southbound PCT, and turn left onto it.

Leave the trail here and climb briefly to a pass on the Cascade crest for a dramatic view of Glacier Peak. White River Glacier is the large snowfield clinging to Peak 8195. A small bench just northwest of this pass offers a very scenic campsite in fair weather with an all-year water source. Imaginative hikers can find other such campsites near the crest in the next two miles.

Continue southward on the PCT above a headwaters bowl of the Little Wenatchee. Schist is the dominant rock in the area. This section of the Cascade crest is a beautiful stroll through patches of mountain hemlock and silver fir, open parks, and meadow-clad slopes.

Three quarters of a mile from the previous junction is another junction at 5,600-foot-high Dishpan Gap, littered with volcanic boulders presumably ejected from a past Glacier Peak eruption. At this four-way junction, trails lead west down the North Fork Skykomish River to a west-side trailhead and northwest for two miles to scenic Blue Lake.

Stay on the southbound PCT, traversing west slopes with fine views to the Monte Cristo Peaks. The trail crosses 5,700-foot Wards Pass and descends along east slopes above a bench through which trickles the infant Little Wenatchee River, beginning its journey to the Columbia.

The trail descends past a few trickling springs, reaching an unmarked junction 1.5 miles from Dishpan Gap. You can continue south on the PCT for half a mile to lovely Lake Sally Ann, a popular campsite set in a timberline basin below Skykomish Peak. No fires or camping are allowed within 200 feet of the lake. For a longer hike follow the PCT four miles south from Lake Sally Ann to Cady Pass and then another 5.25 miles along forested Cady Creek to the trailhead.

Otherwise, bear left onto the vista-filled Cady Ridge Trail, which leads southeast down to a grassy saddle (a good but waterless campsite), and then rises gently along the west slopes of Peak 5816. Along this stretch of the hike, you can enjoy superb views both south and west along the crest of the Cascade Range. Among the varied wildflowers here are pearly everlasting, purple aster, lupine, phlox, Indian paintbrush, false hellebore, fireweed, meadow rue, and western anemone. The abundant huckleberries reach their peak around late September.

A typical ridgeline trail with many ups and downs, this route is best navigated in fair weather. The ridge features meadows, patchy forest, and ever-changing views both east and west once beyond Peak 5816.

After two miles take one last look at mighty Glacier Peak before plunging into the forest, descending quite steeply, and entering a much drier environment. The sparse forest cover of young white pine and Douglas-fir is revegetating the burned-over ridge.

Once switchbacks begin to ease the grade, you enter a moister canyon bottom. The Cady Creek Trail soon joins from the west, and then the trail bridges the Little Wenatchee and climbs quickly to the trailhead, 6.5 miles from the PCT. □

HIKE 50 *ALPINE LOOKOUT*

General description: A ten-mile, round-trip day hike (or overnighter if you pack water) to a panoramic vista point above Wenatchee Lake in Wenatchee National Forest.
Elevation gain and loss: +2,600 feet; -420 feet.
Trailhead elevation: 4,000 feet.
High point: 6,200 feet.
Maps: Wenatchee Lake 15-minute USGS quad; Wenatchee National Forest map.
Season: July through mid-October.
Water availability: There's no water en route, so hikers should bring plenty of drinking water.

Finding the trailhead: Follow U.S. Highway 2 eastbound from Stevens Pass for 17.2 miles to a roadside rest area and southbound Coulter Creek Road. Proceed 0.2 mile to a hard-to-spot junction with northbound Forest Road 6910, just east of mile post 82, and turn left. The dirt road enters an area of residences, bridges Nason Creek, and passes under power lines before climbing timbered slopes. Ignore a closed, right-forking road after 3.1 miles, and bear right onto Road 107 after 4.4 miles. Signs at both junctions point to "trail." This spur road executes a tight right-hand switchback before reaching the signed Round Mountain Trail after 0.2 mile.

The hike: This day hike traverses a portion of a major east-west divide separating the upper Wenatchee River from Nason Creek and the route of U.S. Highway 2. Views of the Wenatchee River drainage, including such major tributaries as the White and Chiwawa rivers, in addition to the snowy cone of Glacier Peak, make the Alpine Lookout a popular and rewarding destina-

With their black saber-like horns, black hoofs, and long, shaggy white hair, mountain goats remain a distinctive, if increasingly familiar, animal in some areas. Forest Service photo.

tion. There's a good chance you'll see mountain goats along the ridge. There's also a chance of encountering mountain bikes here.

With no water en route and much of the trail on open, sunny slopes, you should bring plenty of drinking water. Backpackers who carry water will find many ridgetop campsites and be rewarded with the possibility of enjoying a magnificent Cascade sunrise.

The trail, closed to motor vehicles, leads into a forest of grand fir and Douglas-fir. The varied understory consists of pachystima, ceanothus (variously known as tobacco brush, buckbrush, or sticky laurel), lupine, spirea, huckleberry, thimbleberry, Douglas maple, bracken fern, fireweed, false Solomon's seal, prince's pine, wild rose, Oregon grape, queen's cup, vetch, pearly everlasting, and manzanita—plants adapted to a variety of habitats, each growing in the microclimate it finds most suitable.

The trail rises steadily via switchbacks for 1.6 miles to Nason Ridge. At about 4,500 feet subalpine fir becomes the dominant forest tree.

Turn left upon reaching the Nason Ridge Trail on 5,200-foot Nason Ridge, and then climb an additional 300 feet before beginning a south slope traverse amid scattered whitebark pines and subalpine firs.

The up-and-down ridgetop route proceeds northwestward, passing through a ghost forest of fire-killed trees and an interesting area of small ridgeline depressions.

After three miles the spur trail to Alpine Lookout forks right at an outcrop of boulders composed of schist, a flaky metamorphic rock.

A quick half-mile hike leads to the squat lookout tower set on a rocky 6,200-foot bump on Nason Ridge. Lookout towers are becoming a thing of

HIKE 50 ALPINE LOOKOUT

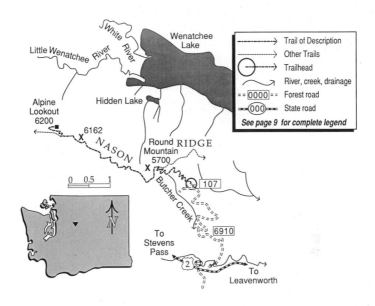

the past, being steadily replaced by aerial surveillance and lightning detection devices.

Trees here, severely stunted by the strong winds and blowing snow that dominate the weather half the year, include five-needled whitebark pine (a common timberline tree east of the Cascade crest), subalpine fir, and, on the colder north side of the ridge, mountain hemlock.

Views are seemingly endless. Westward, Nason Ridge climbs steadily to a group of alpine summits, where numerous cirques shelter several lakes. You can trace the Little Wenatchee River from its broad meanders at the head of Wenatchee Lake to its headwaters on the low Cascade crest, beyond which rise the impressive Monte Cristo Peaks. To the north the milky green White River adds its waters to Wenatchee Lake, contrasting with the crystal clear, nonglacial Little Wenatchee.

Seven miles upstream, the Napeequa River joins the White River. This U-shaped valley in the Glacier Peak Wilderness is perhaps the wildest and most scenic valley in the area.

A series of high ranges—first the White Mountains, then Chiwawa Ridge, the Entiat Mountains, and finally the distant Chelan Mountains—marches eastward for many miles from the backbone of the Cascades, each ridge progressively more arid than the last.

The course of the Wenatchee can be traced far to the southeast, and south beyond the now-silent traffic of Highway 2, the Chiwaukum Mountains rise into the Alpine Lakes Wilderness.

After enjoying the incredible vista, you'll retrace your route back to the trailhead. ☐

HIKE 51 *MAD RIVER—LOST LAKE LOOP*

General description: A moderate 13.3-mile, loop day hike or backpack leading through the pleasant open forests and meadows of the southern Entiat Mountains in Wenatchee National Forest.

Elevation gain and loss: 2,303 feet.

Trailhead elevation: Maverick Saddle, 4,400 feet.

High point: 5,920 feet.

Maps: Chickamin Creek, Silver Falls, and Sugarloaf Peak 7.5-minute USGS quads; Wenatchee National Forest map.

Season: Late June through October.

Water availability: Abundant along initial 5.75 miles.

Finding the trailhead: Drive U.S. Highway 2 west from Leavenworth 14.6 miles to the Lake Wenatchee turnoff, State Route 207, or drive 19.5 miles east of Stevens Pass. Ignore eastbound State Route 209 to Plain at 3.6 miles, and turn right onto Chiwawa Loop Road in another 0.6 mile, just after crossing the Wenatchee River.

Follow this paved county road (No. 22), ignoring turnoffs to Fish Lake, Chiwawa River, and Trinity, to a bridge over the Chiwawa River about 4.6 miles from State Route 207. One half mile beyond, where the road bends south, is a hard-to-spot junction, signed for northbound travelers only ("Lower Chiwawa, Maverick Saddle"). Turn north here onto Forest Road 6100; pavement ends in 0.1 mile. After 1.6 miles is Deep Creek Campground and a junction. Turn right onto Forest Road 6101, avoid several spurs, always following signs to Maverick Saddle.

This good dirt road gets rougher as you approach Deer Camp Campground, where you turn left (north), still on Road 6101, 4.6 miles from the county road.

The road becomes steep, narrow, and even rougher for the next 2.7 miles to Maverick Saddle and a junction with southbound Road 5200 and the northbound spur to the Mad River Trail. Park at the saddle.

The hike: The Entiat Mountains are high, jagged, and snow-clad to the north but gentle and timber-covered to the south, dotted with many large grassy meadows. The forests in the southern Entiats are open, with very little understory. This unique country is a welcome change for hikers used to the dense, overgrown jungles west of the Cascades.

This hike along the upper Mad River in the southern Entiats proceeds through a rolling, meadow-dotted landscape in one of the largest roadless, nonwilderness areas in the state.

Mule deer and black bear roam these mountains, outnumbering the few hikers who visit the area. A major drawback is that weekend motorcyclists disturb the solitude and raise clouds of dust. But on weekdays, and from June to mid-July before the area is opened to trailbikes and pack stock, peace and tranquility prevail. This is the time to hike the Mad River country.

Water is close at hand along the first half of the route, but scarce along the second, ridgetop segment. The trails are good but dusty after midsummer. Backpackers should hang their food to avoid problems with bears.

Wide grassy meadows, lazy streams, and forested mountains greet visitors in the southern Entiat Mountains northwest of Wenatchee. Ron Adkison photo.

From Maverick Saddle, walk 0.3 miles down the rough, narrow road to the trailhead, and then follow the Mad River Trail upstream.

Hike one mile under a shady canopy of spruce and fir, following above the west bank of the tiny Mad River. At this point, the Hi You Trail veers off to the left. This is the return leg of the loop; for now stay right.

Soon the trail bridges the river and meets the Jimmy Creek Trail, leading 3.25 miles to 6,701-foot Cougar Mountain, which offers excellent vistas. You can combine this route with other eastbound trails farther along for a variety of loop trips.

The main trail continues up the Mad River through spruce-fir forest. In early summer, the forest floor is ablaze with wildflowers.

A series of pleasant, narrow meadows begins around the three-mile point. After 3.2 miles, avoid the eastbound Cougar Mountain Trail.

Lodgepole pine, a pioneer in burned areas, dominates the forest beyond that junction.

After 100 yards, the Lost Lake Trail heads west to that lake in 1.5 miles, but save Lost Lake for later.

The route skirts the meadows, passing numerous possible campsites. In fact, this area has such a gentle character that you could camp almost anywhere.

Boulder-hop the river after four miles (a ford during high water). The low, forested ridge to the west is the crest of the Entiat Mountains, where your return trail is located.

After 4.5 miles hop across the Mad River once again via large boulders and meet the eastbound Tyee Ridge Trail, leading to Cougar Meadow and Cougar Mountain among other destinations.

A common shrub in open valleys, the western chokecherry puts forth an impressive floral display in spring and its summer fruit makes excellent jellies and jams. Bob Arrington photo.

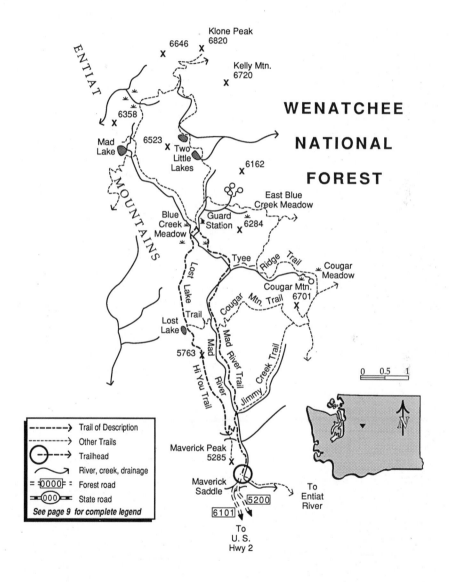

ENTIAT

Klone Peak
6820
6646 X
X

Kelly Mtn.
6720
X

6358
X

WENATCHEE

Mad
Lake
6523
X Two
Little
Lakes

NATIONAL

6162
X

East Blue
Creek Meadow

FOREST

M
O
U
N
T
A
I
N
S

Blue
Creek
Meadow
Guard
Station
6284
X

Tyee
Ridge Trail

Cougar
Meadow

Lost
Lake
Trail
Cougar Mtn.
6701
X

Cougar
Mtn
Trail

Lost
Lake
5763
X

Mad River Trail

Creek Trail

Mad
River

Hi You Trail

Jimmy

Maverick Peak
5285
X

Maverick
Saddle
5200

To
Entiat
River

6101

To
U. S.
Hwy 2

Legend	
– – –→	Trail of Description
·····→	Other Trails
⊖– –→	Trailhead
∿	River, creek, drainage
=:0000:=	Forest road
⊂000⊃	State road

See page 9 for complete legend

0   0.5   1

N

After five miles the trail skirts the eastern edge of large Blue Creek Meadow. Meadows in this region aren't the overgrown fields of shrubs and marshland common west of the Cascades but are inviting expanses of grass and wildflowers. The Mad River, full of tiny trout, meanders through this large flat spread, perhaps the site of an ancient lake. The gentle summits of the Entiat Mountains form a pleasant backdrop to the west.

Near the north end of the meadow, 5.75 miles from the trailhead, the Lost Lake Trail forks left, heading southwest. A lodgepole-pine-shaded campsite with a picnic table lies 100 yards to the north, up the Mad River Trail near the Blue Creek Guard Station, manned in summer only.

Trails lead northwest to Mad Lake in 2.5 miles and northeast to East Blue Creek Meadow in two miles and Two Little Lakes and Klone Peak via a north-bound fork after two miles and 5.25 miles, respectively. Most of these routes can be arranged to make a variety of loop trails.

Follow the much-less-used Lost Lake Trail southwest across the meadow, cross the wide Mad River near the western margin, and climb into a forest of Englemann spruce and subalpine fir, reaching the crest of the southern Entiats after one mile and 250 feet of elevation gain.

Lodgepole pines alternate with the spruce-fir forest as you descend to a junction at shallow, barren Lost Lake, a good summer swimming hole.

Stay right and follow the Hi You Trail south along the undulating crest, first over Peak 5763, then up and over lesser summits, sometimes steeply, offering good views of the Mad River, Cougar Mountain, and points north and east. The forest beyond the Mad River is a patchwork of light green (lodgepoles reforesting burned areas) and dark green (a climax forest of spruce and fir.)

About 3.5 miles from the meadow, a fine vista opens up from Mount Stuart in the southwest to Glacier Peak in the northwest. Wenatchee Lake, and closer at hand, Fish Lake, are also visible as well as the canyon of the Chiwawa River below to the west.

Soon the trail-bike-damaged route descends steeply to a saddle. Turn left (east) at an unmarked junction and quickly switchback down to the Mad River Trail. Turn right onto it and hike one mile back to the trailhead. □

HIKE 52 *HOLDEN VILLAGE TO LYMAN LAKE*

General description: A moderate eighteen-mile, round-trip backpack to a ruggedly beautiful lake basin deep within the vast Glacier Peak Wilderness.
Elevation gain and loss: 2,458 feet.
Trailhead elevation: Holden Village, 3,209 feet.
High point: Lyman Lake, 5,587 feet.
Maps: Holden 15-minute USGS quad (Glacier Peak 15-minute quad necessary for side trips); Glacier Peak Wilderness map; Wenatchee National Forest map.
Season: Mid-July through September.
Water availability: Abundant along entire route.

Finding the trailhead: To reach Holden Village catch the *Lady of the Lake* from Chelan to Lucerne—a three-and-a-half-hour boat ride. The boat runs daily from May 15 through October 15 and costs $18 for a round trip. The Chelan Boat Company dock lies one mile west (toward Wenatchee) of downtown Chelan on U.S. Highway 97. The company charges a parking fee of $3 per night. The boat leaves promptly at 8:30 a.m. Eat a good breakfast before you leave—food on board is expensive. To cut an hour off your cruise, drive twenty-five miles from Chelan to Fields Point Landing. The round-trip fare is the same, and there's also a parking fee.

Upon arrival at Lucerne (Port of Holden), ride the shuttle bus to Holden Village and the trailhead. Round-trip fare is $8.

The hike: This outing begins with a scenic 45-mile boat ride to the trailhead up the narrow, inland fjord of Lake Chelan, a monumental work of glaciation. Its deepest point is 1,586 feet, making it the second-deepest lake in North America. Its bottom is 490 feet below sea level—the lowest point on the North American continent.

This memorable backpack of several days penetrates deeper into the backcountry away from through roads than just about any other hike in the state. Glacier Peak, Washington's largest wilderness area, encompasses 576,865 acres of very rugged mountains, vast ice fields, deep river valleys, and the state's only totally protected volcano. The usual mosquitoes and biting flies are present from early to midsummer. Expect to find quite a few people at Lyman and Hart lakes; there are many isolated nooks, however, where you can find solitude with a modicum of effort. Fishing for cutthroats is only fair in silty Lyman Lake but reportedly more productive for fish in the ten- to twelve-inch range in Hart Lake. No camping or fires are allowed within 200 feet of Lyman Lake.

The shuttle bus from Lucerne to Holden Village will be waiting when you disembark. On your way out, remember to return to the village in time to catch the 1:45 bus back down to Lucerne, or you'll miss the boat.

Holden Village, a nondenominational retreat operated by the Lutheran Church, offers showers, three good meals a day at a reasonable price, and a campground at the end of the road. A nearby hydroelectric power plant supplies electricity to the village.

Once the site of Washington's largest copper mine, Holden was home to as many as 600 people during its heyday in the 1930s. The town boasted a movie theater, bowling alley, and baseball diamond. Ore was transported to Lucerne and Chelan on barges and then shipped to Tacoma for processing. The mining claims are currently owned by Holden Village, Inc.

From Holden Village walk one mile up the road to the trailhead.

The trail undulates for the first mile to a junction with northwestbound Holden Lake Trail. It continues up the U-shaped canyon of Railroad Creek through cottonwood, giant willows, and mixed conifer forest. Much of the canyon was burned in an 1896 fire purposely set by miners. The understory is diverse, including bracken fern, pachystima, red-osier dogwood, Sitka alder, wild rose, thimbleberry, serviceberry, false Solomon's seal, and Douglas maple.

En route up the broad canyon, you'll be able to look south and see various U-shaped waterways surrounded by broken peaks, a contrast to the rounded contours of brush and forest-cloaked slopes on the north side of the canyon. To the west, crags associated with the complicated Bonanza Peak massif will also vie for your attention.

The Cascade Range makes an excellent outdoor classroom for studying the effects of glacial ice. Ron Adkison photo.

After passing a swampy clearing at the head of the first long bench in the canyon, the route ascends brushy slopes to a point overlooking Hart Lake, resting at the east end of the next long bench in the glacial valley. To the west, Crown Point Falls cascades impressively at the head of this bench.

You'll pass a camping area above Hart Lake, partially shaded by small cottonwoods. Then you'll cross a boulder-filled stream. The ford may be difficult before August most years.

Beyond Hart Lake, the route climbs steadily above Crown Point Falls to the third in a series of benches. After leveling off, the trail passes an interesting jumble of granite slabs. Notice how the rock peels away like leaves of lettuce. This is known as exfoliation.

Soon the way passes a mine shaft and then a grass-floored subalpine meadow. From this point on, huckleberries are abundant, reaching their peak in late September.

The route briefly climbs to the next bench, passes a signed southbound spur to Upper Lyman Lakes, and reaches a junction at large, milky-green Lyman Lake. The right fork climbs one mile to Cloudy Pass, and the left fork leads to campsites on the lake's west shore. Other good campsites in subalpine fir forest are located north of the lake.

Keep in mind that no camping or fires are allowed within 200 feet of Lyman Lake. Backpackers should use the more durable sand flats near the trail for campsites rather than the fragile heather areas above the lake. Water issuing from Lyman Glacier is not potable due to an abundance of suspended silt.

From the west shore, views across the lake basin are superb, featuring the

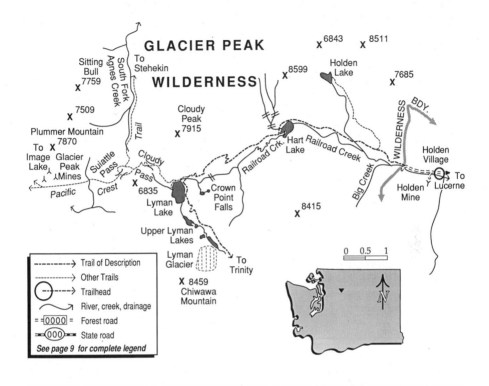

highest nonvolcanic summit in the state, 9,511-foot Bonanza Peak. This peak is composed of resistant gneiss (metamorphosed granite) while its neighbor north of the lake, 7,915-foot Cloudy Peak, is composed of granite, much of which was stripped away by the ancient Lyman Glacier more than 10,000 years ago.

Numerous optional side trips are possible from a Lyman Lake base camp. With a car shuttle, experienced hikers might consider the route over Spider Gap to the Chiwawa River, a relatively easy trail walk in late summer after much of the snow has melted, but an ice axe is recommended for persistent icy sections.

Another possibility is to follow the trail for one mile, climbing 850 feet, to Cloudy Pass (above timberline). From the pass you can see the ice-bound north slopes of mighty Glacier Peak and look down rugged South Fork Agnes Creek. You can spend a full day hiking another six miles west to scenic Image Lake, one of the most-photographed as well as most-frequently-visited spots in the wilderness. The maze of trails around the lake and severe camping restrictions attest to its popularity.

For a more extended trip, you might hike down the South Fork Agnes Creek to the Stehekin River, a total of about twenty-eight miles. You can then catch a shuttle bus to the boat dock in Stehekin.

A side trip to the fascinating Lyman Glacier is a must. Follow the trail signed for Upper Lyman Lakes, climbing over a low ridge to the upper basin. Scattered islands of subalpine fir dot the lower end of this basin, while Lyall larch grows only on hummocks above the glacier-scooped bowl.

The trail passes the remains of an old cabin above the two lowest lakes in Upper Lyman Lakes basin.

Since the end of the Little Ice Age in the early part of the twentieth century, many glaciers have begun an unsteady retreat, advancing and retreating, but mostly retreating. You'll soon come upon evidence of Lyman Glacier's farthest advance this century in a very fresh terminal moraine, a load of rock debris deposited at the tip of the glacier. On the east walls of the basin is a line of red rocks carried from the red peak above and deposited along the side of the glacier's path—a lateral moraine, which illustrates the depth of the glacier. Small trees pioneering that moraine lie below a distinct line of larger trees that escaped the advance of ice.

Proceed southward through the raw landscape, passing a third lake and climbing over a larger terminal moraine created by the latest major advance of the glacier. One more lake lies at the foot of the glacier.

If you climb over Spider Gap you'll stay east of this lake, but stay west and proceed cross-country to investigate the glacier.

The lower part of the glacier is riddled with crevasses, and often you can sit and watch chunks of ice break off and fall into the lake below.

After an informative walk through this spectacular basin, viewing firsthand the great erosive power of a glacier, either continue to Spider Gap or return to Lyman Lake. □

HIKE 53 NORTH FORK SAUK RIVER TO LOST CREEK RIDGE AND LAKE BYRNE

General description: A strenuous twenty-two-mile, round-trip backpack along a scenic ridge on the west side of the North Cascades in the Glacier Peak Wilderness.

Elevation gain and loss: +5,200 feet, -1,400 feet.

Trailhead elevation: 1,900 feet.

High point: 6,000 feet.

Maps: Sloan Peak 7.5-minute USGS quad and Glacier Peak 15-minute USGS quad; Glacier Peak Wilderness map; Mount Baker-Snoqualmie National Forest map.

Season: July through early October.

Water availability: The trail is mostly waterless in late summer, and the ridgetop segment is exposed, so carry an ample water supply.

Finding the trailhead: From State Route 530 in Darrington (twenty-eight miles east of Arlington) turn south onto the Mountain Loop Highway where State Route 530 makes a right angle bend. Pavement ends 8.9 miles from Darrington at a four-way junction. If you plan to return via White Chuck River

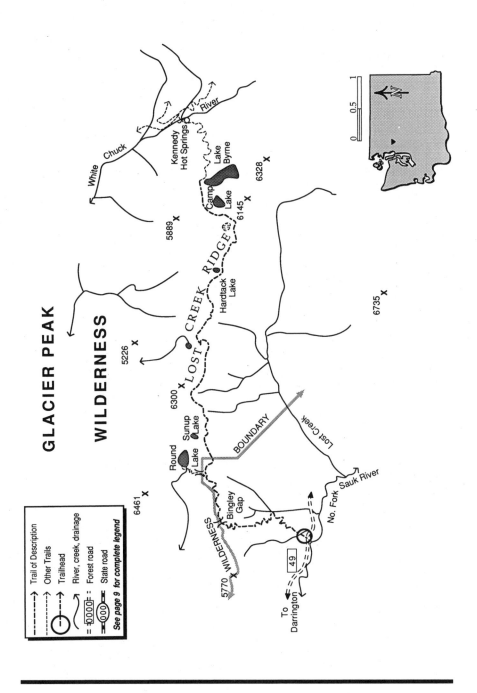

you should turn left at this junction and follow Forest Road 23 east for eleven miles to the White Chuck Trailhead.

Otherwise, continue southeastward on winding dirt Forest Road 20 along the east and northeast banks of the Sauk River. Turn left 15.6 miles from Darrington onto Forest Road 49 where a sign points to Lost Creek Ridge Trail, which is three miles ahead on the north side of the road, just past milepost 3.

The hike: The White Chuck and Suiattle River trails are among the most popular routes into the west side of the vast Glacier Peak Wilderness, Washington's largest roadless area. But the Lost Creek Ridge Trail takes the high route, thousands of feet above those deep river valleys.

This route is quite rigorous, gaining 3,600 feet during the first 4.5 miles, but it's generally easy to follow except when snow covered or foggy. Vistas are expansive and continuous during fair weather, which is the logical time to contemplate such an exposed hike.

The rocky trail climbs gently the first half mile under a shady canopy of red alder and bigleaf maple, a good warm-up before the work begins. Then come switchbacks—moderate at first, becoming steeper later on—through western redcedar, Douglas-fir, and western hemlock. Occasional views of the broad U-shaped North Fork Sauk River and of 7,835-foot Sloan Peak will help to divert your attention from the relentless climb.

At three miles is 4,400-foot Bingley Gap on the southern boundary of the Glacier Peak Wilderness. The route climbs up and away from the densely forested gap, passing openings that allow northward views of isolated Pugh Mountain, White Chuck Mountain, and even distant Mount Baker.

Breaking out of the forest onto south-facing slopes, you'll come into a timberline environment, featuring green slopes carpeted with wildflowers and isolated stands of mountain hemlock and Alaska yellow-cedar, trees of the maritime forest.

Far-ranging vistas begin here, and they get even better as the trail proceeds eastward. The tip of Glacier Peak is visible on the eastern horizon, far to the southeast is the Stuart Range, and south lies the Alpine Lakes country. Peaks in the rugged Sauk River region include Twin Peaks and Mount Forgotten in the southwest.

After 4.5 miles of steady climbing, you'll pass a Glacier Peak Wilderness sign. Ignore the trail to Round Lake, which forks left. It climbs over a 5,600-foot saddle before plunging 500 feet down north slopes to the lake. Those slopes remain snowbound at least until mid-July, but big trout are reputed to lurk in the depths of the popular lake.

The ridge route continues eastward on a gentle grade. Its constant vistas and copious huckleberries are sure to slow you down, however. Snowfields lasting until mid-July may also hamper progress. The undulating ridgeline trail dips into basins and traverses north or south slopes near the upper limit of tree growth. Many possible campsites, scenic but mostly dry, may invite you to call it quits for the first day on the trail.

After 7.5 miles, you'll switchback above a tiny but alluring lake and then negotiate another up-and-down mile to Hardtack Lake, a possible campsite. More campsites, fair but exposed, are 1.25 miles beyond at 5,700-foot Camp Lake.

The trail climbs steeply above the lake, passes through an alpine bench, and then descends to long, deep Lake Byrne. En route enjoy superb vistas of Glacier Peak's rocky western flank, rising over 6,000 feet above the dark forests of the White Chuck valley.

The trail descends from overused Lake Byrne (no fires), and, if you've set up a car shuttle, you can descend past inviting Kennedy Hot Springs to the White Chuck Trailhead, about 8.25 miles from the lake (the shortest route if Lake Byrne is the desired destination).

The best campsites are probably located around Camp or Hardtack lakes, since solitude can be hard to find at Lake Byrne on some weekends. Also, no campfires are allowed within a quarter mile of Lake Byrne.

After enjoying this superb backcountry area, retrace the route to the trailhead. □

HIKE 54 *BOULDER RIVER TO BOULDER FORD CAMP*

General description: An easy eight-mile, round-trip day hike or backpack through virgin lowland forest on the west slope of the North Cascades in the Boulder River Wilderness.
Elevation gain and loss: +750 feet, -300 feet.
Trailhead elevation: 948 feet.
High point: 1,600 feet.
Maps: Granite Falls 7.5-minute USGS quad (trailhead just off map on Oso 15-minute USGS quad); Mount Baker-Snoqualmie National Forest map.
Season: All year.
Water availability: Water is never a problem. En route you pass three springs and four small creeks.

Finding the trailhead: Follow State Route 530 to mile post 41, 8.2 miles west of Darrington Ranger Station and 19.75 miles east of Arlington. Turn south at a hard-to-spot junction onto Forest Road 2010. This dirt road leads past French Creek Campground to a junction after four miles. Turn right here and proceed 100 yards to the trailhead parking area.

The hike: The canyon of the Boulder River cuts a deep trench through the northwestern corner of the wilderness area. Because of its low elevation, the trail along the river remains accessible to hikers year-round. In winter it's wet, but that's a special time to hike the Boulder River, when the high country of Saddle Lake and Goat Flat near Three Fingers, the most frequently visited areas in the wilderness, are buried in white and the river is roaring with runoff.

The trail, open to hikers only, begins at the west end of the parking area. The initial 0.75 mile follows an old road cut into a steep cliff, shaded by red alder, western hemlock, and western redcedar. You can see but not hear roaring Boulder Falls as the route, narrowing to a trail, passes above the remains of an old cabin. A boot-beaten path descends past the cabin site to the river.

After a mile the trail passes above a campsite and reaches the Boulder Falls, indicated by the sign at the trailhead. This ribbon of white water cascades

HIKE 54 *BOULDER RIVER TO BOULDER FORD CAMP*

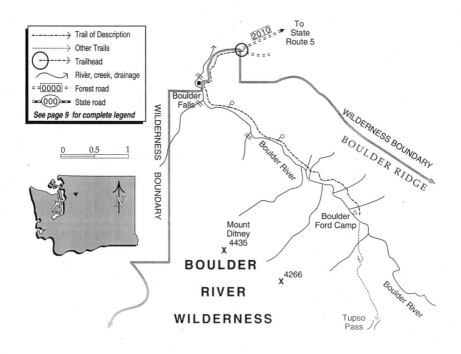

Legend:
- --------→ Trail of Description
- ------------→ Other Trails
- ◯----→ Trailhead
- ～ River, creek, drainage
- ＝［0000］＝ Forest road
- ⊸（000）⊶ State road

See page 9 for complete legend

0   0.5   1

N

2010
To State Route 5

WILDERNESS BOUNDARY

Boulder Falls

WILDERNESS BOUNDARY

BOULDER RIDGE

Boulder River

WILDERNESS BOUNDARY

Boulder Ford Camp

Mount Ditney 4435 x

BOULDER

x 4266

RIVER

WILDERNESS

Tupso Pass

Boulder River

nearly eighty vertical feet into the Boulder River. Many hikers make this the destination of an easy day hike.

The trail continues above the east bank of the river through a lush, low-elevation forest of western hemlock, western redcedar, silver fir, and some very large Douglas-firs. Then, shaded by western hemlock and red alder, it descends to Boulder Ford Camp after four miles.

At the ford you can see up the canyon to a jagged alpine ridge, especially enjoyable since views are infrequent here and limited to forested slopes and ridges.

The trail shown on the map, leading from the ford to Tupso Pass, has been abandoned and is overgrown and difficult to follow. □

HIKE 55 *MOUNT PILCHUCK*

General description: A moderate 3.5-mile hike to the top of 5,324-foot Mount Pilchuck and the restored forest service fire lookout.

Elevation gain and loss: 2,200 feet.

High Point: 5,324 feet.

Length: Seven miles roundtrip.

Maps: USGS Granite Falls; Mount Baker-Snoqualmie National Forest.

Season: June through November.

Water availability: Hikers should bring their own water.

Special attractions: Spectacular views to the west of the Puget Sound Basin and to the east into the Glacier Peak, Boulder River and Henry M. Jackson wilderness areas. The old forest service fire lookout has been restored by the Everett Mountaineers. Sightings of mountain goat are possible.

For more information: USDA Forest Service public service center at Verlot, Granite Falls, WA 98252 (207) 691-7791.

Finding the Trailhead: From Interstate 5 north of Lake Stevens, take a right onto State Road 92 through Granite Falls to the Verlot Pubic Service Center. Go one mile east on 92, which becomes the Mountain Loop Highway, and

HIKE 55 *MOUNT PILCHUCK*

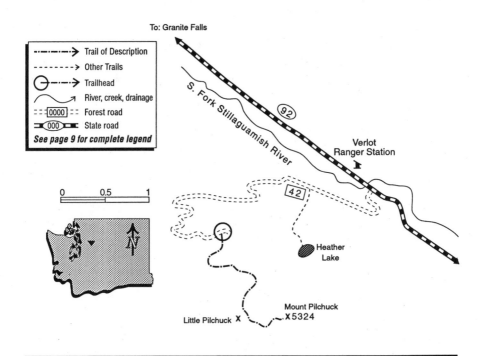

The Mount Pilchuck Lookout offers superb vistas. Cliff Leight photo.

turn right onto the Mount Pilchuck State Park Road #42. Follow this for 6.9 miles to the signed trailhead.

The hike: Mount Pilchuck is the perfect hike for first-time visitors to the area who want a taste of the Cascades, and perhaps want to reach a summit as well. But the hike is not recommended for beginners or hikers with children. Standing atop Pilchuck's broad rocky summit gives one the feeling of having climbed a "real mountain." The 360-degree view from the old forest service fire lookout cabin (restored by the Everett Mountaineers in 1989) is breathtaking. On a clear day, hikers can make out ferries crossing Puget Sound and take in the ragged crest of the Cascades from Mount Rainier to the Canadian border. Not bad for a 3.5-mile hike.

The hike begins on the edges of the old Mount Pilchuck Ski Area. The once-scarred ski-slopes are slowly being reclaimed by ferns, fir and vine-maple. The lower trail, through old-growth forest, can be muddy in the early summer, and hikers traditionally made their own way through the forest. The result was a confusion of trails. Efforts have been made to keep hikers on the main trail. Please help out and don't cut the trail.

Shortly before swinging to the east at about 0.75 mile, the trail touches the eastern edge of a huge clearcut. Near the top of the old ski slopes the trail winds up through heather and over polished rock slabs. Yellow splotches of paint mark the trail through this rocky stretch, a trail-marking system frowned on today.

Just east of Little Pilchuck the trail crosses a saddle onto the south side of the mountain. Above the saddle yellow paint indicates a high route across boulders to the summit. This high trail quickly gains the summit ridge crest and boulder hops to the summit. The main trail continues down and around the south side before switchbacking about 0.5 mile to the summit.

Plan to spend some time on the summit. The restored lookout cabin has a informative historic display, including old forest service photos and panoramic photos that identify the surrounding peaks. Retrace the route back to the trailhead.—*Malcolm Bates* □

HIKE 56 *CASCADE PASS AND SAHALE GLACIER*

General description: A moderate 7.4-mile, round-trip hike (to Cascade Pass) or a strenuous 12.4-mile, round-trip day hike or overnighter in the high country of North Cascades National Park.

Elevation gain and loss: 1,800 feet to Cascade Pass; 4,000 feet to Sahale Glacier.

Trailhead elevation: 3,600 feet.

High point: Cascade Pass, 5,400 feet; Sahale Glacier, 7,600 feet.

Maps: Cascade Pass 7.5-minute USGS quad; North Cascades National Park USGS quad; North Cascades National Park map.

Season: Late July through September.

Water availability: Little available en route to Cascade Pass.

Permit: Required for overnight camping only. Obtain at National Park Service ranger station in Marblemount.

Finding the trailhead: Drive to Marblemount via the North Cascades Highway (State Route 20). Where the highway makes a right angle bend from east to north, turn east onto the Cascade River Road and cross the Skagit River. Pavement ends after 4.6 miles. This wide gravel road (rough due to heavy use) leads to a junction with the right-forking road to the Middle and South Forks of the Cascade River after 16.4 miles. Turn left here onto a narrow dirt road, reaching the large parking area and trailhead after another 6.3 miles. The final two miles are very steep, rough, and narrow—use caution.

The hike: The North Cascades is a land of giant ice-clad peaks rising thousands of feet above deep, densely forested canyons. Generally speaking, this extremely rugged area lies between Snoqualmie Pass and the Canadian border, bounded on the east by the Cascade crest.

It's here that the Cascade Range broadens, reaching 125 miles at its widest point. Incidentally, the North Cascades form the westernmost extension of the longest, unbroken band of east-west mountains in the contiguous United States, stretching 500 miles from the Pacific Ocean to the plains east of Glacier National Park, Montana.

Impenetrable thickets of underbrush, jumbles of fallen trees, icy torrents, vast glaciers, smooth rock walls, and knife-edged ridges limit travel for all but the hardiest mountaineers to the few established trails in the region. The trail to Cascade Pass offers perhaps the easiest route into the heart of the North Cascades, a chance for anyone willing to tread the short path to experience the grandeur of some of the world's most beautiful mountains.

The pass, a historical Indian route, was crossed by Lt. Henry C. Pierce in

Ice-capped Eldorado Peak, 8,868 feet, is the loftiest summit visible from Cascade Pass, one of the shortest and most scenic day-hiking destinations in North Cascades National Park. Ron Adkison photo.

1882 in an epic month-long cross-Cascade journey. Later it was used by miners, whose diggings can be observed in Horseshoe Basin and at Doubtful Lake. The state of Washington had plans in the late nineteenth century to construct a wagon road across the range at Cascade Pass. Even railroad surveys were conducted along the Stehekin River. Eventually, a road was built into Horseshoe Basin to serve the mines there. Fortunately for hikers, plans to extend it over the rugged pass were scrapped, and the road from Cottonwood Camp to Horseshoe Basin was abandoned.

No camping is allowed in the fragile alpine environment of Cascade Pass and nearby Sahale Arm.

The trailhead, surrounded by rock walls and huge glaciers, is perhaps the most beautiful spot accessible by automobile in all the North Cascades. Views from the start inspire the mountaineer in each of us. Johannesburg Mountain and its hanging glaciers loom menacingly to the southwest while ice-capped Eldorado Peak dominates the northwestern horizon. Cascade Pass itself seems but a stone's throw away.

But these impressive sentinels soon fade from view as the wide, easy-to-ascend trail ducks into a stand of silver fir.

En route, you'll be serenaded by a host of waterfalls draining the ice fields

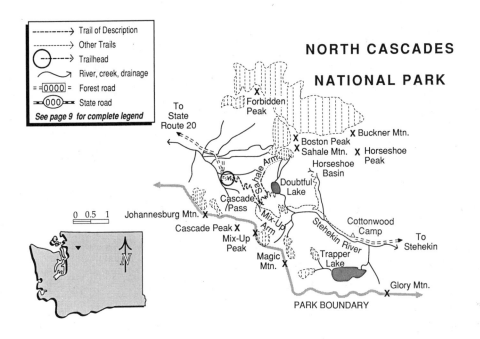

of Cascade Peak as well as startled by the roar of ice crashing down from the hanging glaciers of Johannesburg.

Beyond the switchbacks, the trail passes above timberline and traverses to the pass amid the stunted forms of silver fir and mountain hemlock, trees of the maritime mountains.

Most hikers go no farther than Cascade Pass, enjoying eastward views into Pelton Basin—the headwaters of the Stehekin River, encircled by a jumble of impressive peaks seemingly in the grip of an ice age.

Distant peaks rise farther to the east, as high as those surrounding the pass. Due to the rain shadow created by the North Cascades, those mountains bear little ice on their flanks.

A choice of routes from the pass awaits the adventurous. A trail leads southeast along scenic Mix-Up Arm and then plunges into steep ice fields—the realm of the experienced mountaineer.

The main trail descends east into Pelton Basin (and campsites), passes the spur trail to the mines of Horseshoe Basin, and ends in 5.2 miles at Cottonwood Camp. A shuttle bus serves Cottonwood from the village of Stehekin on Lake Chelan. This is the shortest and easiest trans-Cascade hike in the North Cascades, but highly scenic and rewarding nonetheless.

Another trail leads steeply northeast from Cascade Pass, first climbing grassy slopes before leveling off above a few persistent subalpine firs and mountain hemlocks struggling to survive on Sahale Arm.

Numerous trails crisscross the slopes of the arm above the deep blue oval of Doubtful Lake, which signs indicate are closed for restoration by the park service. One of these trails is open, though, and descends steeply for 800 feet to the lake in one mile. A ribbon of white water drops nearly 2,000 feet into the 5,385-foot lake, draining the Sahale Glacier.

To get to the glacier, continue to follow the trail along gentle Sahale Arm, ending where grass and alpine cushion plants give way to rock—the arctic-alpine life zone. Experienced hikers can continue (although inexperienced hikers, sometimes clad only in tennis shoes and shorts, unwisely proceed beyond the arm) to the Sahale Glacier, 4,000 feet above the trailhead. Several very exposed campsites are situated below the glacier, which provides an ample water supply.

Practiced climbers may contemplate an ascent of Sahale Mountain. The Class 3 summit lies above small but crevasse-riddled Sahale Glacier. The North Cascades National Park map features a photograph taken from the summit, offering further enticement to hikers who thrive on panoramic vistas. □

HIKE 57 *MOUNTAIN LAKE — MOUNT PICKETT LOOP*

General description: A pleasant seven-mile, loop day hike leading through dense forests and passing three glacial lakes in Moran State Park on the largest of the San Juan Islands.
Elevation gain and loss: 846 feet.
Trailhead elevation: 914 feet.
High point: 1,760 feet.
Maps: Orcas Island 15-minute USGS quad; brochure: Your Guide to Moran State Park.
Season: March through mid-December.
Water availability: No potable water en route, available only at trailhead.

Finding the trailhead: Follow directions given in Hike 59 and turn left. Ignore left-forking Mount Constitution Road at one mile, and drive past the Mountain Lake Campground to the boat-launch area at the end of the road.

The hike: Midway between mainland Washington and Vancouver Island, hundreds of landforms rise out of the Pacific, ranging from tiny rocks to large, populated islands.

Once part of the mainland, the San Juan Islands were overridden thousands of years ago by the vast Cordilleran Ice Sheet creeping south from Canada. In addition to rounding the topography of the islands, this ice sheet also formed Puget Sound and the Hood Canal and came close to severing the Olympic Peninsula from the mainland.

One of the more popular recreation sites in the islands, 5,600-acre Moran State Park on Orcas Island features three campgrounds and more than twenty miles of hiking trails. This forested terrain is simply the finest hiking area in the San Juans.

A trip to Orcas Island is not a one-day affair. Most visitors stay in one of the campgrounds and spend several days exploring the island. See Hike 58 for another rewarding day hike.

The Bonnie Sliger Memorial Trail begins north of tiny Mountain Lake Campground at the boat launch and day-use parking area. Proceed northward along the west shore of glacier-gouged, 914-foot Mountain Lake under a canopy of western hemlock, western redcedar, and Douglas-fir. Understory plants in this shady environment are limited to Oregon grape, wild rose, whortleberry, gooseberry, bracken fern, ocean spray, and a variety of grasses.

After one mile, the trail jogs east in a grassy flat shaded by large red alders, and after 1.4 miles it reaches a junction.

The right fork follows the east shore of the lake and loops back to the trailhead, a distance of about four miles. For a longer and more interesting hike, take the left fork, which ascends the course of a small stream and then climbs easily over a low saddle. Sitka spruce make a brief appearance at this 1,100-foot-high saddle, far above the coastal strip they typically inhabit. Numerous large, charred snags recall the huge forests that once blanketed this island.

On the other side of the saddle an imperceptible descent leads to a three-way junction, 2.2 miles from the trailhead. The left fork leads upward for 1.3 steep miles to the ever-popular summit of Mount Constitution. Take the right fork, skirting the southeast end of trout-filled Big Twin Lake (fishing in Mountain Lake is also productive), and quickly reach another junction.

You may either turn left here and loop around Little Twin Lake for a good view to the glacier-smoothed east face of Mount Constitution or turn right and follow the south shore of the lake. Both trails rejoin at the little-used Mount Pickett Trail, ascending a gentle, southeast-trending ridge, viewless due to the dense Douglas-fir forest. The way passes several former ponds, now grass-filled depressions. Keep an eye out for the abundant black-tailed deer that inhabit the area.

You'll reach a destination and mileage sign 0.6 mile from Twin Lakes at the north end of an old road. Continue your trek via this road, topping out on a saddle just east of Mount Pickett after another mile. The 1,765-foot summit lies a few feet to the west, but search as you may, any hint of a vista is obscured by the dense timber. The topo map will inform you that Mountain Lake lies less than one mile west, and the Pacific, rumbling with the motors of numerous watercraft, lies but a mile to the northeast.

Follow the road south as it descends from the saddle, switchbacking at once. A faint trail branches northeastward from this bend, and experienced hikers with the help of the topo map can follow this route as it descends first north, then south along the eastern boundary of the park, and finally west along the southern boundary, rejoining the road part way between Mountain and Cascade lakes.

Most hikers, however, will continue following the course of the old road as it descends, alternating between old-growth forest and younger stands of Douglas-fir and lodgepole pine. The route dips into a 1,000-foot-high saddle just before reaching a junction with a westbound track, 2.2 miles from Mount Pickett.

Turn right (west) at this point, quickly descending to the south end of Mountain Lake. Then turn left and walk to the lower end of the lake, bear right at another junction and cross the lake's outlet just below a small dam. You can enjoy a fine view of Mount Constitution and the summit observation tower from here.

The trail follows the irregular southwest shore, ending on the road opposite a park ranger's cabin, half a mile from the dam. Complete the loop by walking northward on the road for a quarter mile to the trailhead. □

HIKE 58 *CASCADE LAKE TO MOUNT CONSTITUTION*

General description: A moderately strenuous, 8.6-mile round-trip day hike to the highest point on the San Juan Islands in Moran State Park.
Elevation gain and loss: 2,059 feet.
Trailhead elevation: 350 feet.
High point: Mount Constitution, 2,409 feet.
Maps: Orcas Island 15-minute USGS quad; Hiking Trails of Moran State Park map.
Season: March through mid-December.
Water availability: None available.

Finding the trailhead: Follow directions given for Hike 59 to Cascade Lake. The signed Mount Constitution Trail begins on the north side of the road just east of the campground registration booth.

The hike: The not-so-wild 2,409-foot summit of Mount Constitution is the apex of the San Juan Islands. The view from the top, said by one early visitor to be the "finest marine view in North America," takes in the ocean, many islands, and the mountains of two countries.

Most visitors drive the steep, narrow, tortuous, paved road to the summit, but a few take the rewarding, albeit strenuous, hike from the North End Campground on Cascade Lake.

Signed for Cold Spring and Mount Constitution, the trail briefly follows the course of a small cedar-shaded stream opposite the campground before jogging east into the Cold Creek drainage, the realm of gigantic Douglas-firs and western hemlocks. Numerous charred trees tell a silent story of past forest fires.

The route switchbacks steadily upward for 2.3 miles to a junction on Hidden Ridge.

Near the top, the Douglas-fir-and-lodgepole-pine forest is open enough to permit interesting views of Cascade Lake, East Sound, the Turtleback Range, farmlands on the western arm of the horseshoe-shaped island, other San Juan islands, and the distant Olympics.

At the ridgetop junction, turn right, and head southeastward across corrugated slopes, passing two lush meadows—former lakes.

That 0.4-mile stroll ends just beyond the sheltered site of seeping Cold Spring where the trail joins a closed dirt road. Follow this road as it quickly passes a shelter and a picnic area, reaching the Mount Constitution Road beyond the locked gate, 0.1 mile from Cold Spring.

HIKE 57 *MOUNTAIN LAKE — MOUNT PICKETT LOOP*
HIKE 58 *CASCADE LAKE TO MOUNT CONSTITUTION*

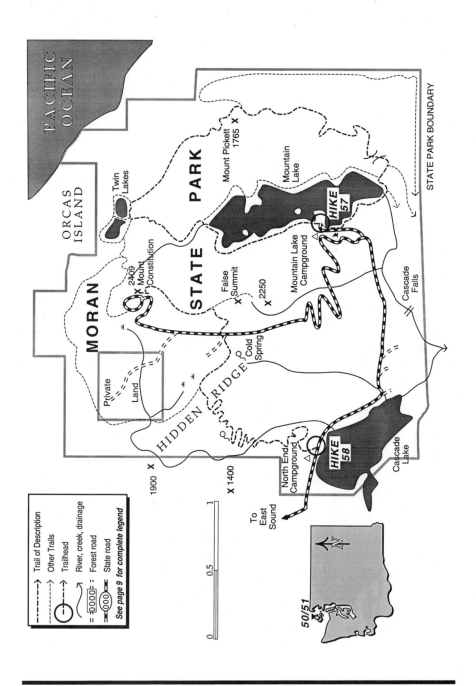

Cross the road and resume hiking the summit trail, ascending steadily for 0.2 mile to yet another junction.

Turn left for the final ascent along or near the ridgetop. The forest is dominated by stunted lodgepole pines. On drier, rocky sites manzanita, Oregon grape, and prince's pine form the understory, but elsewhere salal dominates.

Widening vistas signal the approach to the summit, and the trail soon reaches the road just below the interesting stone observation tower, designed after twelfth-century European watchtowers.

A television relay tower also decorates the rocky summit area, fringed with weather-beaten lodgepole pines and Douglas-firs.

Views are magnificent and far-ranging, including Vancouver Island, the cities of Vancouver, B.C., and Bellingham, Washington, the British Columbia Coast Range, Mount Baker, Twin Sisters Mountain, the North Cascades, and many of the San Juan Islands, including (from northwest to east) Patos, Sucia, Matia, Barnes, and Clark islands. The Olympics raise snowy peaks far above the strait of Juan de Fuca in the southwest, and even Mount Rainier can be seen on a clear day.

Twin Lakes and Mountain Lake lie far below the precipitous east face of the peak, gouged into the land by the Cordilleran Ice Sheet.

Despite its location in the Pacific and its moderate elevation, Mount Constitution receives an average of only twenty-nine inches of precipitation annually. Similar elevations on the west slope of the Cascades may receive two or more times as much precipitation.

From the summit, either retrace the route to Cascade Lake or, if you have arranged for transportation, catch a ride down off the mountain. □

HIKE 59 *OBSTRUCTION PASS BEACH*

General description: An easy 1.2-mile, round-trip day hike or overnighter to a San Juan Island beach.
Elevation gain and loss: -150 feet.
Trailhead elevation: 150 feet.
High point: Trailhead, 150 feet.
Maps: Orcas Island 15-minute USGS quad (trailhead and trail not shown on quad, but map useful for its depiction of landscape.)
Season: All year.
Water availability: None available.

Finding the trailhead: For most people, the only way to reach the San Juan Islands is via the ferry from Anacortes. Drive to the end of State Route 20 in Anacortes, following signs indicating San Juan Ferries. Take the ferry to Orcas Island. (In summer 1987, twelve daily ferries left Anacortes bound for Orcas Island. Round-trip fares were $16.60 per vehicle plus $4.65 per person— by no means a cheap trip but certainly a spectacular one.)

From Orcas Landing, follow the main road north and then east through East Sound Village, turning right toward Rosario and Moran State Park after 9.2 miles. Enter Moran State Park, passing Cascade Lake and the trailhead for

HIKE 59 *OBSTRUCTION PASS BEACH*

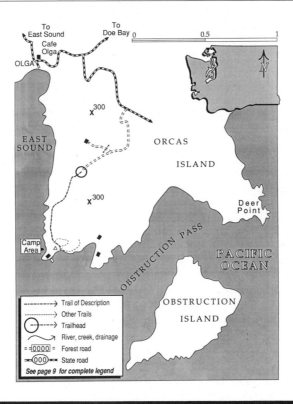

To East Sound
Cafe Olga
OLGA

To Doe Bay

0   0.5   1

x 300

EAST SOUND

ORCAS ISLAND

Deer Point

x 300

Camp Area

OBSTRUCTION PASS

PACIFIC OCEAN

OBSTRUCTION ISLAND

- - - - - - → Trail of Description
- - - - - - → Other Trails
◯ - - - → Trailhead
〜 ↗ River, creek, drainage
= [0000] = Forest road
(000) State road
See page 9 for complete legend

Mount Constitution, and bear right 0.9 mile beyond the campground registration booth toward Olga, where the Mountain Lake road forks left. Turn left after another two miles at Cafe Olga, signed for Doe Bay and Obstruction Pass. Travel half a mile and turn right toward Obstruction Pass. You'll reach another junction within 0.9 mile, indicated by a trailhead sign. Turn right onto this dirt road, which leads to the road's end and the trailhead after 0.8 mile. You'll have traveled a total of 5.1 miles from Cascade Lake.

The hike: To experience the San Juan Islands, you must climb their mountains, explore their forests, and walk their beaches.

But beaches are a precious commodity in the San Juans. They're either privately owned or they don't exist; much of the coastline of Orcas Island is quite rugged, with broken cliffs plunging into the clear, cold Pacific.

This short but rewarding hike to the campground and narrow beach at Obstruction Pass Park, administered by the state Department of Natural Resources, is a fine addition to anyone's Orcas Island itinerary.

No fresh water is available, but the campground boasts picnic tables, firepits and a toilet. The site is occasionally used by boaters who anchor just offshore.

From the parking area, the hiker-only trail proceeds into a forest composed of red alder, western redcedar, Douglas-fir, the broad-leaved Pacific madrone (common on dry coastal sites), bigleaf maple, grand fir, willow, and vine maple. Understory plants consist of sword fern, salal, blackberry, gooseberry, and wild rose.

The trail gently descends through the forest, soon nearing the edge of a cliff plunging 100 feet into the clear ocean waters. A short detour to the brink of this precipice reveals fine views northwestward up East Sound, which nearly divides the two arms of horseshoelike Orcas Island. Visible up the east coast of the sound is the village of Olga, and beyond is the Rosario resort.

After half a mile you'll stroll into the campground. A narrow pebble beach fronts the camp area, creating a fine spot to enjoy the view and soak up the sun. Private land lies a short distance east and west of this site, so act accordingly during explorations.

To the east of the campground, you can follow a faint trail along the rim above the shoreline to more isolated campsites—without trespassing on private land. The water is very clear, but you may consider it too cold for a comfortable swim.

Shore pine (a subspecies of lodgepole pine), Douglas-fir and Pacific madrone hug the rocky shoreline.

Offshore views reach as far as the snow-clad Olympics, more than fifty miles away. More immediate features include Obstruction Island beyond narrow Obstruction Pass. More massive Blakely Island rises beyond Obstruction, crowned by 1050-foot Blakely Peak. Beyond Blakely from left to right are a point of Decatur Island, isolated Frost Island, and Lopez Island and its prominent point, Humphrey Head.

Ferries plying the waters between islands as well as the drone of private water-craft are more likely to lull campers to sleep than the lapping of miniscule waves at the shoreline.

There's a quarter-mile loop trail (so signed) in the campground, but it's hard to follow because it's easily confused with several unofficial paths worn by visitors using the campground. □

HIKE 60 *SWAMP CREEK TO GOLD RUN PASS AND TOMYHOI LAKE*

General description: A eight-mile, round-trip backpack to a large lake in the Mount Baker Wilderness at the heart of the North Cascades' Chilliwack Range.
Elevation gain and loss: +1,800 feet, -1,700 feet.
Trailhead elevation: 3,600 feet.
High point: Gold Run Pass, 5,400 feet.
Maps: Mount Skuksan 15-minute USGS quad; North Cascades National Park USGS quad.
Season: Late July through September.
Water availability: Abundant north of Gold Run Pass.

Finding the trailhead: Follow paved Mount Baker Highway (State Route 543) east from its junction with State Route 547 at Kendall, passing the ranger station

Mount Baker from just below Gold Run Pass. Cliff Leight photo.

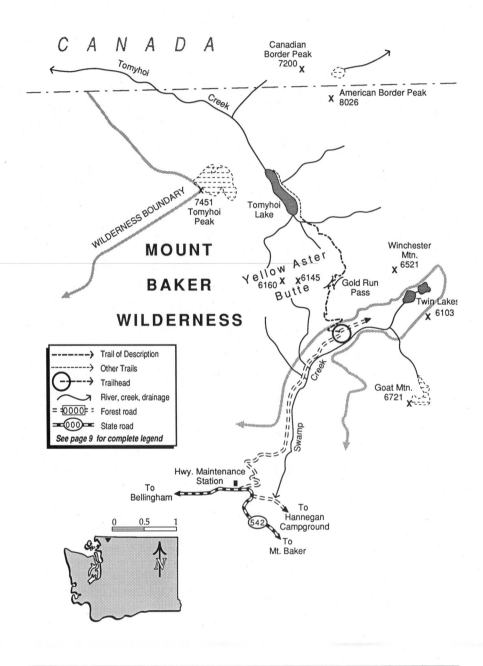

CANADA

Tomyhoi

Canadian
Border Peak
7200 X

American Border Peak
X 8026

Creek

WILDERNESS BOUNDARY

X 7451
Tomyhoi
Peak

Tomyhoi
Lake

Winchester
Mtn.
X 6521

MOUNT

Yellow Aster
X 6160   X X6145
Butte

Gold Run
Pass

Twin Lakes
X 6103

BAKER

WILDERNESS

Creek

Goat Mtn.
6721
X

Trail of Description
Other Trails
Trailhead
River, creek, drainage
0000 Forest road
000 State road
See page 9 for complete legend

Swamp

Hwy. Maintenance
Station
To
Bellingham

To
Hannegan
Campground

542

To
Mt. Baker

0   0.5   1

N

after 10.5 miles. Continue another 12.4 miles to Twin Lakes Road, immediately beyond the highway maintenance station. Turn left here and follow this steep and narrow gravel road, avoiding a left turn after 2.8 miles, to the trailhead, signed for Tomyhoi Lake Trail, 4.5 miles from the highway at the switchback just below an "end of maintained road" sign.

The hike: The North Fork Nooksack River country contains some of the most uniquely scenic mountains in all the North Cascades. The highest and most prominent peaks in the drainage—Mounts Baker and Shuksan—host the only extensive glacier systems. Other peaks, rising to nearly 8,000 feet, host small ice fields on their shadiest flanks.

These scenic, grassy mountains, lying south and west of the Chilliwack River and north of the North Fork Nooksack River, are known as the Chilliwack Range. The range is divided almost in half by the international boundary. Canada's half has been logged, with roads penetrating most drainages as far as the border. South of the border much of the range was protected from similar development with the creation of the Mount Baker Wilderness and North Cascades National Park.

Mile-long Tomyhoi Lake rests in a deep valley in the heart of the Chilliwacks, encircled by some of the highest, most impressive peaks in the range. This fish-filled lake lies at nearly the same elevation as the trailhead, but to get there you must negotiate a steep trail over timberline Gold Run Pass. Most hikers simply day-hike to the pass for the memorable view.

Water is abundant north of the pass, and as usual mosquitoes and biting flies are thick until August in most years. Anglers will be interested in the abundant rainbows and browns that lurk in the depths of the 3,700-foot-high lake.

From the trailhead, the route climbs steadily through a forest of silver fir and mountain hemlock, levels off after 1.25 miles on a subalpine bench, and then resumes climbing, gaining 600 feet in the final half mile to 5,400-foot Gold Run Pass.

Northwestward from the pass, a series of alpine benches stair-steps down toward the narrow lake, which rests below the east wall of 7,451-foot Tomyhoi Peak. The prominent peak in the distance is 6,620-foot Mount McGuire. The clearcut abuts the international border on the Canadian side.

Above the logging scar to the right (east) is 7,200-foot Canadian Border Peak. To the south 8,026-foot American Border Peak rises more than 4,000 feet above the shores of Tomyhoi Lake. South of that giant crag is 7,868-foot Mount Larrabee, and due east of the pass rises 6,521-foot Winchester Mountain, destination of a popular day hike from Twin Lakes. To the southwest is snowy Mount Baker, and, if you leave the trail and walk eastward from the pass, you'll enjoy an unobstructed view of Mount Shuksan's ice-encrusted bulk.

From the scattered hemlocks and wildflower meadows of the pass, the trail switchbacks down a north slope, upon which snow lingers into August some years. The final mile to the lake drops steeply, reaching fair campsites at the south end. The level of the lake can drop considerably in late summer, particularly during dry years. Other campsites, sheltered by a thick forest of silver fir and mountain hemlock, can be found along the east shore of the lake. ☐

HIKE 61 *PTARMIGAN RIDGE*

General description: A ten-mile, round-trip day hike or overnighter along an alpine ridge in the Mount Baker Wilderness under the shadow of the northernmost Cascade volcano in Washington.
Elevation gain and loss: 960 feet.
Trailhead elevation: 5,040 feet.
High point: 6,000 feet.
Maps: Mount Shuksan and Mount Baker 15-minute USGS quads; Mount Baker-Snoqualmie National Forest map.
Season: Late July through September.
Water availability: A few small streams cross the route, but you should carry an ample supply.

Finding the trailhead: Follow paved Mount Baker Highway (State Route 543) east from Kendall for 33.5 miles to its end at the large parking area at the trailhead on Kulshan Ridge. Views from the trailhead are magnificent, including Mount Shuksan, Mount Baker, and a host of surrounding peaks.

The hike: The trail along Ptarmigan Ridge is arguably the most scenic ridge walk in the Mount Baker area. Constant glorious views of either Baker's vast fields of ice or the complicated mass of Mount Shuksan will accompany you all along the route.

Elevations en route are high, and the trail is generally not passable until late July or August. Even then, several permanent snowfields remain. Many hikers go only a mile or two to the first snowfields, which may be small in late summer but still quite steep. A misstep could lead to disaster. Sturdy, lug-soled boots are highly recommended. Despite the snowfields, many attempt the Ptarmigan Ridge Trail, sometimes wearing tennis shoes!

There are few bugs on the ridge, but carry ample drinking water. Sunscreen is recommended. No campfires are permitted anywhere on Ptarmigan Ridge, so carry a backpack stove.

Beginning at the timberline trailhead, follow the Chain Lakes Trail westward, ignoring the ridgeline route to Table Mountain.

The trail traverses the open, south-facing slopes of Table Mountain, which is a large alpine plateau isolated from its surroundings by the erosive forces of glaciation.

Views are impressive, featuring inescapable Mount Baker and its satellite summit, Sherman Peak. Baker's main summit, 10,778-foot Grant Peak, a nearly flat, ice covered plateau, is separated from 10,000-foot Sherman Peak by the Sherman Crater. This crater is the most active volcanic feature in the Cascades with the exception of Mount St. Helens. Increasing thermal activity in the crater beginning in 1975 caused geologists to worry about an impending eruption.

Other views from this south-slope traverse are superb. Southward, beyond a nearby stream-dissected bench, Swift Creek's canyon opens up to reveal a portion of Baker Lake. Beyond rises Glacier Peak and a host of other icy North Cascade crags. West of Glacier Peak is a cluster of three especially prominent peaks—Sloan Peak, Pugh Mountain, and White Chuck Mountain.

You'll enter the Mount Baker Wilderness at an isolated stand of mountain

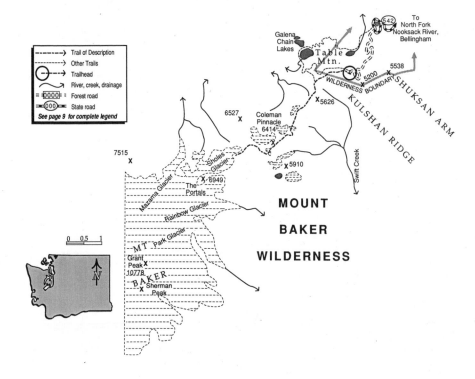

The Ptarmigan Ridge trail is alpine in character from beginning to end and features continuous vistas of rugged North Cascades wilderness, including towering Mount Baker, elevation 10,778 feet. Ron Adkison photo.

From trail's end on Ptarmigan Ridge, an austere landscape of rock and ice frames 10,778-foot Mount Baker, the centerpiece of 20 square miles of glacial ice. Ron Adkison photo.

hemlock. After a mile of easy walking, you'll see the Chain Lakes Trail fork right. That trail forms a popular semiloop, passing the Galena Chain Lakes and then crossing a 5,300-foot saddle before descending past two more alpine lakes and ending near Picture Lake—a total of about seven miles.

Stay left at that junction and descend into the headwaters bowl of Wells Creek to avoid permanent snow. From this point, grassy Skyline Divide and icy Chowder Ridge form the western horizon.

Much of this sheltered bowl was recently vacated by Little Ice Age glaciers, as evidenced by a fresh moraine you must cross before climbing back to the ridge crest. A superb view of the cliffs, buttresses, pinnacles, and ice fields of 9,127-foot Mount Shuksan, one of the classic peaks of the Cascade Range, unfolds from the top of the ridge.

Soon the trail jogs southward, traversing east-facing slopes with constant inspiring vistas of alpine wilderness. The first major permanent snowfield blocks the trail 1.75 miles from the previous junction. Thus far, the hike is a rewarding stroll, and average hikers should be content to stop here.

More experienced hikers will cross the snowfield (an ice axe may aid the unsteady) and then round a ridge emanating from Peak 5841, featuring more fine vistas.

A southwestward traverse leads to another, larger snowfield on the flank of Coleman Pinnacle, its smooth, tree-clad south slopes a stark contrast to its ice-chiseled north face. About a mile to the southeast lies a milky green, 5,500-foot-high alpine lake, reached via gentle, snowy slopes. This lake would make a superb alpine campsite.

Ahead, the trail crosses more snow while traversing a headwaters bowl of Rainbow Creek. The route plunges hikers into an isolated stand of stunted subalpine fir and crosses a few tiny creeks, more snowfields, and wildflower-decorated fells before climbing briefly to a boulder-littered volcanic bench where the trail ends.

Just below the bench to the west lies the crevasse-riddled Sholes Glacier. The crevasses were created when the glacier flowed over uneven terrain and the resulting stress caused the ice to split and crack.

Ahead, to the southwest, are The Portals, passageways between a group of volcanic crags leading to the Rainbow and Mazama glaciers and Mount Baker itself. Only seasoned mountaineers should continue beyond trails-end on this bench.

Although fully exposed to the often merciless, changeable weather of the North Cascades, this bench and the aforementioned alpine lake are the best choices on this hike for an overnight stay. ☐

HIKE 62 *RUTH CREEK TO COPPER RIDGE*

General description: A twenty-mile, round-trip backpack along a grass-covered timberline ridge, featuring vistas that reach deep into the North Cascades wilderness.
Elevation gain and loss: +4,100 feet, -1,400 feet.
Trailhead elevation: 3,100 feet.
High point: Copper Ridge Lookout, 6,260 feet.
Maps: Mount Shuksan and Mount Challenger 15-minute USGS quads; North Cascades National Park USGS quads; North Cascades National Park map.
Season: Late July through September.
Water availability: Abundant for first four miles; intermittent thereafter.
Permit: A backcountry permit is needed for overnight camping in North Cascades National Park; you can get one at the Glacier Public Service Center, 10.5 miles east of Kendall.

Finding the trailhead: Follow the Mount Baker Highway (State Route 542) east from Kendall for twenty-three miles to eastbound Forest Road 32, signed for Hannegan Pass Trail. Follow this narrow and sometimes rough dirt road (the Forest Service plans to widen it eventually), ignoring right-forking Road 34 (but not the glorious view of Mount Shuksan) at 1.3 miles. You'll reach the camping area and trailhead at the road's end, 5.2 miles from the highway.

The hike: This exceptionally scenic hike penetrates the wilds of the Chilliwack Range, a friendlier group of mountains than the jagged, icy peaks that make up most of the North Cascades. The contours of the Chilliwacks are generally more gentle and their slopes covered with more grass and timber than those of glaciated neighbors to the south and east.

As you hike along scenic Copper Ridge you'll cross timberline parks not commonly found in the North Cascades. But continuous vistas of some of the state's most rugged peaks—Shuksan, Baker, Challenger and the Picket Range—will serve to remind you of where you are.

Water seems ever-present in the North Cascades, but after the first four miles of this hike, beyond Hannegan Pass and as you ascend dry Copper Ridge, it becomes a precious commodity. A small lake at seven miles and Egg Lake at eight miles provide the best sources of water. The only other water source on the ridge is Copper Lake, 11.5 miles from the trailhead.

Camping restrictions are in effect on Copper Ridge. Three campsites are available at Egg Lake, three at Copper Lake, and two at Silesia Camp, a dry site perched on Point 5689 above Egg Lake. Remember that no camping is allowed within 0.25 mile of trails except at established sites. No fires are permitted anywhere along the trail. Weekdays are the best time to hike the ridge if you're looking for quiet and solitude.

From the trailhead, the shrub-lined trail quickly enters Mount Baker Wilderness and proceeds southeastward up the U-shaped Ruth Creek drainage, climbing steadily after one mile.

On your right you'll see the glacier-scoured north face of Nooksack Ridge, laced with numerous cascading creeks draining alpine snowfields. It provides marked contrast to the wooded slopes of the Skagit Range to the north of the

Ruth Creek to Copper Ridge is exceptionally scenic. Cliff Leight photo.

trail. Soon the ice-sheathed dome of 7,100-foot Ruth Mountain will come into view at the head of the canyon.

Numerous hanging valleys high on Nooksack Ridge illustrate the depth of the ancient Ruth Creek Glacier, which removed the lower portions of those drainages.

After 3.5 miles of hiking through discontinuous stands of mountain hemlock and silver fir, you'll pass just north of a subalpine bench and small stream. Campsites here are good but should be avoided—they are too close to the trail. Instead, enjoy the excellent views down Ruth Creek and to Ruth Mountain.

The trail presently climbs through meadows and timber to 5,050-foot Hannegan Pass. Views from this grassy saddle, partially clothed in silver fir and mountain hemlock, include portions of Copper Ridge to the northeast and several impressive peaks on the northeast horizon.

Several spur trails climb the ridge crest southeast from the pass leading to scenic campsites (avoid the sites within 0.25 mile of the trail), a small pond, and huckleberry-clad slopes with an unforgettable view of Mount Shuksan.

From the pass, the trail descends via switchbacks to the headwaters of the Chilliwack River. Below the switchbacks, you'll cross an alluvial fan that bears a variety of rock—metamorphic, granitic, breccia—from the layered slopes of 6,186-foot Hannegan Peak.

You'll reach a junction and the boundary of North Cascades National Park one mile and 600 feet below the pass. Boundary Camp next to the infant Chilliwack River lies below this junction; it's the last campsite with water until Egg Lake, three miles distant.

Take the left fork bound for Copper Ridge. Some hikers, after traversing Copper Ridge, loop back via the Chilliwack River Trail, a strenuous backpack of three or more days. Even more ambitious hikers have used either trail to cross the North Cascades to Ross Lake. Plan a week for that unforgettable trek.

As you head onto Copper Ridge, you'll climb 1,000 feet in 1.75 miles, first through forest and then through meadows and discontinuous timber. You'll cross the precipitous upper end of Hells Gorge before attaining the ridge crest dividing Silesia Creek from the Chilliwack.

From this point views are breathtaking, and they improve as you progress toward the lookout. You'll see the incredible north side of Shuksan, its jagged tooth-like crags rising above a sea of ice; the overbearing hulk of Mount Baker; and in the southeast the Picket Range, a ridge of some of the most precipitous peaks in the nation, many of them clad in perpetual ice.

A small alpine lake lies a quarter of a mile north of the ridge on a bench, reached by a faint spur from the main trail.

Presently the undulating trail follows the crest of Copper Ridge, carpeted with numerous alpine cushion plants: red heather, white heather, huckleberry, and partridge foot among them. Scattered clumps of mountain hemlock, stunted and tortured by severe North Cascades weather, offer a modicum of shelter during inclement weather, which is all too common in the region.

You'll pass the spur trail to Egg Lake after eight miles and then reach ridgetop Silesia Camp. Campers there must rely on Egg Lake for their water. Both of these sites are excellent choices for an overnight stay, but they're fully exposed to the weather.

The trail climbs up and over yet another hump in the ridge before the final stiff climb of 1,000 feet to the 6,260-foot Copper Ridge Lookout, which stands

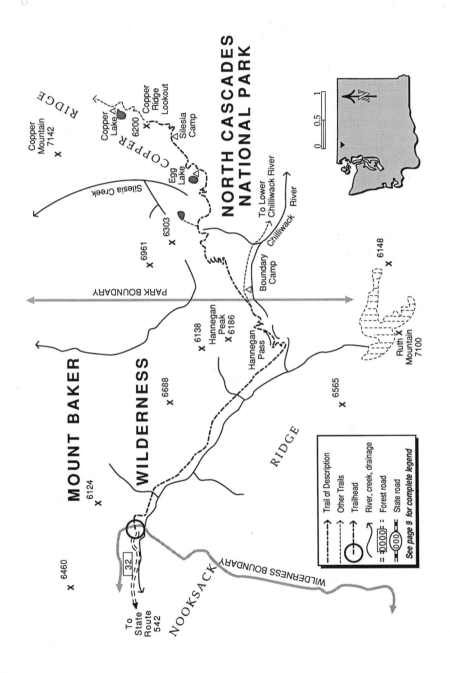

above timberline except for the ground-hugging mountain hemlocks surrounding the summit.

The views you'll enjoy all along Copper Ridge culminate in the sublime spectacle of the most ruggedly beautiful mountain wilderness in the contiguous United States. Looking northwestward from the lookout, you can gaze down Silesia Creek (Slesse Creek north of the border with Canada) to one of the classic crags of the Cascades, 7,800-foot Slesse Mountain, two miles north of the border. To the east across the timbered depths of the Chilliwack River you'll see striking 8,956-foot Mount Redoubt, 7,942-foot Bear Mountain, 7,131-foot Indian Mountain, and 7,000-foot Red Face Mountain. To the southeast are the Pickets, crowned by another classic Cascade summit, Mount Challenger. To the southwest are the more familiar but equally impressive summits of Ruth, Shuksan and Baker. Even the distant Coast Range of British Columbia, rocky and snow-clad, appears far to the northwest.

You have a number of options after leaving the lookout, which is base camp for the summer ranger. If you're ambitious you can follow the Copper Ridge Trail northward into the Chilliwack for 8.5 miles and then loop back via that river and Hannegan Pass—a hike of about twenty-nine miles, best spread out over three or four days.

Copper Lake, 1.5 miles north of the lookout, makes a fine base for exploration of Copper Ridge to the northwest. Or you can return to the trailhead via Copper Ridge. □

HIKE 63 *BAKER RIVER TO SULPHIDE CAMP*

General description: A five-mile, round-trip day hike or overnighter, leading through rain forest to the southern foot of Mount Shuksan in North Cascades National Park.
Elevation gain and loss: About 100 feet.
Trailhead elevation: 800 feet.
High point: Sulphide Camp, 880 feet.
Maps: Mount Shuksan 15-minute USGS quad; North Cascades National Park USGS quad; North Cascades National Park map.
Season: March through mid-December.
Water availability: Abundant but silty at Sulphide Camp and Baker River.
Permit: Backcountry permit required for overnight stay in North Cascades National Park; available at ranger stations in Marblemount and Sedro-Woolley.

Finding the trailhead: Drive to the Baker Lake Road turnoff on State Route 20 (see Hike 64) and drive north. Follow this excellent paved road, Forest Road 11, generally northeastward, avoiding numerous signed turnoffs. Pavement ends 0.3 miles beyond a junction with the right-forking road to Baker Lake resort and left-forking Park Creek Road, twenty miles from the highway. Take the middle fork, signed for Baker River. Drive around the north shore of Baker Lake and turn left onto Forest Road 1168, signed for Baker River Trail, after another five miles. This rough dirt road leads northeastward through shady red alders, forks right after 0.3 mile and ends at the large gravel parking area after 0.2 mile.

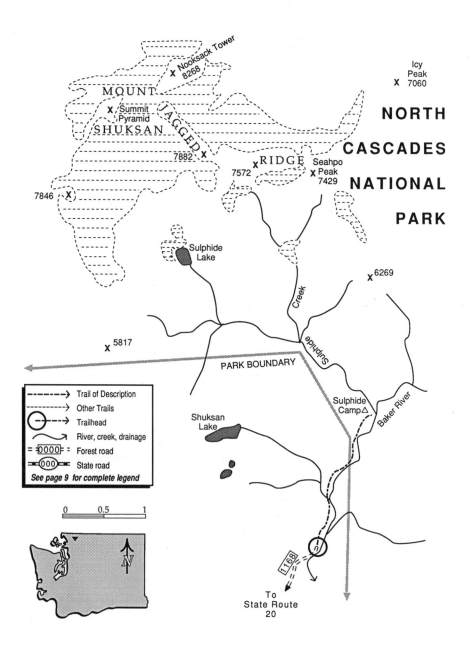

The hike: From the Picket Range to the Skagit River, the Baker River cuts a deep swath through the western North Cascades, draining the south slopes of the two preeminent peaks of the region, Mounts Baker and Shuksan. Its upper reaches are wild and trailless; its lower section is followed by roads and impounded in two large reservoirs.

A short trail follows the river from above Baker Lake to a backcountry campsite on Sulphide Creek, below the enormous emptiness of the Sulphide Creek cirque. Above the camp, Seahpo Peak and aptly-named Jagged Ridge soar more than 6,000 feet from the rain forests of the canyon bottom to alpine heights.

This easy and scenic 2.5-mile hike is suitable for families with young children, since the way gains little elevation. The rain forests along the Baker River are probably the best example of this type of environment in the Mount Baker area, and the contrast between nearby icy crags and the moist forests is dramatic.

Sulphide Creek offers a year-round water source, but the rock particles suspended in the creek may be a little rough on some hikers' insides. Nearby Baker River also carries a silty load from glaciers above.

The hiker-only trail begins at the west side of the parking area and heads north through a stand of young Douglas-firs to the west bank of the boulder-strewn river bed. It then enters a moss-draped rain forest of red alder, bigleaf maple, western redcedar (some of which are very large), vine maple, and western hemlock. At times you'll enjoy distant views up the river to the northeast, as well as to Mount Blum and other crags which tower to the east.

After one mile, silver fir joins the forest, indicating that you've reached the upper limits of the rain-forest zone. Silver fir is a very common tree on the west side of the Cascades up to an elevation of about 6,000 feet. Its bark is silver to gray with white blotches, and resin blisters on mature trees. The needles are blunt and notched at the tip, and they point forward along the branches. Two white lines on the underside of each needle give the tree a silvery appearance. The tree commonly attains a height of 100 to 160 feet, averages two to three feet in diameter, and is spire-shaped and quite symmetrical. Even botanists sometimes have difficulty distinguishing between species of true fir, and the silver fir may be confused with subalpine fir where their ranges overlap.

The trail proceeds through the lush forest with a few minor ups and downs, enters the park after passing a flooded area with many cedar snags—possibly an old beaver pond—and finally ends at the edge of wide, swift Sulphide Creek. If you're adventurous you may choose to ford that difficult stream and proceed up the wild Baker River. But Sulphide Camp is hard to resist, pleasantly shaded by such large trees as bigleaf maple, silver fir, and western hemlock. A fine view from the camp reaches up into the deep bowl at the head of Sulphide Creek—the largest cirque on Mount Shuksan. Jagged Ridge, crowned by toothed summits, and nearby Seahpo Peak rise northward above a thick hanging glacier. □

HIKE 64

General description: Three short day hikes or overnighters in the high country east of Baker Lake in the Noisy-Diobsud Wilderness: 1) Anderson Butte Lookout site, four miles round-trip; 2) Watson Lakes, 4.4 miles round-trip; and 3) Anderson Lakes, 4.6 miles round-trip.

Elevation gain and loss: 1) 1,120 feet; 2) +650 feet, -750 feet; and 3) +650 feet, -550 feet.

Trailhead elevation: 4,300 feet.

High point: Lookout site, 5,420 feet; lakes, 4,900 feet.

Maps: Lake Shannon 15-minute USGS quad; Mt. Baker-Snoqualmie National Forest map.

Season: July through early October.

Water availability: Abundant at lakes; carry water to lookout site.

Finding the trailhead: From State Route 20, 14.5 miles east of Sedro-Woolley or fifteen miles west of Rockport, turn north onto Baker Lake Road. Follow this highway through the Grandy Creek drainage, turning right after 11.9 miles at a Baker Lake sign. Shortly after the snowy cone of Mount Baker comes into view, turn right onto Forest Road 1106 where a sign points to Baker Dam and Kulshan Campground, 13.4 miles from State Route 20. Pavement quickly ends on Forest Road 1106, and you'll reach a junction just beyond Kulshan Campground after 0.9 mile. Avoid the left and right forks and bear straight ahead toward the Watson Lake Trail. The road crosses Baker Dam and reaches another junction two miles from Baker Lake Road. Turn left here onto Forest Road 1107. This good but sometimes narrow dirt road climbs steadily, offering superb views of Mount Baker (for passengers only). Avoid a left fork to a wood-cutting area 10.5 miles from Baker Lake Road, and you'll reach the trailhead spur road just before milepost 10, after 11.6 miles. Turn left here and drive a half mile up the spur road to the trailhead.

The hike: East of Baker Lake and adjacent to the western boundary of North Cascades National Park lies the 14,300-acre Noisy-Diobsud Wilderness, which protects the drainages of Noisy and Diobsud creeks. The wilderness is rugged and generally inaccessible, except for the trail to Anderson and Watson lakes on the western edge of the area.

These short hikes start high and stay high, providing access to three fishable lakes and broad vistas from the Anderson Lookout site. These attractions combine to make the area a justifiably popular destination. Many hikers will simply choose one destination, but because the trails are short and concentrated in one area, they're all described here.

The hiker-only trail winds upward through forested slopes, climbing steeply from its start in a typical west-slope forest of silver fir and western hemlock to a grassy, 4,800-foot saddle after one mile. Views are good from the saddle—Mount Baker, Ptarmigan Ridge, and beyond to distant Tomyhoi Peak.

At the south end of the long saddle, the trail to the lookout site forks left (east). To get to the lookout and enjoy far-flung vistas, turn left and traverse

HIKE 64   FOREST ROAD 1107 TO ANDERSON BUTTE LOOKOUT SITE, WATSON AND ANDERSON LAKES

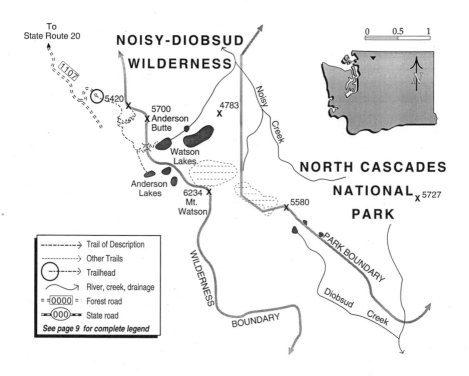

easily toward a talus slope before switchbacking steeply through forest, red heather, and huckleberries to the ridge crest between the lookout site to the north and rugged Anderson Butte to the south. The trail turns north, following the ridge to the 5,420-foot summit, one mile from the junction.

An inviting and seldom-visited timberline basin with a limited water supply lies immediately below to the east. It can be easily reached and makes a scenic campsite.

The view from the lookout is breathtaking. Mounts Shuksan and Baker dominate the north and northwest. Shuksan is especially striking from here, with its distinctive summit pyramid rising above the vast, crevasse-riddled Sulphide and Crystal glaciers.

Far to the southwest are the Olympics, and closer at hand is Baker River's deep valley, with Twin Sisters Mountain rising above, forming the western horizon. In the northeast are peaks such as Redoubt and Bear Mountain, Hagan and Blum. The impressive southern Picket Range and Crescent Creek Spires loom boldly to the east, and beyond them is the isolated crag of Mount Triumph.

On the southern skyline, more prominent peaks rise above a sea of lesser mountains. A cluster of three jagged peaks is particularly noticeable—Sloan Peak, White Chuck Mountain, and Pugh Mountain. Isolated Whitehorse Mountain near Darrington bears the westernmost glacier in the North Cascades south of the Skagit River. Even Mount Rainier can be seen on a clear day.

To reach the lakes, return to the junction and proceed southeastward, crossing a sloping, hemlock-and-fir-rimmed meadow. You'll lose elevation at first and then climb to another saddle slightly higher than the last. Rugged Anderson Butte soars skyward directly above.

From this saddle (featuring a great view of Mount Baker) the trail enters forest and descends 300 feet to a junction in yet another subalpine grassland, 0.6 miles from the previous junction. Turn left to reach Watson Lakes, climbing several switchbacks to a watershed divide between Noisy and Anderson creeks. You'll get a fine view of Twin Sisters Mountain from the top of the climb at another 4,800-foot saddle. Then you'll descend 300 feet through a forest of mountain hemlock and silver fir, within site of the two Watson Lakes and of jagged North Cascade summits, including glacier-cloaked Bacon Peak nearby to the southeast.

Here you'll enter the wilderness and complete the descent to the highest and westernmost lake. You'll find good campsites near the lake's outlet, but you may prefer to go on to the larger, more isolated lake, set on a bench to the east over a low grass-and-heather-clad ridge. Fishing is productive for pan-sized trout in both lakes.

To reach Anderson Lakes, proceed southward from the second junction, through the meadow and over a boulder-and-hemlock-dotted saddle. The rocky trail drops 100 feet to lower Anderson Lake at 4,500 feet, 0.7 mile from the junction.

Rugged Mount Watson forms an alpine backdrop, while subalpine meadows encircle the lake on three sides. Choose a campsite well away from the fragile shore of this very scenic lake. Secluded sites can be found in the basin to the south. Keep in mind that no camping is permitted within 0.25 mile of Watson and Anderson lakes, except at established sites.

Two other lakes rest in cirques 500 feet above the lower lake to the east, and experienced hikers can reach them by scrambling through rock and meadow. □

HIKE 65 *THORNTON LAKES*

General description: A rigorous 10.5-mile, round-trip backpack leading into a timberline lake basin in western North Cascades National Park.
Elevation gain and loss: +2,360 feet, -485 feet.
Trailhead elevation: 2,600 feet.
High point: 4,960 feet.
Maps: Marblemount 15-minute USGS quad; North Cascades National Park USGS quad; North Cascades National Park map.
Season: Mid-July through early October.
Water availability: Abundant along route.
Permit: Backcountry permit required; obtain at Marblemount ranger station.

Evidence of glaciation, both past and present, awaits hikers who travel through the backcountry of North Cascades National Park. Ron Adkison photo.

Finding the trailhead: Follow the North Cascades Highway (State Route 20) east from Marblemount for eleven miles to the signed Thornton Creek Road, just past milepost 117. Turn left (northwest) and follow this very steep and rough gravel road as it switchbacks 4.9 miles to the road's end. Parking is limited to about five or six vehicles.

The hike: This scenic but strenuous hike is unusual for North Cascades National Park in that it leads to three subalpine lakes. Lakes are few and far between in the park, and very few have established trails leading to them. It may seem unusual that so few lakes exist in such a heavily glaciated area. However, the number would probably double if the present-day glaciers melted.

Campsites are limited to the lower lake, but exploration of the upper lakes and surroundings ridges, including Trappers Peak, offers plenty of diversions for a weekend in the park.

Water is fairly abundant along the route, and huckleberries are plentiful along the final half of the hike. Fishing can be productive in the lower lake, but the water's very deep. Pack in a rubber raft or wait until fall when the fishing is better. No campfires are permitted here; so bring a backpacking stove along. You must camp in designated sites in the park.

At its beginning, the trail traces the route of a closed logging road. This area was logged between the early 1950s and late 1960s, before the national park and national recreation area were established.

The route heads toward a crossing of Thornton Creek below a barren, granite crest. Instead of ascending the Thornton Creek drainage as you might expect, the route climbs the timbered slopes east of the creek, fortunately passing several springs on an otherwise dry slope. Views up and across the Skagit River are superb as the trail bends into, then out of, the Thornton Creek drainage, passing large, revegetated clearcuts.

After two easy miles, the trail leaves the roadbed and climbs through a shady forest of fir, hemlock, and some cedar—a typical mid-elevation forest on the west slope of the North Cascades. The way becomes quite steep, passes numerous reliable springs, and finally reaches level ground after 3.5 miles. Here, at 4,150 feet, is a subalpine bench crossed by a small stream and blanketed by a timberline forest of mountain hemlock and Alaska yellow-cedar. Possible campsites are nearby.

The trail winds through this pleasant basin and then resumes climbing. Soon a skyline ridge becomes visible, and you may be lured into believing that the end of the climb is near. You'll realize you've been deceived as the trail continues the steady ascent, passing into the national park and heading up a series of benches plucked out of the bedrock by the large glacier that over-rode the ridge ahead. The same glacier gouged out the Thornton Lakes.

Before you reach the ridge crest, you'll notice a well-worn trail that forks right from the main trail. A "Thornton Lakes" sign points left. The righthand trail climbs 1,000 feet in about one mile to 5,964-foot Trappers Peak, offering a breathtaking panorama to anyone with the energy to get there. For now, continue to the left through huckleberry thickets (hikers in September will surely linger here) to the ice-smoothed bedrock ridge, featuring splendid vistas, both near and far.

Below the ridge to the north is the lowest and largest of the Thornton Lakes, elevation 4,475 feet. The soaring crag of Mount Triumph looms above the

HIKE 65 *THORNTON LAKES*

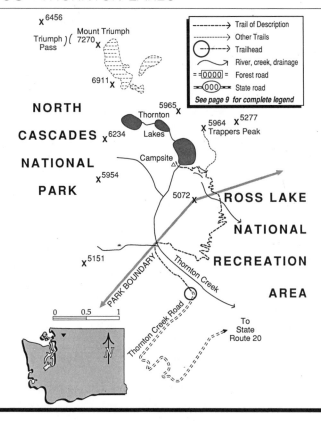

See page 9 for complete legend

middle lake, but the upper lake isn't visible.

Far to the southwest, Whitehorse Mountain rises in bold relief above the valley of the Stillaguamish River. Closer at hand are the peaks beyond the nadir of the Skagit River. Closest is 7,055-foot Big Devil Peak, visible from almost every point along the route to this ridge. Just like all other peaks of more than 6,000 feet elevation in the North Cascades, Big Devil has its share of snowfields and hanging glaciers.

Ice-capped Eldorado Peak stands above one of the largest concentrations of glaciers in the park. Jagged summits such as Tepeh Towers, Klawatti Peak, Austera Peak, Austera Towers, and Primus Peak barely reach above the sea of ice, among the more than 300 active glaciers in the park. The North Cascades host approximately 756 glaciers, more than half the active ice fields in the contiguous United States.

Other impressive sights to the east up the Skagit River include Snowfield Peak, the western lobe of the ridge-straddling Neve Glacier, the interesting tower of Paul Bunyan's Stump, and Pinnacle Peak. North of the river's canyon are the drier summits of Crater and Jack mountains. Although these are the highest peaks visible—even higher than perpetually white Eldorado—they lie in the rain shadow of the North Cascades and so shelter snowfields only on their shadiest flanks.

You may notice stunted trees clinging to rocky ribs above the two upper lakes, while the intervening concave slopes are barren of vegetation. Most likely, these slopes held ice during the Little Ice Age, which ended early in the twentieth century. The buttresses and ribs that rose above the ice were not stripped bare of vegetation, allowing the ancient, gnarled timber to stand as silent witnesses to remarkable geologic processes.

From the ridge, descend partially forested northwest slopes for 485 feet in half a mile to the camp area just beyond the outlet of the lower lake. Return to the trailhead via the same route. □

HIKE 66 *PANTHER CREEK TO THUNDER CREEK*

General description: A moderate 10.7-mile, point-to-point backpack south of Ross Lake in Ross Lake National Recreation Area, surveying some of the finest forests and most striking peaks south of the Skagit River.
Elevation gain and loss: +2,300 feet, -2,890 feet.
Trailhead elevation: 1,840 feet.
High point: Fourth of July Pass, 3,500 feet.

Maps: Ross Dam and Crater Mtn. 7.5-minute USGS quads; North Cascades National Park USGS quad; North Cascades National Park map.
Season: Late June through October.
Water availability: Abundant along most of route.
Permit: Backcountry permit required for overnight camping. Eastbound drivers should obtain their permit at the National Park Service station in Marblemount, thirty-three miles west of the Panther Creek trailhead. Westbound drivers can obtain theirs at the Early Winters Information Station on State Route 20, twenty miles west of Winthrop.

Finding the trailhead: Since this is a point-to-point hike, there are two trailheads to locate, both just off the North Cascades Highway (State Route 20).

The hike begins at the Panther Creek trailhead. To get there, follow the North Cascades Highway to the East Bank Trailhead parking area east of Ross Lake, and park there. The trail begins east of the Panther Creek Bridge on the south side of the highway, 0.2 mile east of the parking area.

The hike ends at the Colonial Creek Campground (south segment) on the Thunder Arm of Diablo Lake. Park in the large parking area just beyond the campground registration booth. This trailhead (eight miles west of Panther Creek) is about four miles east of Diablo Dam and twenty-five miles east of Marblemount. The trail ends at the west end of this parking area.

The hike: The North Cascades area is not only a land of high, rugged peaks and perpetual snow. It's also a land of deep canyons, big rivers, and dense

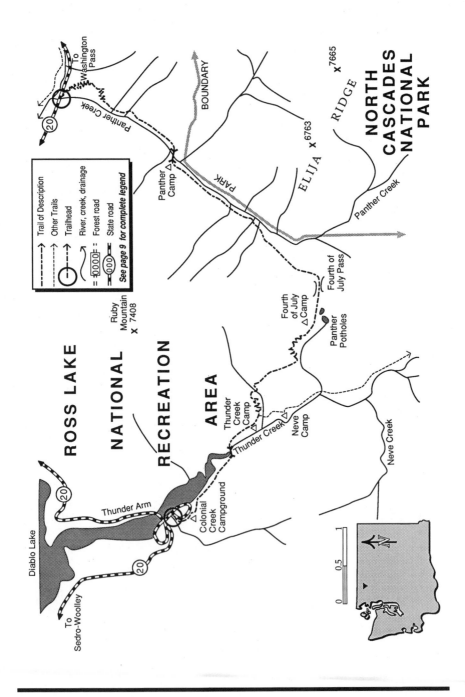

forests. This interesting backpack trip of two or more days offers a glimpse of both sides of the North Cascades' character.

The hike surveys two very different drainages—one a deep, narrow defile in a west-side rain shadow created by towering mountains; the other a broad, flat, densely forested valley draining a host of immense ice fields. The trail crosses a low divide between the drainages, and a nearby campsite boasts views to the tremendous, ice-encrusted mountain peaks so common in the other half of the North Cascades.

The hike is rigorous, but three widely spaced trail camps, each in its own unique setting, allow you to plan your hike according to your ability and the type of experience you seek.

Finding water is no problem along much of the route. You can expect to see many more hikers along the second half of the hike; Panther Creek is seldom crowded.

From the trailhead, the route switchbacks upward through a moss-carpeted forest of Douglas-firs and western hemlocks (the state tree of Washington). The forest alternates with more open stands of lodgepole pine, recognizable by its scaly bark and needles in bundles of two, which typically pioneers burned areas and is fairly common east of the Cascades.

The trail gains 700 feet during the first mile to avoid the rugged reaches of lower Panther Creek. Then it descends 600 feet into the canyon, where the noise of highway traffic is—thankfully—no longer audible.

Towering more than a mile above the narrow canyon bottom is 7,408-foot Ruby Mountain. The undulating trail follows along the rushing creek through mossy forest, bridges the creek after three miles, and then reaches isolated Panther Camp on the west side of the creek, shaded by a canopy of western hemlocks and western redcedar.

You'll leave the stream bank on a southwestward traverse and cross numerous springs and small creeks before climbing dry, hemlock-covered slopes toward Fourth of July Pass. The trail levels out and crosses a small creek before entering the broad, hemlock-and-silver-fir-clad saddle of Fourth of July Pass, elevation 3,500 feet, six miles from the trailhead.

The trail then heads west through the pass, crosses above the emerald-green Panther Potholes (two tiny lakes below the pass), and proceeds briefly downhill to the spur trail to Fourth of July camp.

This superb, scenic campsite lies on a sunny western slope decorated with scattered lodgepole pines, Douglas-firs and hemlocks. Campfires are allowed at this and the other two trail camps en route, and water is available nearby in this otherwise dry area. The outstanding features of this campsite are the views across Thunder Creek to Snowfield Peak and the eastern lobe of the ridge-straddling Neve Glacier, and the pyramids of Primus and Tricouni Peaks in the southwest.

Experienced and determined peak-baggers will want to scale the timbered ridge northward to Ruby Mountain, a superb vista point 3.5 miles above.

Beyond the camp, the trail descends 2,100 feet in 2.5 miles, alternately crossing dense and open forest, to the Thunder Creek Trail, an old miners' route. During a final series of switchbacks near the canyon bottom, you can enjoy a superb view across Diablo Lake to the glaciated peaks beyond.

As you turn right (northwest) at a junction onto Thunder Creek Trail, you'll pass through a moist forest of redcedars and silver firs. You'll reach the spur trail to Thunder Camp after 0.3 mile. The camp is a very pleasant site surrounded by huge trees and situated next to the large, silty creek. It's a choice location for families with young children.

The final two miles to the trailhead proceed through the forest, crossing the milky-green, river-like creek via an impressive suspension bridge after half a mile. The route then contours above murky Thunder Arm of Diablo Lake.

Upon reaching a junction with a nature trail, take the middle fork to reach the parking area below at Colonial Creek Campground, passing through a walk-in camp area en route. □

HIKE 67 NORTH CASCADES HIGHWAY TO MCALESTER LAKE

General description: A pleasant fourteen-mile, round-trip backpack in the high country of the North Cascades crest in Okanogan National Forest, North Cascades National Park, and Lake Chelan National Recreation Area.
Elevation gain and loss: +1,700, -710 feet.
Trailhead elevation: 4,510 feet.
High point: McAlester Lake, 5,500 feet.
Maps: McAlester Mtn. and Washington Pass 7.5-minute USGS quads; North Cascades National Park USGS quad; Okanogan National Forest map.
Season: July through September.
Water availability: Abundant along route.
Permit: A permit is required for overnight camping. See Hike 66 for instructions.

Finding the trailhead: This obscure trailhead lies in a grassy clearing on the north side of the North Cascades Highway (State Route 20), 1.2 miles east of Rainy Pass or 3.4 miles west of Washington Pass, and just west of milepost 159. If you're eastbound, you'll find the trailhead after crossing Bridge Creek (signed) for the second time. If you're westbound, you'll find it just before crossing Bridge Creek for the first time. The trail begins on the south side of the highway, opposite the parking area.

The hike: The scenic North Cascades Highway, completed in 1972, offers motorists a unique opportunity to experience the North Cascades—from the moist forests of the west to the drier, rain-shadow forests of the east, from the shady depths of river canyons to the rugged grandeur of the Cascade crest. The summit of the highway between Rainy Pass and Washington Pass is, perhaps, the highlight of this spectacular route.

You can access a variety of trails from this area, from a delightful stroll to an alpine lake to the famous Pacific Crest Trail (PCT), a 2,600-mile link between Canada and Mexico.

This particular backpack trip leads through rain-shadow forests at the headwaters of Bridge Creek, a major tributary to the Stehekin River. The destination is a beautiful, subalpine lake boasting a healthy trout population. If you're seeking a longer wilderness trek, you can continue on, taking the Rainbow

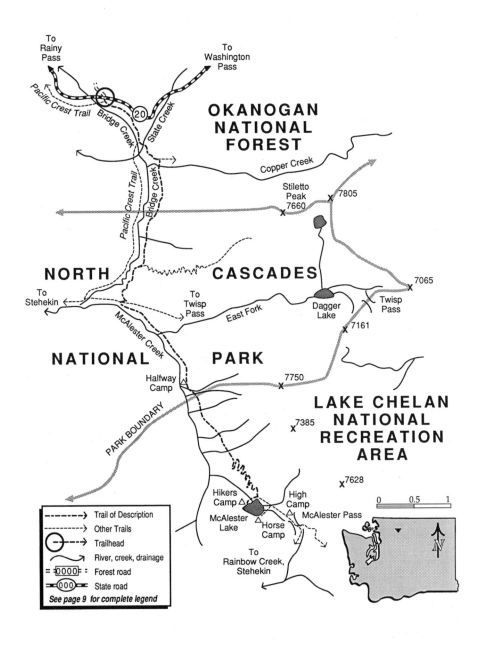

To Rainy Pass

To Washington Pass

Pacific Crest Trail

Bridge Creek

State Creek

20

OKANOGAN NATIONAL FOREST

Copper Creek

Pacific Crest Trail

Bridge Creek

Stiletto Peak 7660
× 7805

NORTH   **CASCADES**

To Stehekin

To Twisp Pass

East Fork

Dagger Lake

Twisp Pass
× 7065

× 7161

McAlester Creek

NATIONAL   **PARK**

Halfway Camp

7750 ×

LAKE CHELAN NATIONAL RECREATION AREA

× 7385

PARK BOUNDARY

× 7628

Hikers Camp △

High Camp △

McAlester Lake △ Horse Camp

McAlester Pass

To Rainbow Creek, Stehekin

Trail of Description

Other Trails

Trailhead

River, creek, drainage

=0000= Forest road

(000) State road

See page 9 for complete legend

0   0.5   1

N

Creek-Bridge Creek loop, or making a point-to-point hike to Stehekin at the head of Lake Chelan.

The trail is easy to follow, and water is available along much of the route. Deer are fairly abundant in the Bridge Creek headwaters.

From the bulletin board at the beginning of this trail, walk briefly to the PCT and turn left, paralleling the noisy highway for half a mile. Then stroll easily downhill for 0.9 mile through a subalpine forest of spruce and fir, typical of the east side of the range. Turn left at the junction and part company with PCT hikers.

You'll pass a campsite and then boulder-hop across State Creek, a difficult ford in early summer. Soon you'll reach an old mileage sign and an abandoned segment of the PCT. Bear left, quickly reaching another trail sign and the faint eastbound trail leading to Copper Pass and Twisp River.

Bear right here, hop across Copper Creek after a quarter of a mile and another unnamed stream 0.6 mile farther. White pine and Douglas-fir will have joined the spruce and fir forest, indicating a slightly drier, warmer environment.

You'll enter North Cascades National Park 2.25 miles from the trailhead. The trail beyond descends steadily through an increasingly dry forest, passing the climbing, seldom-used eastbound trail to Stiletto Peak 2.8 miles in.

The eastbound Twisp Pass Trail, also leading to the road's end on the Twisp River, is reached after another 0.7 mile, but you should turn right, quickly coming to the trail to McAlester Lake. The westbound path leads to campsites on Bridge Creek and the PCT within half a mile.

In a rain-shadow forest of Douglas-fir and lodgepole and white pine, the nearly viewless trail begins ascending McAlester Creek, crossing its east fork after 0.8 mile. You'll pass shady, inviting Halfway Camp in another 0.8 mile. It boasts a picnic table, fire pits, and the beauty of nearby McAlester Creek.

Shortly beyond the camp the trail breaks into the open in a large, avalanche-scoured meadow. Here you'll get a fine view of timberline mountains at the head of the McAlester drainage. But all too soon the trail re-enters the spruce and fir forest, becoming very steep before a series of switchbacks begins to ease the grade. En route, you'll be entertained by glimpses of inviting cirque basins and rocky ridges lined with ribbons of stunted timber.

You'll pass a good, reliable source of drinking water—a creek free from upstream pollution—at the beginning of the switchbacks.

A total of 6.8 miles from the highway, a spur trail branches right (west) to a hiker's camp and the lower end of McAlester Lake. Pleasant campsites amid mountain hemlock and fir are numerous at the northwest end of the small, 5,500-foot-high lake. Fishing for eight-to-ten-inch cutthroats is usually productive.

Peak 7628, pointed and cloaked with scrub timber, rises east of the lake, while broken cliffs rise to the west below ridges decorated with the statuesque Lyall larch. McAlester Pass, 6,000 feet, is the notch to the southeast below Peak 7628. It's home to High Camp, a fine subalpine campsite in timberline parkland.

If you're itching for more, you can continue on and make the popular thirty-mile Rainbow Creek-Bridge Creek loop. Many hikers following the loop stay their first night at McAlester Lake. Otherwise, return to the trailhead the same way you came. □

HIKE 68 *RAINY PASS TO SNOWY LAKES*

General description: A rigorous twenty-two-mile, point-to-point backpack along a spectacular but unprotected segment of the Cascade crest east of North Cascades National Park in the Okanogan National Forest.
Elevation gain and loss: +2,964 feet, -3,110 feet.
Trailhead elevation: 4,855 feet.
High point: 6,880 feet.
Maps: Mount Arriva and Washington Pass 7.5-minute USGS quads; Okanogan National Forest map.
Season: July through September.
Water availability: Water limited to one mile west of Cutthroat Pass and the Snowy Lakes.

Finding the trailhead: Follow the North Cascades Highway (State Route 20) to Rainy Pass, 50.2 miles east of Marblemount or forty-three miles west of Winthrop. Opposite a picnic area at the pass, turn north onto a spur road that leads 0.3 mile to the northbound Pacific Crest Trail (PCT).

To reach the Cutthroat Creek Trailhead, follow the North Cascades Highway east from Washington Pass for 4.5 miles to the Cutthroat Creek Road, and turn left (west). Follow this one-lane pavement for a mile to the trailhead. Or drive thirty miles west from Winthrop to the Cutthroat Creek Road.

The hike: The PCT crosses the Cascade crest at Rainy Pass. From there it heads southward to Lake Chelan and northward into the Pasayten Wilderness.

Between Rainy and Harts passes is a spectacular section of the Cascade crest, dominated by the sawtoothed ridges and summits of the Golden Horn Batholith, the youngest granitic rocks exposed in Washington. The dominant erosive force responsible for shaping these jagged rocks (in addition to past glaciation) is a process known as frost-wedging: moisture seeps into cracks in the rock, wedging them apart as the water freezes and expands.

Somehow this highly scenic roadless area was overlooked for inclusion in the wilderness system. It's the only remaining roadless section of the Cascade crest not formally designated as wilderness, and this grave error ought to be corrected.

This is a rigorous hike, and the only campsites with available water are one mile west of Cutthroat Pass, in the bowl below Snowy Lakes, and at the lakes themselves. The route is high and exposed; so carry plenty of water and try to avoid bad weather. There are no fish in the lakes, but the panoramic views you'll have of a wide range of North Cascades terrain make the hike worthwhile.

For the most scenic trip (west to east), arrange for transportation home from the Cutthroat Creek Trailhead. It's a mile farther from Cutthroat Pass to Cutthroat Creek Trailhead than it is to the Rainy Pass Trailhead, but outstanding scenery makes the extra distance worth hiking.

To begin your adventure, proceed northward from the Rainy Pass Trailhead into fir forest. You'll cross a small stream after 0.75 mile, just below a delightful, two-tiered mini-waterfall. Looking westward you'll be able to see Black Peak which, at 8,970-feet, is one of the highest summits in the Skagit River drainage.

Snowy Lakes. Cliff Leight photo.

The divide upon which Black Peak rests is a granitic intrusion predating the Golden Horn Batholith you're traversing. If you look southward before the trail bends into the Porcupine Creek drainage, you'll see Lyall Glacier and the basin of Rainy Lake.

You'll pass a variety of forest trees on this slope: mountain hemlock and silver fir from the west slope of the Cascades, and Englemann spruce and subalpine fir from the drier, colder east slope.

Just before the trail bridges Porcupine Creek, you'll cross a smaller creek below a campsite, 1.5 miles from the trailhead. Granitic Dome 7520 looms boldly to the northwest. Then you'll negotiate three switchbacks to reach more open slopes, cross two small-but-year-round streams, and enjoy fine views up the canyon to broad Cutthroat Pass, standing at timberline on the eastern skyline.

This country is dominated in higher elevations by the tough Lyall larch, which grows in exposed sites above all other trees. It seems to thrive in the harshest mountain conditions. This interesting deciduous conifer, cousin to the western larch more common at lower elevations east of the Cascades, puts on a showy display of fall color, brightening even the cloudiest days in late September and early October.

The trail continues traversing south-facing slopes, crosses one more reliable creek, and then crosses the headwaters bowl of Porcupine Creek and a signed camping area. It then negotiates a series of switchbacks, rising toward the pass. The view improves as you leave behind a few persistent larches and reach the pass after 5.1 miles. There you'll find a ribbon of weather-tortured trees: Lyall larch, subalpine fir, Englemann spruce, mountain hemlock, and whitebark pine.

Views from this pass are superb and far-ranging. Far to the southwest lies

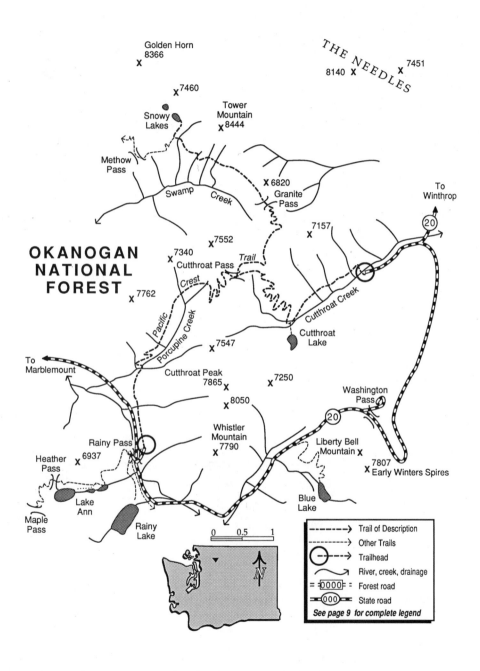

Golden Horn
8366
X

THE NEEDLES
7451
X
8140 **X**

X 7460

Snowy
Lakes

Tower
Mountain
X 8444

Methow
Pass

X 6820
Granite
Pass

Swamp   Creek

To
Winthrop

20

7157
X

X 7552

**OKANOGAN
NATIONAL
FOREST**

7340
X
Cutthroat Pass

Trail

Crest

X 7762

Pacific

Porcupine Creek

Cutthroat Creek

Cutthroat
Lake

X 7547

To
Marblemount

Cutthroat Peak
7865 **X**

X 7250

Washington
Pass

X 8050

Whistler
Mountain
X 7790

20

Liberty Bell
Mountain **X**

7807
X Early Winters Spires

Rainy Pass

Heather
Pass

X 6937

Lake
Ann

Blue
Lake

Maple
Pass

Rainy
Lake

0   0.5   1

N

	Trail of Description
	Other Trails
	Trailhead
	River, creek, drainage
=0000=	Forest road
(000)	State road

See page 9 for complete legend

Occupying a granite cirque scraped bare by ancient glaciers, the Snowy Lakes are a highly scenic alpine destination in the as-yet-unprotected high country north of Rainy Pass in the North Cascades. Ron Adkison photo.

ice-encrusted Dome Peak, visible through the notch of Maple Pass. Corteo Peak rises just northwest of that pass. Although Dome and Corteo peaks reach similar elevations, Corteo hosts only a few persistent snow patches in late summer—a fine example of the rain-shadow effect. In the southeast a jumble of impressive, toothed summits will meet your gaze. Due east is 8,876-foot Silver Star Mountain. South of it is jagged Kangaroo Ridge and the smooth dome of Liberty Bell, all composed of Golden Horn granodiorite.

Just east of the pass, the Cutthroat Creek Trail forks right. This is the route you'll take to reach Cutthroat Creek Trailhead after you visit the Snowy Lakes.

The fragile alpine environment at the pass has been used as a camping area, but you'll have to carry water and use minimum-impact camping techniques to the fullest if you stop here.

Remnants of glacial polish on exposed bedrock surfaces nearby indicate the glaciers overrode the Cascade crest here.

Proceed northward on the PCT, traversing below broken cliffs and above larch-clad benches. Northeast views will soon include the aptly named Needles, and distant alpine ridges of the Pasayten country, a land that more closely resembles the Rockies than the Cascades.

After strolling 1.3 miles from the pass, ignore a descending, right-forking trail, which dead-ends within 100 yards.

The PCT soon rounds a shoulder, and you'll get a grand view northwestward along the crest, dominated by 8,444-foot Tower Mountain.

Views from the trail near Granite Pass. Cliff Leight photo.

To the left of that peak is 8,366-foot Golden Horn, the namesake of this country.

A series of short, tight switchbacks ensues above the classic U-shaped valley of Swamp Creek. You'll reach Granite Pass 2.4 miles from the junction with the Cutthroat Creek Trail. There are campsites here at 6,290-feet, but expect to search eastward for a quarter mile or more to find water in late summer.

Ahead you can see the PCT traversing open, south-facing slopes, and you'll press on through a timberline stand of subalpine fir and whitebark pine, crossing numerous dry, precipitous gullies. The presence of pine mat manzanita on these slopes is an indication of their dryness. Penstemon growing here may be confused with manzanita, after the bloom, but it doesn't have the manzanita's shredding bark.

Two miles from Granite Pass, the trail enters a scenic subalpine bowl, crosses a tiny but reliable stream, and reaches a fragile alpine meadow frequently used by careless campers who've left lasting scars. Turn right at a junction above the campsite, 9.7 miles from the trailhead, and climb 550 feet on a well-worn path through spotty clumps of timberline trees.

The path finally levels out next to the beautiful alpine tarn of lower Snowy Lake. Only scattered larches and heather grow here; all else is bare rock. The outlet of this lake usually ceases to flow by late summer. A campsite lies near the outlet, but it's completely exposed. Tower Mountain looms ominously above to the east.

The trail continues a quarter of a mile to the upper lake, which is slightly larger and deeper, but not deep enough to support fish. Foolish, uninitiated hikers have built fires here, and firewood is scarce, with the few trees being widely scattered. Minimum-impact hikers would never build a fire in such a fragile alpine environment, except during an emergency.

Snowy Lakes Pass rises just above the upper lake. A climb to the pass yields rewarding vistas across the upper Methow River to the stark pinnacle of Mount Hardy, seen rising abruptly from broad Methow Pass, as well as to a host of snowier North Cascades peaks.

West of the pass, but still east of the Cascade crest, is a broad bench with water and more sheltered campsites than at the lakes.

To complete this hike, backtrack 5.3 miles to Cutthroat Pass and turn left. You'll descend easy switchbacks, first across open slopes and then through a timberline forest of Lyall larch, Engelmann spruce, and subalpine fir.

After two miles the route levels off on a waterless bench shaded by huge larches. Then it resumes its steady descent through a forest, where picturesque snags are as numerous as live trees. Huckleberry and manzanita carpet the slopes down to the canyon bottom. Below lies Cutthroat Lake; above the lake rises a number of jagged granitic summits.

After four miles you'll reach a junction with the short spur to beautiful Cutthroat Lake, where no overnight camping is permitted. Bear left, pass a spur trail to creekside campsites, and then descend the glacier-shaped valley of Cutthroat Creek for two miles amid mixed conifers. You'll cross the creek just before the trailhead. □

HIKE 69 NORTH CASCADES HIGHWAY TO BLUE LAKE

General description: A moderately easy 4.6 mile round trip day hike to a timberline lake on the Cascade crest near Washington Pass in the Okanogan National Forest.

Elevation gain and loss: 1,100 feet.

Trailhead elevation: 5,200 feet.

High point: 6,300 feet.

Maps: Washington Pass 7.5-minute USGS quad; Okanogan National Forest map.

Season: July through September.

Water availability: Spring at one mile point; abundant at the lake.

Finding the trailhead: Follow North Cascades Highway (Highway 20) fifty-four miles east from Marblemount or thirty-nine miles west from Winthrop to the signed Blue Lake Trailhead parking area, which is located on the south side of the highway. The trailhead lies 0.8 mile west of Washington Pass, and 3.8 miles east of Rainy Pass.

HIKE 69 NORTH CASCADES HIGHWAY TO BLUE LAKE

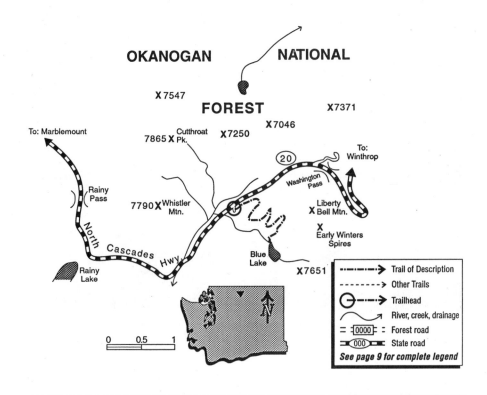

A September snowfall gives Blue Lake a dusting of frosty whiteness. Ron Adkison photo.

The hike: Few short hikes from the North Cascades Highway rival Blue Lake for fabulous scenery and ease of access. Nestled in a high cirque in the shadow of the granite dome of Liberty Bell Mountain and Early Winters Spires, Blue Lake offers a peaceful, scenic destination of a one-to-two-hour hike. The lake hosts a good population of pan-sized trout. The good trail maintains a steady, moderate grade throughout its length, making the hike suitable for most hikers, even families with young children.

The hike begins in a cool silver fir forest, initially passing small meadows and a pond before climbing forested slopes beneath Liberty Bell Mountain. As the trail gains elevation, the forest thins and dramatic views unfold at every bend in the trail. Across the glacial valley of State Creek are the bold crags of Whistler Mountain and Cutthroat Peak to the west and northwest, while the sheer cliffs of Liberty Bell and Early Winters Spires jut skyward directly above the trail.

After 1.7 miles the trail crosses a boulder field, ignore the climber's trail that branches left. The hiking trail then curves around the small cirque, its slopes carpeted in heather and huckleberry. Lyall larch and mountain hemlock now dominate the timberline forest.

The narrowing path proceeds through increasingly rocky terrain as it contours to Blue Lake's outlet creek next to a dilapidated cabin. Campsites are scarce around the sloping shores of this timberline lake, so hikers must be content to enjoy the magnificent surroundings for an afternoon before returning to the trailhead. □

HIKE 70 *CEDAR CREEK FALLS*

General description: An easy four-mile round trip day hike to a roaring waterfall on the east slope of the North Cascades in the Okanogan National Forest.
Elevation gain and loss: 500 feet.
Trailhead elevation: 3,000 feet.
High point: 3,500 feet.
Maps: Mazama 15-minute USGS quad; Okanogan National Forest map.
Season: June through October.
Water availability: Abundant at the end of the hike.

Finding the trailhead: From Highway 20 (the North Cascades Highway), 17.7 miles west of Winthrop and 2.6 miles west of the Early Winters Information Station, or 13.4 miles east of Washington Pass, turn south onto Forest Road 200, signed for Cedar Creek Trail. This one lane dirt road, rough in places, leads another 0.9 mile to the large trailhead parking area.

The hike: Cedar Creek, born on the flanks of the towering granite crags of Silver Star, North Gardiner, and Gilbert mountains, flows nine miles through a rugged and lonely canyon 3,000 to 4,000 feet deep. Scenery in this splendid canyon ranges from lofty, ice-encrusted summits to peaceful forests of Douglas-fir and ponderosa pine. The length of the canyon, the grandeur of its scenery, and its remoteness combine to make Cedar Creek an attractive backpacking destination.

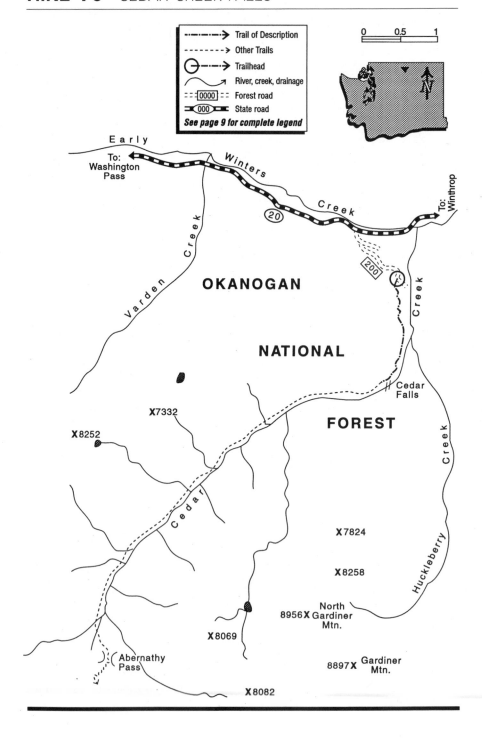

Trail of Description
Other Trails
Trailhead
River, creek, drainage
0000 Forest road
000 State road
See page 9 for complete legend

0   0.5   1

Early
To:
Washington
Pass

Winters

Creek

To:
Winthrop

20

200

Varden Creek

OKANOGAN

NATIONAL

Cedar
Falls

FOREST

Creek

Huckleberry Creek

X7332

X8252

Cedar

X7824

X8258

North
8956 X Gardiner
Mtn.

X8069

Abernathy
Pass

8897 X Gardiner
Mtn.

X8082

Cedar Creek Falls plunge off granite cliffs. Ron Adkison photo.

The hike to Cedar Creek Falls is a fine introduction to this canyon, and is the destination of most hikers. Actually a double waterfall, Cedar Creek plummets over two thirty-foot granite ledges—just two of several waterfalls in the canyon's lower reaches—two miles from the trailhead.

The hike is suitable for families with children, but children must be closely supervised near the falls.

From the trailhead the trail climbs to a fine view of the sheer gray cliffs of Goat Wall and the lookout-capped knob of Goat Peak to the north.

The trail ahead climbs gently through a pleasant forest of ponderosa pine and Douglas-fir high above the lower canyon of Cedar Creek. There are occasional tree-framed views south up the canyon of North Gardiner Mountain more than a mile above. The lofty ridges that embrace the canyon will be ablaze with the golden colors of Lyall larches in autumn.

Further up the trail Douglas-fir comes to dominate the forest, and occasionally, western red cedars drape their fan-like branches over the trail.

The roar of Cedar Creek increases along the last mile to the falls, and after two miles you reach a fair campsite among the boulders just above Cedar Creek Falls. Use caution on the slippery granite boulders when viewing the falls.

After enjoying this pleasant locale, retrace the route to the trailhead. □

HIKE 71 *SLATE PEAK— WEST FORK PASAYTEN RIVER LOOP*

General description: A moderate twenty-two-mile, loop backpack along the Cascade crest in the western Pasayten Wilderness.
Elevation gain and loss: 3,830 feet.
Trailhead elevation: 6,800 feet.
High point: 7,320 feet.
Maps: Slate Peak and Pasayten Peak 7.5-minute USGS quads; Okanogan National Forest map.
Season: July through September.
Water availability: Limited along the crest, abundant along West Fork Pasayten River.

Finding the trailhead: From State Route 20, seventeen miles east of Washington Pass or 17.5 miles west of Winthrop, turn north to Mazama. After 0.4 mile, turn left and pass the Mazama General Store. Follow this road westward up the course of the Methow River. Pavement ends after 6.6 miles, but becomes good dirt road. At numerous junctions, follow signs to Harts Pass. The road climbs steadily and becomes quite narrow in places; drive with care. Ignore an unsigned left fork 15.8 miles from Mazama and you'll reach a junction at Harts Pass after 18.3 miles. Bear right at this junction, pass a Forest Service guard station, and then turn right onto the Slate Peak Road. The trailhead is at the first switchback in the road, 1.3 miles from Harts Pass. Parking is limited to only about four vehicles.

The hike: North of the Methow River, the crest of the Cascade Range assumes an entirely different character. Here, the crest is a series of gentle timberline summits separated by many low saddles, grassy and timber-clad. The open grassy slopes are decorated by a host of colorful wildflowers, and vistas are boundless. This is pleasant, friendly hiking country, unburdened by overbearing crags and glaciers.

Although this backpack trip covers more than twenty miles, it passes quickly because of the gentle nature of the trails. Water is scarce along the Pacific Crest Trail; you'll find it only at three easily accessible creeks—at two, 4.2, and 8.3 miles. The second half of the trip follows the West Fork Pasayten River, where water is always close at hand, and where there is good fishing for pan-sized rainbows.

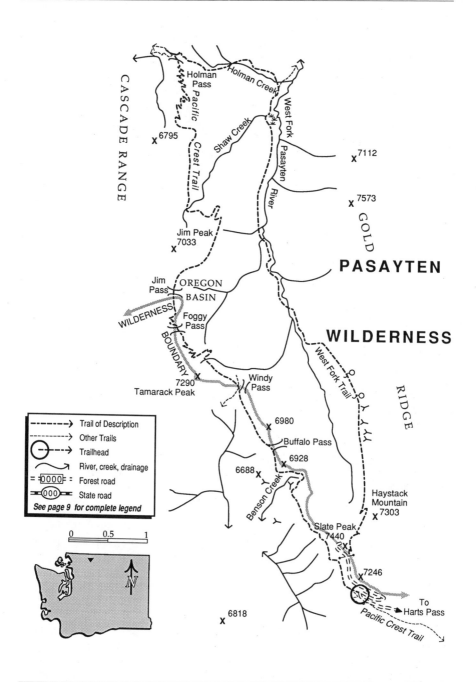

Holman Pass

Holman Creek

CASCADE RANGE

Pacific Crest Trail

x 6795

Shaw Creek

West Fork Pasayten River

x 7112

x 7573

GOLD

Jim Peak
7033
x

Jim Pass

OREGON BASIN

WILDERNESS

Foggy Pass

BOUNDARY

PASAYTEN

WILDERNESS

West Fork Trail

RIDGE

7290 x
Tamarack Peak

Windy Pass

x 6980

Buffalo Pass

6928

6688 x

Benson Creek

Haystack Mountain
x 7303

Slate Peak
7440
x

x 7246

x 6818

To Harts Pass

Pacific Crest Trail

Legend

- - - - - → Trail of Description
- - - - → Other Trails
⊖- - → Trailhead
～～～ River, creek, drainage
=□0000□= Forest road
=○000○= State road

See page 9 for complete legend

0   0.5   1

N

Much of this hike is along very exposed slopes, which should be avoided if inclement weather is imminent.

From the trailhead, begin by following the righthand trail through scattered Lyall larches for 0.1 mile to the PCT and turn right. The view from here is exceptional; it includes domineering Silver Star Mountain and its small glacier to the south, along with other prominent peaks such as The Needles, Tatie Peak, Mount Hardy, Fisher Peak, Azurite Peak and Mount Ballard. Beyond are peaks of North Cascades National Park: Snowfield Peak, Paul Bunyan's Stump, Bacon Peak, and the isolated crag of Mount Triumph. Closer at hand in the west are the dark masses of Crater Peak and Jack Mountain. Beyond them are distant North Cascades summits west of Ross Lake, and finally, the snowy cone of Mount Baker.

The trail traverses the west slopes of Slate Peak's lookout-crowned summit, passing subalpine fir in krummholz form and flowers such as yarrow, lupine, false dandelion, meadow rue, blue harebell, buckwheat, stonecrop, purple aster, red Indian paintbrush, phlox, figwort, wild pink, and anemone. Beyond the slopes of Slate Peak, trailside vegetation becomes less diverse and timber (stunted and widely scattered) includes subalpine fir, whitebark pine, Engelmann spruce, and Lyall larch.

After two miles, you'll pass above an inviting larch-clad bench at the head of Benson Creek, a mere trickle late in the season. Ahead, the trail traverses around the south and west slopes of Peak 6928. Notice the abrupt change in the forest: the south-slope forest of subalpine fir and spruce gives way abruptly on the north slopes to cold-tolerant larch.

You'll pass Buffalo Pass after 2.7 miles and then descend another mile to broad, 6,280-foot Windy Pass.

As you hike, you won't be able to help noticing the scars of past mining activity and the town site of Barron, below to the west. This area is part of the productive Slate Creek mining district, where ores of gold, silver, zinc, lead, and copper were extracted around the turn of the century. The road over Harts Pass (formerly Slate Pass) was built in the 1890s to serve the area.

At Windy Pass, ignore a left-forking jeep trail and a right-forking, northwest-bound path and follow the PCT into the Pasayten Wilderness, one of Washington's largest and most isolated wild areas. You'll cross a stream 4.2 miles from the trailhead and half a mile from Windy Pass, crossing between trailside campsites amid a ground cover of huckleberry, red heather, and anemone. Soon, four switchbacks will bring you onto a northeast-trending ridge emanating from Tamarack Peak. Subalpine firs atop the ridge hug the ground, while nearby Lyall larches and whitebark pines stand erect, defying the elements.

The route descends into a timberline bowl, reaching forested Foggy Pass two miles from Windy Pass. You'll briefly leave the wilderness during the west-slope traverse to 6,280-foot Jim Pass and then re-enter it on east slopes above wooded Oregon Basin.

The route descends rocky Devils Backbone, a ridge emanating from Jim Peak, and then traverses a north-facing cirque where the infant Shaw Creek is crossed at 8.3 miles.

A protracted, forested traverse leads to a descent of 1,000 feet, which in turn leads to wooded Holman Pass, elevation 5,050 feet. Turn right at the pass, parting company with PCT trekkers, and descend gently for 1.6 miles along Holman Creek to the West Fork Pasayten River Trail, and turn right (south).

You'll enter a broad, U-shaped valley densely forested with Engelmann spruce and subalpine fir. The Pasayten River eventually empties into British Columbia's Fraser River.

You'll cross the West Fork after 3.2 miles, just beyond a good campsite. Soon the trail leaves the valley bottom, climbing briefly before beginning an easy timberline traverse of the west slopes of Gold Ridge. You'll pass two springs—one is 1.4 miles and the other is 1.75 miles from the river crossing.

When you've traveled 2.25 miles from the river crossing, you'll pass a trail leading to several old diggings. But the main route proceeds southward across open slopes and through spotty timber. Lyall larches soon appear, and the trail switchbacks above timberline to the scree slopes of rounded Haystack Mountain.

Soon you'll pass just below a tiny but permanent snowfield; Slate Peak and its lookout loom above. You'll leave the Pasayten Wilderness when you reach the Slate Peak Road, eight miles from the junction of the West Fork Pasayten River and Holman Creek trails. If you seek broad panoramas, stroll the short distance to Slate Peak for your reward.

You'll stride past a locked gate on the Slate Peak Road and walk an easy 1.2 miles before reaching your vehicles at the trailhead. □

HIKE 72 *GOAT PEAK*

General description: A moderate 4.5-mile round trip day hike to a commanding viewpoint on a lookout-capped peak in the Okanogan Cascades.
Elevation gain and loss: 1,400 feet.
Trailhead elevation: 5,600 feet.
High point: Goat Peak, 7,001 feet.
Maps: Mazama 15-minute USGS quad: Okanogan National Forest map.
Season: July through September.
Water availability: None available; carry an adequate supply.

Finding the trailhead: From the North Cascades Highway State Route, 20, seventeen miles east of Washington Pass or 17.5 miles west of Winthrop, turn north to Mazama. After 0.4 mile turn right, drive southeast for two miles to the Goat Creek Road and turn left.

This one lane dirt road, rough in places, climbs steadily for 2.7 miles to a junction. Turn left again; a sign indicates the Goat Peak Lookout Trail is nine miles ahead.

This good dirt road leads 6.2 miles to signed Forest Road 200. Bear right here and proceed another three miles to the small trailhead parking area on the ridge at a three-way junction.

The hike: If Goat Peak did not boast incredible vistas from its summit, the hike would nonetheless be a worthwhile excursion, passing among wind-flagged forests and stands of Lyall larch that flame with autumn color. But it's the vistas that attract hikers to this prominent peak—vistas that are unsurpassed from any trail in the region. Ranging from the green fields of the Methow Valley to the rolling ridges of the Okanogan Cascades and from the bare 8,000-foot

The fire lookout on Goat Peak stands above scrub timber. Ron Adkison.

summits of the Pasayten Wilderness to the great ice-encrusted peaks of the North Cascades, the view from Goat Peak is truly breathtaking.

The trail is steep and rocky in places, and the peak is subject to strong winds and lightning strikes; so avoid the hike if thunderstorms threaten.

The trail begins by climbing a rocky ridge among subalpine fir and wind-torn Douglas-firs. Views are good from the start, reaching from the Cascade crest to the high peaks of the western Pasayten Wilderness. The trail rises moderately at first but soon climbs steeply upon the north slopes of Peak 6849. Nearing the top of that rocky knob, switchbacks begin to moderate the grade.

HIKE 72 *GOAT PEAK*

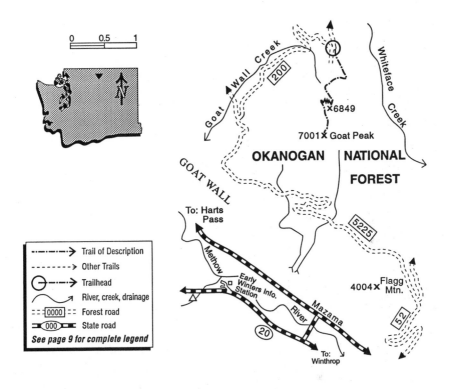

From the top of the knob, a broad panorama of majestic mountain scenery unfolds, a view that is surpassed only from Goat Peak itself.

The trail ahead follows the undulating ridge, passing stunted groves of Lyall larch, whitebark pine, and subalpine fir.

Then the trail climbs the final steep pitch among small larches to the lookout-capped summit.

After absorbing one of the finest vistas in Washington, retrace the route to the trailhead. □

HIKE 73 *BILLY GOAT LOOP*

General description: A week-long, fifty-mile loop backpack into the heart of the Pasayten Wilderness.

Elevation gain and loss: 10,160 feet.

Trailhead elevation: 4,800 feet.

High point: 7,500 feet.

Maps: Billy Goat Mountain, Ashnola Pass and Ashnola Mountain 7.5-minute USGS quads; Okanogan National Forest map.

Season: July through September.

Water availability: Abundant along much of the route.

Finding the trailhead: From State Route 20 at the west end of Winthrop, turn northwest onto West Chewuch Road, just west of the bridge over the Chewuch River. You can get last-minute information at the Winthrop Ranger Station; to reach it, turn right after 0.3 mile.

This paved road follows the valley of the Chewuch River for 9.6 miles to a junction with left-forking Forest Road 5130. Turn left here where the sign indicates Billy Goat and Buck Lake.

Avoid several signed spur roads as you follow the winding pavement of Forest Road 5130 up the Eightmile Creek drainage. The pavement ends after 5.3 miles, but the dirt portion of Forest Road 5130 remains wide and smooth, except for the final rough mile to the trailhead, which is 16.6 miles from the Chewuch River and 26.2 miles from Winthrop.

The hike: Pasayten country is big, lonely country, unlike any other wildland in the state. Although the land is punctuated by a few sharp peaks, it's primarily gentle and rolling. Broad U-shaped valleys rise easily to friendly ridges. Although many peaks in the Pasayten rise above 8,000 feet, most are simple walkups; no special skills are needed to attain their summits. This landscape more closely resembles the Rockies than the Cascades.

This country is old; its contours have been rounded and subdued by eons of erosion. Glacial cirques and U-shaped valleys indicate the land has been carved by ancient glaciers. But this is rain-shadow country; it receives a third less precipitation than the North Cascades farther west.

The Pasayten is prime hiking country. The region is crisscrossed with trails, and off-trail hiking is easy and rewarding. The wilderness is so big (approximately forty miles from east to west and twenty miles from north to south) that you can walk for two weeks and not cross a single road.

This week-long, fifty-mile backpack trip tours fishable lakes, subalpine forests and parkland, alpine ridges and cirque basins, and eight passes, two of which must be recrossed on the return trip. Travelers are few and far between in this country. You're more likely to meet horse packers than other hikers.

Fishing for pan-sized cutthroats is good in all the lakes passed en route, and wildflowers, vast mountainscapes, and brilliant displays of fall color, thanks to an abundance of Lyall larch at timberline, are all major attractions in a region often overlooked by Washington hikers.

A closed road quickly leads to the trail. Soon the Eightmile Pass Trail forks left, a popular route leading eventually to the Hidden Lakes along the Lost

A typical timberline bowl in the Pasayten Wilderness offers sheltered campsides and scenic diversity. Bob Arrington photo.

River. You should bear right, switchbacking into an open Douglas fir and subalpine fir forest from which you'll have good views across Eightmile Creek to the jumbo crag of Big Craggy Peak, one of the most rugged mountains in the area.

The trail eventually bends into another drainage, continuing to climb through subalpine forest and increasingly rocky terrain. It passes a reliable spring and climbs another half mile to 6,600-foot Billy Goat Pass, 2.75 miles from the trailhead on the boundary of the Pasayten Wilderness.

Beyond the pass, the trail quickly descends past southeastbound Burch Mountain Trail, which leads to that 7,782-foot peak in two miles, a fine destination for a day hike.

Proceed downward through flower-filled meadows and open timberline forest, crossing a few small creeks and possible campsites. Massive Billy Goat Mountain, its granitic ramparts studded with Lyall larch, looms menacingly to the west.

The trail steadily descends to a lodgepole-shaded crossing of Drake Creek, passes a few trailside campsites, climbs past reliable Two Bit Creek, and then splits with the Drake Creek Trail, 2.25 miles from Billy Goat Pass. If your time is limited, you might consider turning downstream along that trail, reaching the trail to Eightmile Pass after three miles and looping back to the trailhead via that four-mile-long trail.

To continue this hike, bear right at the junction and climb across the slopes of an old burn decorated with many standing snags. Whitebark and lodgepole pine, Englemann spruce and subalpine fir are steadily reforesting the area.

The trail leads through fascinating Three Fools Pass, a series of three low saddles. In the northwest you'll be able to see Two Point Mountain, and looking back you can see Billy Goat Pass. As you descend from Three Fools Pass you'll reach the junction with the return leg of the loop, 7.2 miles from the trailhead. Bear left, hop across Diamond Creek (this may be difficult in early summer) and begin a sunny westbound traverse across rocky slopes clothed in aspen and Douglas fir.

The route jogs north into a forest of young lodgepole pines, open enough to allow fine views down Diamond Creek to massive Many Trails Peak. Ignore a left-forking trail 1.5 miles from the previous junction. It leads to Dollar Watch Pass. Instead, stroll another mile to a bridge across Larch Creek. Another trail to Dollar Watch Pass forks left west of the bridge.

The main trail proceeds upstream along Larch Creek through meadows and a forest of young lodgepole pines, passing campsites along the way. Then, abruptly, spruce forest supplants the lodgepoles, and the trail crosses back to the east bank of Larch Creek. It soon bridges a westward-flowing tributary and then briefly switchbacks before jogging northwest.

At the head of Larch Creek, you'll pass a series of subalpine meadows decorated with high-country wildflowers. The small stream tends to dry up in the upper meadows by late summer. You'll also pass a scenic campsite before squishing through the mud of a seeping spring and negotiating one long switchback to attain 7,200-foot Larch Pass, clad in stunted Lyall larch forest. Another small spring seeps across the trail about a quarter mile below (south of) the pass.

North of the pass is a world of open parks and alpine grasslands. You should be sure to go at least this far, but the major attractions lie ahead.

Southward views from the pass feature a host of bald, gently sloping alpine

A side trip from Park Pass on the Billy Goat Loop leads to one of the many concrete monuments placed at intervals all along the international boundary. Ron Adkison photo.

mountains. Northwest of the pass is the broad alpine mesa of Ashnola Mountain, and on the western skyline are rugged summits of the distant North Cascades.

The trail contours across rocky slopes north of Larch Pass into beautiful McCall Gulch, passing a few seeping springs and the last islands of timber set amidst flower-filled alpine meadows. The gulch is a popular camping area, with a small but year-round stream nearby.

Ignore the left-forking trail eventually leading to Hidden Lakes, 0.75 mile from Larch Pass. Your trail gains 400 feet and reaches a 7,500-foot saddle, the highest elevation attained on this trip.

The popular Corral Lake Trail forks right at the pass, leading one mile to campsites and only fair fishing at the 7,152-foot lake. A very faint track forks left from the pass, crosses over Ashnola Mountain and heads 1.5 miles into Whistler Basin, named for its population of whistling marmots. The basin is a beautiful alpine bench offering all-year water and a secluded camping area.

The main trail descends briefly along a spur ridge above isolated Crow Lake (good fishing and off-the-beaten-track campsites) before dropping into very scenic Timber Wolf Basin. Notice the small islands of stunted trees here. This basin collects copious amounts of snow, blown from surrounding ridges in winter. Only on the hummocks in the basin does the snowpack remain shallow enough for trees to grow. The thinner snowpack melts sooner, aided by the heat absorbed by the dense groves, thus providing a longer growing season in a basin that ordinarily wouldn't be able to support trees.

Hiking through the basin, you pass groves of Lyall larch, Englemann spruce, subalpine fir, and whitebark pine that shelter numerous scenic campsites. Abundant water flows nearby. The trail soon heads northwest, contouring above the basin, leading to an east-trending spur ridge emanating from Sand

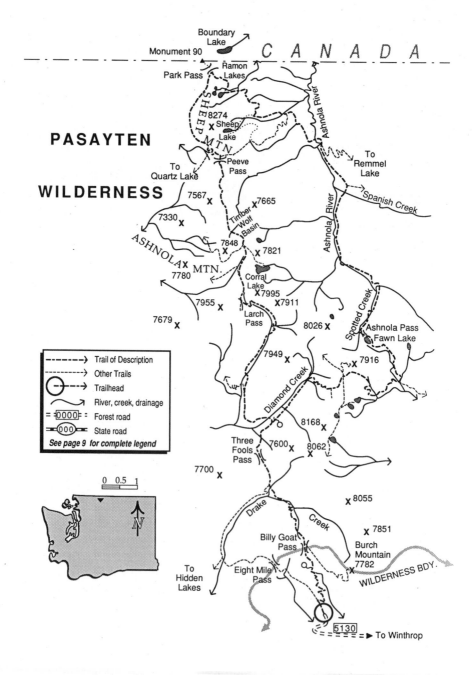

Boundary Lake
Monument 90
CANADA
Park Pass
Ramon Lakes
PASAYTEN
SHEEP MTN
8274 X
Sheep Lake
Ashnola River
To Remmel Lake
Peeve Pass
To Quartz Lake
Spanish Creek
WILDERNESS
7567 X
7330 X
Timber Wolf Basin
7665 X
Ashnola River
7848 X
ASHNOLA MTN.
7821 X
7780 X
Corral Lake
7995 X
Spotted Creek
7955 X
7911 X
Larch Pass
8026 X
Ashnola Pass
Fawn Lake
7679 X
7949 X
7916 X
Diamond Creek
8168 X
Three Fools Pass
7600 X
8062 X
7700 X
8055 X
Drake
Creek
7851 X
Billy Goat Pass
Burch Mountain 7782
Eight Mile Pass
WILDERNESS BDY.
To Hidden Lakes
5130
To Winthrop

Legend:
- Trail of Description
- Other Trails
- Trailhead
- River, creek, drainage
- = {0000} = Forest road
- ▬(000)▬ State road
- *See page 9 for complete legend*

0 0.5 1

N

Ridge, 2.25 miles beyond the last pass. Views from this point are excellent across the deep canyon of the Ashnola River to a series of high peaks and alpine plateaus. Among the more prominent landmarks visible in the east are craggy Cathedral Peak and the broad plateau of Bald Mountain.

For an even better view, leave the trail and follow a faint tread up the spur ridge to wide, grassy Sand Ridge, only a quarter mile away. The view from here extends westward beyond the peaks of the Cascade crest. You'll be able to see the bold, ice-clad crag of 8,928-foot Jack Mountain rising east of Ross Lake in the westernmost reaches of the Pasayten Wilderness.

Beyond the ridge, the trail descends into yet another scenic alpine basin, featuring running water and isolated trees. Then it descends easily amid increasing timber to 6,900-foot Peeve Pass and a junction, eighteen miles from the trailhead. The right fork descends 4.5 miles to the Ashnola River, passing a northbound spur to Sheep Lake after one mile.

Follow the left fork, signed for Hidden Lakes and Pasayten River, descending 300 feet in 0.4 mile to another junction.

Scenic Quartz Lake rests in a deep cirque 1.5 miles down the left-forking trail. But you should turn right, beginning a protracted 2.75-mile undulating traverse of the west slopes of 8,274-foot Sheep Mountain. You'll hike first through timber and then across open, grassy slopes that boast numerous springs.

Vistas from this mountainside are superb, reaching southwestward across the vast Pasayten Wilderness to glaciated Jack Mountain and the peaks of the Cascade crest. Westward lies the swath cut through the forest marking the international boundary. To the northwest and just north of the border is a burned area of forest that has been salvage-logged—the first sign of man after twenty miles of hiking.

Eventually, the trail descends through scattered timber and grassy slopes to 7,000-foot Park Pass, 2.75 miles from the last junction and more than twenty-one miles from the trailhead. The rounded, grassy mountain north of the pass lies across the border in Canada, and as you proceed beyond the pass the border swath again comes into view, making a beeline eastward toward Cathedral Peak.

An interesting side trip begins at Park Pass. Ascending moderately steep, grassy slopes northwestward for 0.75 mile, you can climb to Monument 90 along the U.S.-Canada boundary. The concrete monument is one of many erected all along the border, and views from it are excellent; you can see Boundary Lake lying in a cirque below to the northeast. There's good fishing for cutthroats in this Canadian lake, but to fish it you'll need a British Columbia fishing license.

Most of the high country lies south of the border, while to the north the landscape consists of a vast, forested plateau. Little sign of logging or other development is visible, although it undoubtedly exists.

Back at Park Pass, follow the main trail southeast through grassland to a low ridge and then down to the lowest and largest of the Ramon Lakes via a very faint tread. The lake basin is quite scenic, surrounded by grassy slopes clad in a sparse forest of Lyall larch, Englemann spruce, whitebark pine and subalpine fir. The trees shelter numerous possible campsites. Sheep Mountain rises steadily above the basin in the west. Fishing is productive in the lower lake for pan-sized cutthroats.

Two small upper lakes rest on a bench above to the west at timberline. There are secluded, very scenic campsites there, but the lakes are shallow and don't support fish, and their outlet streams will likely be dry by late summer.

To continue, follow the outlet of the lower lake downstream along its south bank. Soon the trail crosses a lower basin amid well-watered meadows before angling over a low ridge into another shallow basin. Vistas from this lovely park are excellent eastward across the Ashnola River, but the tread soon disappears.

Head southeastward, aiming for the distant upper reaches of the Ashnola River between Bald Mountain and Fred's Mountain; there may be ducks to lead the way. Once upon the next ridge, follow it briefly downhill. With luck you'll meet the trail just after descending into a grove of small lodgepole pines. Turn right and descend steeply into the Martina Creek drainage.

Upon reaching the canyon bottom, 23.5 miles from the trailhead, you'll have to look hard to locate the trail that reportedly climbs to Sheep Lake at the head of the drainage. At its junction with the main trail, turn left (east) and descend one mile through the forest to a crossing of Martina Creek and a junction with the trail coming down from Peeve Pass.

Bear left again, descending 800 feet in 1.75 miles to the Ashnola River. After fording it, you'll find a log lean-to shelter in the lodgepole forest. Beyond this shelter, the trail jogs south for 0.2 mile to a junction with an eastbound trail to Remmel Lake.

From this junction, you can gaze northwestward to the slopes rising west of the Ashnola. Burned in spots years ago, they host a patchwork forest of young, light-green trees (lodgepole pines) and darker stands of mature trees (spruces and firs). Lodgepole pines are typically the first trees to pioneer burned areas, while the spruces and firs represent an older climax forest.

Bear right at this junction, hiking another 1.5 miles through the timber to meet the Spanish Creek Trail heading southeastward in the lower reaches of Spanish Creek, an Ashnola tributary. Incidentally, the Ashnola is a tributary of the Okanogan River, which eventually empties its waters into the Columbia.

Turning right again, bridge Spanish Creek near a campsite and continue southward. Deer and moose frequent this route more than hikers.

The trail crosses the bouldery bed of the Ashnola River 2.25 miles beyond Spanish Creek. Here, spruce and fir begin to supplant the lodgepole forest. Avoiding a boggy meadow, the route soon crosses back to the east bank, passing a series of wet meadows and a few scattered campsites.

Hop across the infant Ashnola four miles from Spanish Creek (or twenty-nine miles from the trailhead) and begin ascending the course of small Spotted Creek along a narrow meadow being overtaken by lodgepole pines. You'll have good views up the canyon to rugged Diamond Point.

The muddy trail crosses and recrosses the small creek and then climbs steeply away from it to the low ridge of Ashnola Pass, beyond which lies tree- and rock-encircled Fawn Lake, elevation 6,201 feet.

The impressive pyramid of Diamond Point rears up mightily beyond the lake, which boasts numerous campsites all around its shores and good fishing for cutthroats up to a foot long. Beyond the lake the trail crosses over a rocky rise erroneously signed as Ashnola Pass and begins a steady descent of Lake Creek.

After two rugged miles from Fawn Lake, you'll cross small Newland Creek via a rotten log bridge. At a junction, turn right (west) toward Diamond Creek (so signed). You'll immediately hop across Lake Creek and begin climbing on a much smoother trail.

After the initial climb, the trail levels off on a bench, crosses several small streams and passes a single small campsite. Switchbacks ensue, but the trail shortly reaches the level of a second bench, clad in subalpine forest. No water is available nearby.

After hiking 3.25 miles, you'll reach a 7,100-foot saddle 1,800 feet above Lake Creek. From this timberline saddle, trails lead north to Diamond Point in 1.25 miles and south toward Fox Lake and Fool Hen Lake.

Briefly follow the main trail south along the ridgeline and turn right after about 100 feet, descending toward a massive alpine mountain in the southwest. After 0.75 mile, avoid a left-branching trail and descend via switchbacks into the depths of Diamond Creek, leveling off next to a roofless cabin and passing a few trailside campsites near a small creek.

You'll soon pass a beautiful meadow and campsite resting at the foot of Peak 7949. Traverse above the creek along the foot of a talus slope and cross a small, reliable stream 2.5 miles from the pass. Then stroll downhill through the woods past a rocky spring for one more mile to a junction, where you'll turn left and retrace your route through Three Fools and Billy Goat passes for 7.25 miles to the trailhead. □

HIKE 74 *BLACK LAKE*

General description: A moderate eight-mile round trip backpack or day hike to a large canyon lake in the Pasayten Wilderness.
Elevation gain and loss: 785 feet.
Trailhead elevation: 3,200 feet.
High Point: Black Lake, 3,982 feet.
Maps: Mount Barney 7.5-minute USGS quad; Okanogan National Forest map.
Season: Mid-June through early October.
Water availability: Abundant along much of the route and at the lake.

Finding the trailhead: Follow directions given in Hike 73 to Forest Road 5130, the Eightmile Creek Road, and continue straight ahead on the paved West Chewuch Road. This road turns to one-lane pavement after another 1.4 miles.

After another 10.3 miles and immediately after bridging Lake Creek, turn left onto the one-lane dirt road an drive 2.5 miles to the trailhead parking area.

The hike: Most hikes into the Pasayten Wilderness require a backpack of several days to a week or more to enjoy the unique landscapes of this eastern Cascade wild area.

But the short hike to Black Lake, one of the gems of the Pasayten, can be enjoyed by either a day hike or weekend backpack. In addition to good fishing this 0.8 mile long lake rests in a beautiful setting; its forest and rock-rimmed shores lie at the foot of lofty ridges soaring more than 3,000 feet above. The

Black Lake is tucked away in the Pasayten Wilderness. Ron Adkison photo.

low elevation of the lake gives this hike a longer season than most other trails in the Pasayten.

Don't forget to carry an effective insect repellant in summer and, anglers should bring a variety of fishing gear for this deep lake.

The hike to Black Lake is a pleasant jaunt up the forested canyon of Lake creek. The trail gains minimal elevation, and alternates from the banks of the noisy, boulder-strewn creek to the quiet forested slopes above. Water is almost always close at hand, either from the creek itself or from any of the ten spring-fed creeks crossed en route.

The often shady, sometimes open forests of the canyon consist of ponderosa, lodgepole, and white pine, Douglas-fir, Englemann spruce, and subalpine fir. Understory shrubs are also abundant and diverse, including red-osier dogwood, pachystima, false Solomon's seal, thimbleberry, spirea, serviceberry, and Douglas maple. Riparian trees include aspen, water birch, black cottonwood, and Sitka alder.

Views en route reach to the subalpine forests of the 7,000-foot ridges far above that embrace the canyon. In autumn the brilliant orange-yellow patches of foliage on the ridges are Lyall larches; their needles nipped by September frosts.

HIKE 74 *BLACK LAKE*

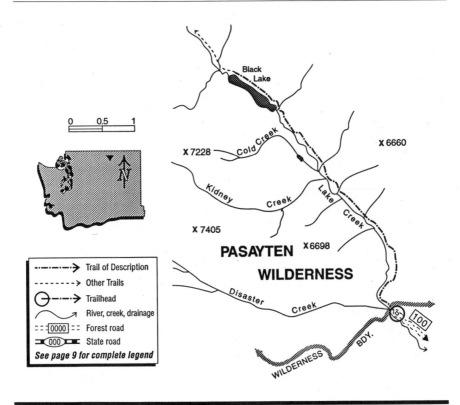

Upon reaching the outlet of the lake, look for good campsites near a spring. The view from here up the canyon of Lake Creek is superb. There are several fair campsites below the trail along the northeast shore of the lake and still more sites in the forest above the lakes's inlet.

After enjoying this short but scenic hike, retrace the route to the trailhead. If time and energy allow, several timberline lakes lie another day's hike away near the head of Lake Creek canyon (See Hike 73). □

HIKE 75 *FREEZEOUT PASS TO TIFFANY MOUNTAIN*

General description: A moderate five-mile, round-trip day hike to a peak in the Okanogan Cascades.
Elevation gain and loss: 1,742 feet.
Trailhead elevation: 6,500 feet.
High point: Tiffany Mountain, 8,242 feet.
Maps: Tiffany Mountain 15-minute USGS quad; Okanogan National Forest map.
Season: July through early October.
Water availability: None available.

Finding the trailhead: From State Route 20 at the west end of Winthrop, turn north onto West Chewuch Road, following it for 6.9 miles along the Chewuch River. Then turn right, bridge the small river and turn left (north) onto Forest Road 37 after 0.2 mile.

Follow Forest Road 37 along the east bank of the Chewuch River for 1.3 miles, turning right into the Boulder Creek drainage where a sign indicates Roger Lake, among other destinations. Bear right after another 6.3 miles at the end of pavement.

After another 5.7 miles, turn left off Forest Road 37 and onto Forest Road 39. This good gravel road leads northward past the Roger Lake turnoff to Freezeout Pass and the trailhead, 3.3 miles from Forest Road 37.

The hike: To reach the high, open ridges and summits of the Okanogan Cascades, you must usually walk many miles. But not everyone has the time or inclination for such extended treks.

This short hike to the crest of Tiffany Mountain—just outside the Pasayten Wilderness—offers great rewards for a minimum of effort. Three nearby lakes and several cirque basins invite backpackers to linger.

Tiffany Mountain is part of a large roadless area along the divide between the Chewuch and Okanogan rivers. A road up the Chewuch severs its link with the Pasayten. The entire region from the Okanogan River westward to the Cascade crest is known as the Okanogan Cascades, a unique and rewarding place to hike.

From Freezeout Pass, the trail proceeds eastward along boulder-littered Freezeout Ridge through an open forest of lodgepole and whitebark pine, subalpine fir and Englemann spruce. A variety of flowers decorate otherwise open slopes: lupine, arnica, yarrow, stonecrop, whortleberry, senecio, purple aster, pearly everlasting, whorled penstemon, buckwheat, and red Indian paint-

HIKE 75 *FREEZEOUT PASS TO TIFFANY MOUNTAIN*

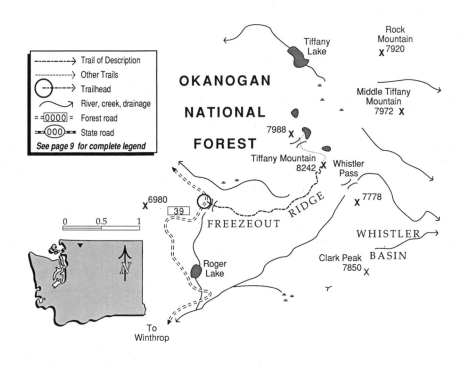

Trail of Description
Other Trails
Trailhead
River, creek, drainage
Forest road
State road
See page 9 for complete legend

OKANOGAN

NATIONAL

FOREST

Rock
Mountain
x 7920

Tiffany
Lake

Middle Tiffany
Mountain
7972 X

7988 x

Tiffany Mountain
8242 x   Whistler
Pass

x 6980
39
FREEZEOUT   RIDGE

x 7778

0   0.5   1

WHISTLER

Roger
Lake

Clark Peak   BASIN
7850 x

To
Winthrop

brush. After one mile of steady climbing, the trail breaks out into open meadows and passes scattered, increasingly stunted trees. Soon the route becomes faint; if you lose it, simply head northeastward up the broad slopes of Tiffany Mountain.

Upon reaching the foot of the mountain, the route climbs steep, grassy slopes, littered with granite boulders and a few persistent, ground-hugging whitebark pines and Englemann spruces. You'll finally reach the flat, rocky summit area after 2.5 miles of pleasant high-country walking.

Views from the mountain are far-reaching, including the vast rolling landscape of the Okanogan Cascades to the west, north and south. Far to the east is the Okanogan Valley, the only major interruption in a chain of mountains stretching 500 miles from the Pacific Ocean in northwest Washington to the High Plains east of Glacier National Park, Montana.

Nearby are other grassy, alpine summits, beckoning you in summer with the promise of solitude, broad vistas, and fields of grass and flowers.

Skiers will be lured back to this country in winter, when open slopes and usually-excellent, dry snow conditions combine to make the high country of the Okanogan Cascades a wilderness skier's paradise.

Below the summit to the northeast is an inviting timberline lake in a deep cirque at 7,300 feet. To the north, Tiffany Lake sits amid the marshlands of upper Tiffany Creek.

Invisible from the summit is Little Tiffany Lake, elevation 7,400 feet. To get to that isolated tarn, you must walk north from the summit via the gentle alpine ridge for half a mile to a broad saddle. The lake lies in a tiny cirque just north of the saddle.

After enjoying this fine, easily accessible high country, retrace the route to the trailhead. □

HIKE 76 *TIFFANY LAKE*

General description: A very easy two-mile round trip hike to a beautiful mountain lake in the Okanogan Cascades.
Elevation gain and loss: -200 feet.
Trailhead elevation: 6,750 feet.
High point: Trailhead, 6,750 feet.
Maps: Tiffany Mountain 15-minute USGS quad; Okanogan National Forest map.
Season: Late June through early October.
Water availability: Available from several springs along the trail and at the lake.

Finding the trailhead: Follow directions given in Hike 75 to Freezeout Pass

Tiffany Lake lies beneath its namesake, Tiffany Mountain, the highest point in the Okanogan Cascades. Ron Adkison photo.

and continue on Forest Road 39 for another 4.1 miles to Tiffany Spring Campground. Parking is available at the campground entrance, and the signed trail begins on the opposite side of the road.

The hike: The Tiffany Mountain massif is the highest, and arguably, the most scenic feature of the Okanogan Cascades beyond the boundaries of the Pasayten Wilderness. Here are five, lofty peaks, timberline forests of pine, fir, and larch, glacier-carved cirques, and three high lakes.

The stroll to Tiffany Lake—downhill all the way—is a fine choice for families with small children. The lake, hosting a good population of hungry trout, rests in the forested valley between the cliffs of Tiffany Mountain and the alpine slopes of Rock Mountain.

More adventurous hikers have several side-trip opportunities, including the ascent of Rock or Middle Tiffany mountains for far-ranging vistas and a scramble to the timberline tarns of Little Tiffany lakes.

HIKE 76 *TIFFANY LAKE*

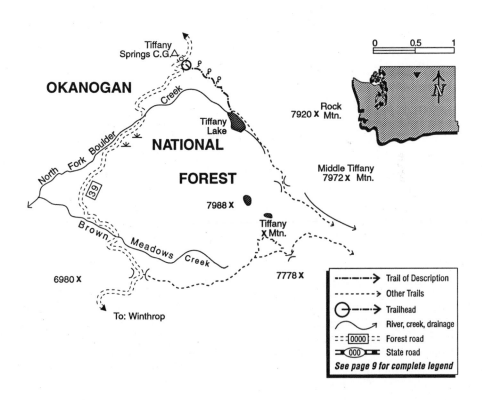

The trail begins on grassy slopes among scattered lodgepole pines. Views reach into the peak-rimmed cirque in which Tiffany Lake lies, as well as to the southwest and west toward the bold, snow-streaked crags of the Sawtooth Range and the North Cascades.

The wide trail enters a pine and spruce forest, descending slightly past several good springs. The forested jaunt continues to the forest and meadow-fringed shores of Tiffany Lake, only one mile from the campground. A few good campsites are located near the lake's outlet, but are seldom used. The smooth, rounded slopes of Rock Mountain rising above timberline to the east, contrast markedly with the gray cliffs and boulder-littered slopes of Tiffany Mountain south of the lake. Those slopes host stands of Lyall larch, which offer a fine display of golden autumn color in September. □

HIKE 77 *CRATER LAKES*

General description: A 7.8-mile, round-trip backpack to a larch-cloaked lake basin east of Lake Chelan in the Okanogan National Forest.
Elevation gain and loss: 2,209 feet.
Trailhead elevation: 4,760 feet.
High point: Upper Crater Lake, 6,969 feet.
Maps: Martin Peak 7.5-minute USGS quad; Okanogan National Forest map.
Season: July through mid-October.
Water availability: Abundant at Crater Lakes.

Finding the trailhead: From Pateros on the Columbia River, follow State Route 153 northwest for 16.4 miles to Gold Creek Road and turn left, following the west bank of the Methow River upstream. The river road continues north-west, leading back to State Route 20 in 1.6 miles. Travelers from Winthrop can reach this point in 21.5 miles. Turn left again after 0.8 mile, where a sign indicates Crater Creek Camp, among other destinations.

After one mile, bear right onto Forest Road 4340, and stick with this road at subsequent junctions. Avoid a left fork after another 1.75 miles, and reach the end of pavement 4.9 miles from the river.

Turn left onto Road 300, marked by a "Crater Trailhead" sign, 6.5 miles from the river. Follow this switchbacking road for 4.4 miles to the trailhead parking area, signed "Eagle Lakes Trail."

The hike: Washington's backcountry areas are well-endowed with lakes. Repeated episodes of glaciation have carved and gouged the mountain land-scape into sharp crests and pointed peaks which rise above broad cirques and U-shaped valleys.

But although this glacier-created scenery is widespread throughout the state, each region has its own unique character based on rock type, vegetation, climate, and other factors.

The Sawtooth Range east of Lake Chelan is one of the easternmost subranges of the Cascades. Its forests are open and dry. Rugged granite peaks attaining

HIKE 77 *CRATER LAKES*

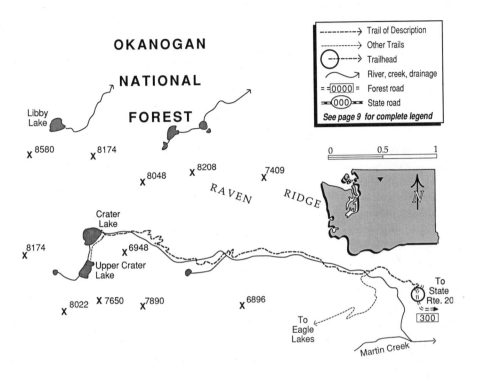

OKANOGAN

NATIONAL

FOREST

Libby
Lake

x 8580   x 8174

x 8048   x 8208   x 7409

R A V E N   R I D G E

Crater
Lake

x 8174   x 6948

Upper Crater
Lake

x 8022   X 7650   x 7890   x 6896

To
Eagle
Lakes

To
State
Rte. 20

300

Martin Creek

Trail of Description
Other Trails
Trailhead
River, creek, drainage
0000 Forest road
000 State road
See page 9 for complete legend

0   0.5   1

heights upwards of 8,000 feet rise above a series of cirque basins on the north-east slope of the range.

This rewarding hike into the Crater Lakes will lead you through the upper reaches of an eastside drainage to a peak-rimmed lake basin, clothed in timberline forests of Englemann spruce, Lyall larch, whitebark pine (trees almost exclusive to the east side of the Cascades), and subalpine fir. Camp-sites are numerous, and fishing for pan-sized trout in both lakes is productive.

From the trailhead, proceed on an easy grade through an open, grass-floored forest. You'll soon reach a viewpoint that offers glimpses into the Martin Creek drainage in the southwest and the Crater Creek drainage in the west—the latter is your destination.

After 0.6 mile, the trail bridges Crater Creek, and you'll reach a junction. Thus far, motorcycles are allowed to use this trail, and they can continue up the left fork to the Eagle Lakes, four miles distant. But most non-motorized recreationists turn right onto Crater Lake Trail which, although beyond the boundaries of the Lake Chelan-Sawtooth Wilderness, remains closed to motor vehicles.

This trail climbs moderately through a spruce and fir forest with limited views for two miles. Then it executes three steep switchbacks, where you may pause to enjoy a fine vista to the pine and grass-covered hills of the Methow Valley and beyond to the Columbia Basin.

Ahead, the canyon opens up as the trail briefly reaches the level ground of the first in a series of step-like benches so typical of glacial valleys. Views are good up the canyon to rugged granite peaks. A small unseen tarn lies at the head of the bench at an elevation of 6,200 feet.

The trail presently leaves that bench and climbs steeply at times for .8 mile to another bench at 6,800 feet. This second bench features a lovely meadow and a campsite frequented by horse packers.

Now in a subalpine forest, the trail climbs gently to 6,841-foot Crater Lake. This scenic lake is shallow but supports a stable population of pan-sized trout. Good, little-used, campsites are located along the eastern shore amid a timberline forest of Lyall larch, Englemann spruce, whitebark pine, and subalpine fir. Beyond is a backdrop of rugged, craggy peaks shaped by glacial plucking and frost-wedging. Mount Bigelow, 8,450 feet, rises southwest of the basin, shining brightly with the morning sun but somber-gray in the waning daylight hours.

An even more secluded lake lies above, reached by a sketchy trail that climbs up from the southeast shore of Crater Lake for 0.3 mile. Set on a bench surrounded by stunted timber and encircled by high peaks, this lake is an excellent choice for the solitude-seeker. Like the lower lake, it boasts a healthy population of pan-sized trout. Blue gentian, red heather, and white heather are among the alpine cushion plants present at the 6,969-foot lake.

Another tiny lake lies 500 feet above on an alpine bench below Peak 8174. You can reach it in a tough but rewarding scramble. Many of the peaks encircling this basin can be reached in the same way.

From the lakes, notice the south slopes of Raven Ridge, densely clad with stunted whitebark pines. These trees contrast with the cold-tolerant larches, spruces and firs that prefer the cooler, glacier-scoured basin. □

HIKE 78 NORTHSIDE TRAILHEAD TO MOUNT BONAPARTE

General description: A eight-mile round-trip day hike (or overnighter if you carry water) to an isolated subalpine peak featuring panoramic vistas in Okanogan National Forest.
Elevation gain and loss: 2,778 feet.
Trailhead elevation: 4,480 feet.
High point: Mount Bonaparte, 7,258 feet.
Maps: Mount Bonaparte 15-minute USGS quad; Okanogan National Forest map.
Season: Late June through early October.
Water availability: None available.

Finding the trailhead: From U.S. Highway 97 at the north end of Tonasket, turn right where a sign indicates Havillah and Sitzmark Ski Area. Follow this paved county road through hills and rangeland to the tiny settlement of Havillah, 15.5 miles from Tonasket. Turn right (east) here onto West Lost Lake Road. At the end of pavement, after 0.8 mile, turn right (south) onto gravel Forest Road 33. Avoiding numerous signed spur roads, drive another 3.25 miles and turn right (south) again, onto Forest Road 300. A sign here indicates Bonaparte Trail. Follow this dirt road 1.2 miles to a destination-and-mileage sign, and park just before the road crosses a small creek.

If you're driving from the east, follow State Route 20 west for twenty miles from Republic and turn right (north) where a sign indicates Bonaparte Recreation Area. Follow this paved road (Road 32) for 8.25 miles and then turn left onto Forest Road 33, signed for Lost Lake. Pavement ends at a four-way junction after another 5.2 miles. Stay on Forest Road 33 for another 6.2 miles and then turn left (south) onto Forest Road 300. You'll reach the lower trailhead in 1.2 miles. Bear left here and drive another 0.8 mile to the upper hiker's trailhead.

The hike: Isolated Mount Bonaparte, one of the westernmost peaks of the Rocky Mountains in the United States, commands a far-reaching, panoramic view of northeastern and north-central Washington, from Idaho's Selkirk Crest in the east to peaks of the eastern North Cascades to distant ranges in southern British Columbia.

The unobstructed vista available from this summit makes it an ideal site from which to detect fires. This fact was recognized by the Forest Service years ago, and the original fire-lookout house (built circa 1914), minus the crow's nest viewing platform, still stands on the summit. The newer lookout tower is still in use, despite the increasing use of aerial fire patrols and lightning detection systems.

Carry water and don't be surprised to encounter motorcycles on this trail.

From the trailhead, the trail enters a virgin forest of lodgepole pine, Douglas fir, and western larch. Pause here to enjoy an over-the-shoulder look at hilly rangeland and distant peaks across the border in Canada.

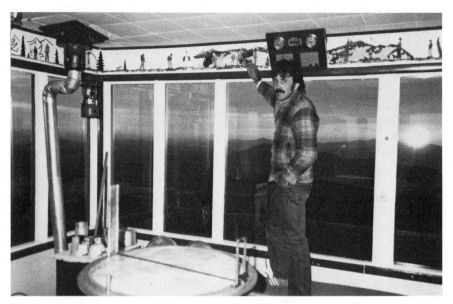

Not only does the lookout tower atop Mount Bonaparte in Washington's Rocky Mountains offer panoramic vistas, but the mural painted by the lookout-on-duty during 1986 and 1987 atttracts many visitors as well. Ron Adkison photo.

You may notice an ash-like substance at times along the trail cut. Some geologists believe it's a result of Glacier Peak's most recent major eruption, approximately 12,000 years ago. They think the eruption may have blanketed a vast region of the Pacific Northwest with pumiceous ash.

Bear right at the junction with the Southside Trail, quickly passing a right fork to Lookout Spring. Don't expect to find water here after mid-September. Then proceed steadily upward through lodgepole-dominated forest. You may find glass insulators, remnants of the telephone line that served the lookout until the 1960s.

One-and-a-half miles of steady climbing are required to reach westbound Antoine Trail, seldom used because it begins on private land. By now the forest has changed, showing signs of the short growing season on this cold, shady north slope. You'll see mostly Englemann spruce, subalpine fir and whitebark pine—trees characteristic of timberline environments. The understory consists of grouse whortleberry, mountain azalea, and red heather.

Continue another half mile to the broad summit of Mount Bonaparte. You may notice an old trail crossing and recrossing the newer trail, which climbs more gradually.

In addition to the two lookouts on the summit, a "forest" of shrublike trees manages to survive the extremes of cold, wind, and snow here. Primarily subalpine fir and whitebark pine, this type of tree is known to botanists as *krummholz*, after the German for "crooked wood." Granite boulders also litter the summit area.

The far-ranging vista includes summits of the eastern North Cascades, from Sawtooth Ridge east of Lake Chelan in the southwest to Chopaka Mountain

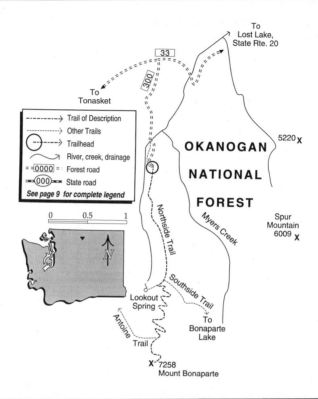

and the Canadian Cascades in the northwest. The latter rise abruptly westward from the depths of the arid Okanogan Valley.

Osoyoos Lake is visible in the northwest, straddling the border between Washington and British Columbia. To the east are ranges of the Rockies, from the Kettle Range to the distant Selkirk Crest in Idaho.

A few small campsites have been cleared below the lookout tower; one even has a picnic table and fire pit. A cistern has been constructed to catch rainwater, but this is the sole source of water for the lookout on duty; so be a good neighbor and bring your own.

About 150 people visited Mount Bonaparte during the 1987 fire season, but the job of a fire lookout is a lonely one. Often, many days elapse between visits. To help pass the time during the summers of 1986 and 1987, the lookout stationed here painted a beautiful mural on the inside of the lookout house. It depicts various outdoor scenes such as hiking, snowshoeing, and firefighting. Even if the day is cloudy, you may want to climb Mount Bonaparte just to see this work of art.

From the lookout, return the way you came. □

HIKE 79 KETTLE CREST NORTH TRAIL

General description: A moderate fifteen-mile round-trip day hike or backpack along the backbone of the Kettle River Range in the Colville National Forest.
Elevation gain and loss: +2,224 feet, -850 feet.
Trailhead elevation: 5,500 feet.
High point: Peak 6874.
Maps: Sherman Peak 15-minute USGS quad; Colville National Forest map.
Season: Late June through early October.
Water availability: Limited to two springs, one at 2.75 miles and the other at 6.5 miles.

Finding the trailhead: Follow State Route 20 to Sherman Pass, seventeen miles east of Republic or 24.75 miles west of Kettle Falls. Turn north onto Road 495, signed for Kettle Crest Trail, and you'll reach the trailhead parking area within 0.1 mile.

The hike: The Kettle River Range is one of Washington's westernmost Rocky Mountain ranges. This distinctive range is composed of a large granite batholith rising north and east of the Columbia, and bounded on the west by the valley of the Sanpoil River.

East of the confluence of the Okanogan and Columbia rivers, a nearly continuous wall of mountains rises from the sunbaked grasslands and basalt plateaus of the east-to-west-trending Columbia along a major fault zone extending eastward nearly to Helena, Montana. These are Washington's Rocky Mountains, and they remain largely unexplored by the majority of Washingtonians.

By Cascade standards, these aren't high mountains; the highest summits barely exceed 7,000 feet. But this is excellent hiking country with a character entirely different from that of other wildlands in the state. Feelings of remoteness and isolation accompany hikers into these mountains—a delightful change for those weary with the crowded trails and campsites so common in more well-known areas.

The forty-two-mile-long Kettle Crest Trail traverses much of the rolling crest of the range, protected within the Kettle Range Limited Access Area. State Route 20 cuts across this wild trail at Sherman Pass, dividing the route into a southern segment of 13.1 miles and a northern segment of 28.9 miles.

The crest is more rugged south of the pass, but northward rises a series of rolling summits from which you're treated to a variety of wide-ranging vistas.

This rewarding hike traverses the initial 7.5 miles of the Kettle Crest North Trail. It features subalpine forests and parkland, broad views, and precious solitude. Water is available only at two springs on this hike, each with nearby campsites. You should carry an adequate water supply.

From the trailhead parking area, walk southward back down the road to the signed trailhead and turn right (west). The trail winds upward under a canopy of western larch, lodgepole pine and subalpine fir, passing under power lines before attaining the boulder-dotted crest of the range. You'll maneuver a series of switchbacks, alternating between the east and west sides of the crest amid open forest and boulders of granite and schist. You'll see

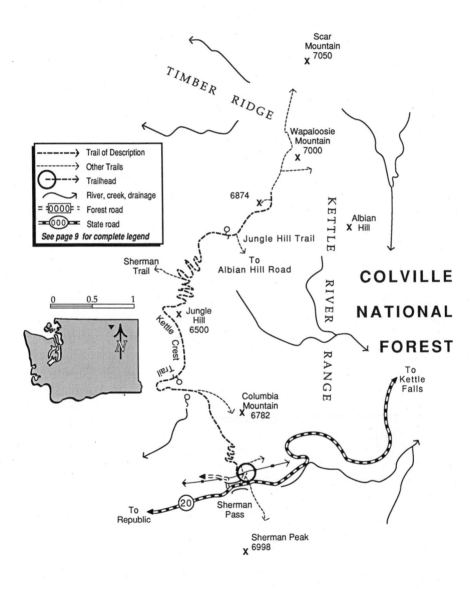

7,011-foot Sherman Peak rising abruptly to the south of Sherman Pass. Much of the forest south of Sherman Pass was consumed by the 20,000-acre White Mountain Fire of 1988 but, fortunately, the vast forests along the North Trail escaped that destructive blaze.

After one mile of steady ascent, you'll traverse the west slope of Columbia Mountain, reaching the Columbia Mountain Trail after another 0.75 mile. Westward views from this slope extend beyond Mount Bonaparte to the easternmost peaks of the North Cascades. If your time and energy are limited, you might consider following the 0.75-mile spur trail to Columbia Mountain for rewarding vistas and then returning to the trailhead.

Otherwise, bear left at the junction and, soon after rounding a west-trending ridge, you'll enter a cool, north-slope forest. Water is available year-round from the piped spring you'll encounter a mile from the previous junction.

The trail drops to a 6,200-foot saddle and a small campsite a quarter of a mile beyond the spring. Then it rises once again, passing just west of the summit of 6,544-foot Jungle Hill. En route, the trail crosses glacier-smoothed granite bedrock where remnants of glacial polish and scratch marks can be observed.

North of Jungle Hill, a series of gentle switchbacks will lower you to a junction in a narrow, 5,800-foot saddle. Ignore the little-used Sherman Trail, which forks west. Bear right instead. Now the switchbacks will lift you up and away from the saddle along viewless pine- and fir-clad slopes. Finally, the grade eases where the route begins an eastbound traverse under the Kettle Crest. Occasional vistas toward the Columbia River Valley in the east and the Kettle Range in the south help pass the time.

After 6.5 up-and-down miles, skirt the northern edge of a cattle-trampled meadow and pass another piped spring—the last water en route, and its purity is questionable. Fifty yards to the east, shaded by scattered pines, is a fair campsite with a fine view.

Quite soon, the signed Jungle Hill Trail will fork right, but its invisible tread is hard to locate. That route leads three miles eastward to the Albian Hill Road. It's just one of many spur trails offering quick access to the Kettle Crest.

Now your trail passes open, grassy slopes and stunted, discontinuous subalpine firs and whitebark and lodgepole pines. Soon, you'll enter a ghost forest of weathered, wind-polished snags framing distant Rocky Mountain ranges. Go north along the east slope of Peak 6874.

The next summit to the north along the crest is 7,018-foot Wapaloosie Mountain, and its timber-clad crown obscures what otherwise might be panoramic vistas. For the best views, leave the trail after it bends north and stroll through tall grass to Peak 6874. From here, peaks of the North Cascades form the western skyline, marching northward into British Columbia. To the north, the Kettle River Range loses elevation and merges with other mountains in southern British Columbia. Eastward are the Selkirks, extending into Idaho and northward into Canada, a major range of the Rocky Mountains. Far to the southeast, near the southern end of the Selkirks, is the broad dome of Mount Spokane, seventy-five miles away.

Views southward across the Kettle River Range are outstanding, highlighted by vast stands of yellowing western larch after the first frosts of autumn.

Eventually, you'll have to pull yourself away from the tremendous panorama and backtrack to the trailhead. □

HIKE 80 *SHERMAN PASS TO SHERMAN PEAK*

General description: A moderately strenuous 6.6-mile round trip day hike to a prominent Kettle Crest peak in the Colville National Forest.
Elevation gain and loss: +1,710 feet; -200 feet.
Trailhead elevation: 5,500 feet.
High point: Sherman Peak, 7,011 feet.
Maps: Sherman Peak 15-minute USGS quad; Colville National Forest map.
Season: Late June through early October.
Water availability: Small spring one mile from the trailhead.

Finding the trailhead: Follow directions given in Hike 79.

The hike: South of Sherman Pass the Kettle Crest rises abruptly to a series of rugged and rocky summits—Sherman and Snow peaks, Bald and White mountains—that contrast markedly with the gentle, rolling uplands to the north. Here the granite and gneiss bedrock core of the Kettle Dome is fully exposed, and the Kettle Crest South Trail, although well designed and constructed, is more demanding than the North Trail, as it climbs rocky slopes up and around these rugged peaks.

Although the steep and rocky flanks of Sherman Peak jut skyward less than one mile south of Sherman Pass, the Kettle Crest South Trail offers easier access to the peak for most hikers. The final half-mile to the summit is a cross-country route upon a steep rocky ridge and should be attempted only by more experienced hikers.

In August of 1988 several lightning strikes near the south end of the Kettle Crest ignited the 20,000-plus-acre White Mountain Fire. That destructive blaze consumed much of the pine and fir forests of the southern Kettle Crest but, fortunately, was stopped just north of Highway 20, sparing the northern Kettle Crest.

Much of this hike passes through the charred remains of these forests, but hikers will notice nature's quick response to fire, which was once a natural and occasional event before the advent of organized firefighting. The openings created by the fire now host a lush carpet of grasses, and small shrubs and tree saplings are growing once more. This fresh new greenery is attracting an increasing number of mule deer into the area, which hikers are likely to see.

Caution: Hikers should avoid this hike during high winds when snags are likely to topple.

From the parking area, walk south back down the road to the Kettle Crest Trail and turn left (east). The trail descends into lodgepole pine forest for 100 yards to a signed junction. Bear right and continue downhill into a shady draw and ascend switchbacks to the highway.

Use caution crossing the highway and resume walking in the trail on the opposite side; the trail then climbs steadily amid granite boulders under a shady canopy of lodgepole pine, western larch, Douglas-fir, and subalpine fir. The blue diamond markers on trees indicate that this is a cross-country ski trail in winter.

HIKE 80 *SHERMAN PASS TO SHERMAN PEAK*

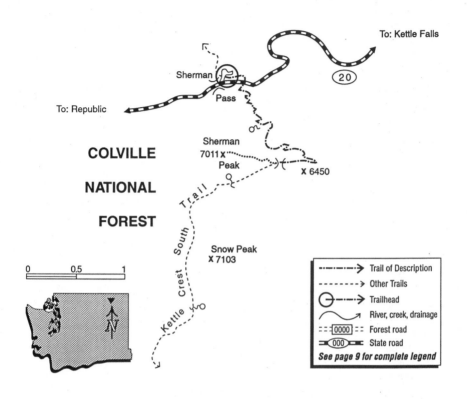

The rocky trail climbs at a moderate grade with occasional switchbacks beneath the looming north slopes of Sherman Peak. About 0.7 mile from the highway, the trail bridges a small, spring-fed creek—the only water available en route. After another 0.2 mile, you curve around the shoulder of a low ridge and enter a forest of charred and bleached snags, then contour into a small cirque basin.

Curving around the basin, the trail switchbacks four times, eventually topping out on a 6,300-foot saddle, about a half mile east of Sherman Peak and 2.8 miles from the trailhead. Trailside snags frame your first view of rugged Snow Peak. Barnaby Buttes, and White Mountain to the south.

Leave the trail at the saddle and climb westward up the increasingly steep ridge among charred snags and live trees. The ridge is composed of loose, rubbly gneiss near the summit; be cautious.

Labor past lichen encrusted boulders and a few stunted pines and prostrate junipers to reach the summit where a commanding 360-degree panorama unfolds.

Sherman Peak's central location in northern Washington between the Cascades and the Idaho line offers interesting perspectives of mountains that most Washington hikers have never enjoyed. On the western horizon, beyond the rolling mountains of the Okanogan Highlands, lies the abrupt eastern escarpment of the Okanogan Cascades; the jagged peaks of the Sawtooth Range stand in the southwest. Eastward, beyond the impoundment on the Columbia River, the Selkirk Mountains march off toward the horizon, seventy-five miles distant in the Idaho panhandle. And northward, beyond the rolling highlands of the Kettle Crest, ranks of high ranges stretch into British Columbia's interior. □

HIKE 81 *DEADMAN CREEK TO HOODOO CANYON AND EMERALD LAKE*

General description: A moderate 5.6-mile, round-trip day hike or overnighter to a striking glacial canyon at low elevation in northeastern Washington's Kettle River Range in Colville National Forest.
Elevation gain and loss: +950 feet, -800 feet.
Trailhead elevation: 2,850 feet.
High point: Hoodoo Overlook, 3,750 feet.
Maps: Sherman Peak 15-minute USGS quad (trail not shown on quad); Colville National Forest map.
Season: Mid-April through October.
Water availability: None available en route; carry an ample supply.

Finding the trailhead: Follow State Route 20 west from Kettle Falls for 21.5 miles to northbound Albian Hill Road (Road 2030). Eastbound drivers will find this turnoff 4.1 miles east of Sherman Pass where the highway executes a horseshoe bend from north to southeast.

Follow that gravel road northward 3.8 miles to the junction with eastbound Road 9565 (Deadman Creek Road). Then turn right. You'll reach a large clearing on the south side of the road where a sign indicates Hoodoo Canyon Trail after 8.8 miles from the previous junction. Park here.

The hike: Hoodoo Canyon—deep, narrow, and glacier-carved—lies within the Kettle River Range, a group of mountains essentially unknown to most Washingtonians. The trails of this range are seldom trod, but most lead into extraordinary country. Once hikers discover this range, they're drawn back time and again.

Diverse flora and views into spectacular Hoodoo Canyon are the major attractions of this moderate day hike. Carry ample water, as none is available en route.

The trail begins at the south side of the large clearing at the trailhead. It immediately drops past a trail register to a bridge across Deadman Creek, shaded by a typical northern Rocky Mountain forest of lodgepole pine, western larch, western redcedar, Englemann spruce, Douglas-fir, and alder. Other plants in this moist forest environment include serviceberry, huckleberry, oregon grape, bunchberry dogwood, prince's pine, Douglas maple, and thimbleberry.

The trail soon ascends a north-facing draw east of Hoodoo Canyon, passing through a vast array of plant life, including thimbleberry, wild rose, ocean spray, willow, mallow ninebark, huckleberry, alder, aspen, serviceberry, Douglas maple,

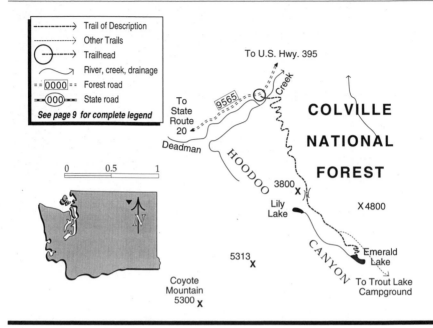

birch, pachystima, kinnikinnick, and red Indian paintbrush. Granite boulders litter these shrubby slopes.

As the trail gains elevation (950 feet in 1.75 miles), it re-enters a forest composed of lodgepole pine, western larch, Douglas fir, and some redcedar. The trail crests in a saddle at 3,750 feet. Views are good from this point into the narrow chasm of Hoodoo Canyon, where precipitous granite cliffs rise abruptly from the valley floor. This scenic overlook has been used as a dry campsite, and it's surrounded by boulders and outcrops of granite. Scattered Douglas firs and ponderosa pines offer a modicum of shade on hot summer days.

The east wall of 5,313-foot Coyote Mountain soars 2,000 feet above the canyon bottom to the west—its rugged, glacier-smoothed granite walls only partially timber-clad. But to get the best view of the canyon, leave the trail before it crests the saddle and plunge westward into the timber to a rocky knoll. The southeastward view down Hoodoo Canyon from this point reveals Emerald Lake, and beyond, Trout Lake. This cross-country route is recommended only to experienced hikers.

Beyond the saddle, follow the good, wide trail as it contours southeast through open forests and among scattered granite boulders. About a third of a mile from the saddle, you may begin to notice the beautiful pink blooms of clarkia, with its four pink petals, each petal divided into three lobes. It usually blooms by early August. This flower was named in honor of Captain William Clark of the Lewis and Clark Expedition. This is its westernmost limit, but it's fairly common in parts of Idaho and western Montana.

About 0.3 mile from the saddle, at a junction, bear right and descend. The

True-to-its-name Emerald Lake lies near the upper end of the Hoodoo Canyon Trail, one of the most interesting hikes in the Kettle River Range of northeastern Washington. Bob Arrington photo.

left fork is a new trail leading 2.5 view-filled miles down the canyon to Trout Lake Campground.

Your trail traverses through the forest to the brink of the canyon, where four short switchbacks lead to aptly-named Emerald Lake, 2.8 miles from the trailhead. No fish live in this shallow lake, but swimming is a major attraction. Campsites are limited, and the lake is the only water source. The shoreline is rocky and irregular, and cliffs soar skyward from the water's edge.

Return to the trailhead via the same trail. □

HIKE 82 *ALBIAN HILL ROAD TO COPPER BUTTE*

General description: A strenuous 6.5-mile day hike, following part of Washington's oldest state highway to the highest summit on the Kettle Crest in the Colville National Forest in northeastern Washington.
Elevation gain and loss: 1,635 feet.
Trailhead elevation: 5,500 feet.
High point: Copper Butte. 7,135 feet.
Maps: Sherman Peak 15-minute USGS quad; Colville National Forest map.
Season: Late June through early October.
Water availability: None; carry an adequate supply.

Finding the trailhead: Follow directions given in Hike 81 to the Deadman Creek Road, and continue straight ahead (north) on Forest Road 2030, a narrow undulating mountain road. After driving another 3.6 miles, turn left where a sign indicates the Old Stage Road Trail, and follow this spur for 250 yards to the trailhead parking area.

The hike: In 1892 the State of Washington passed legislation authorizing the construction of the state's first official state highway, linking Marblemount and Pacific coast ports with Marcus and the busy riverboat traffic on the Columbia River. The most difficult task of the project required carving the road over the lofty divide of the Kettle Range. When completed this segment of the road remained impassable to freight wagons; and with the heavy snows

This gate marks the trailhead to the Old Stage Trail to Copper Butte. Ron Adkison photo.

HIKE 82   ALBIAN HILL ROAD TO COPPER BUTTE

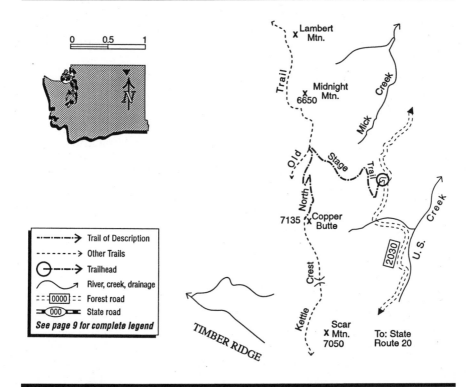

of winter, passage over the range even on horseback was often impossible.

By 1898 when a better route was established over Sherman Pass to the south, the Old State (or Stage) Trail was abandoned. Today only seven miles of this historic route remains, and this fine day hike traces 1.7 miles of the road on the westbound grade to the Kettle Crest.

The remainder of the hike, to a former lookout site on Copper Butte, follows one of the steepest section's of the Kettle Crest Trail. But panoramic vistas are the reward for your efforts.

The Old Stage Trail, closed to motorized vehicles, maintains a steady yet gentle-to-moderate grade as it climbs through thick forests of subalpine fir and lodgepole pine to the Kettle Crest, 1.7 miles from the trailhead. It is not difficult to imagine the arduous journeys of stagecoaches and pack trains as they struggled over this steep and lonely wilderness road.

Upon reaching the crest, follow the old road southwest and downhill for fifty yards, then turn left onto the Kettle Crest Trail. From the start the trail climbs very steeply through a thick lodgepole pine forest, which restricts views to occasional vignettes.

Without respite the trail climbs for 1.2 miles to the summit area of Copper Butte where the grade abates. The final 0.3 mile winds among groves of stunted whitebark pine and subalpine fir to the old lookout site.

Views are far-reaching and panoramic, including the Columbia River (impounded in Franklin D. Roosevelt Lake) and the Selkirks stretching into Idaho in the east, ranks of lofty British Columbia ranges to the north, to the escarpment of the Okanogan Cascades in the west, and southward to the prominent summits of the Kettle Crest.

After absorbing the tremendous vista, retrace the route to the trailhead. □

HIKE 83   *KETTLE CREST SOUTH TRAIL TO BARNABY BUTTES*

General description: A moderately strenuous twelve-mile round trip day hike or backpack along the scenic Kettle Crest, leading to a former lookout site and panoramic vista.
Elevation gain and loss: +2,000 feet; -750 feet.
Trailhead elevation: 5,250 feet.
High point: 6,750 feet.
Maps: Sherman Peak 15-minute USGS quad; Colville National Forest map.
Season: Late June through early October.
Water availability: Two small springs at 1.3 and three miles.

Finding the trailhead: Follow State Route 20 to the east end of South Sherman Road (Forest Road 2020) 12.2 miles east of Sherman Pass and fifteen miles west of Kettle Falls. The turnoff is located between mileposts 331 and 332. Follow this good gravel road, with a washboard surface in places, west up South Sherman Creek for 6.6 miles, then turn left onto Barnaby Creek Road #2014. Follow this good dirt road 4.1 miles and turn right at the junction with Forest Road 250 which is signed for White Mountain and the Kettle Crest Trail.

This narrow dirt road, with occasional turnouts, climbs steadily through forest and past clearcuts to a four-way junction on Onion Ridge after another 4.4 miles. Turn right into the spacious parking area at the White Mountain Trailhead.

The hike: This is an enjoyable but demanding hike following the Kettle Crest South Trail north from its terminus to remote Barnaby Buttes, a former lookout site. The trail is steep and rocky along the initial four miles leading up and over White Mountain, also a former lookout site.

This is where several lightning strikes in August, 1988, grew into the destructive White Mountain Fire, thus the trail leads through both charred and virgin forests along the edges of the burn.

Caution: Avoid this hike during strong winds when snags are likely to fall.

The spring at 1.3 miles is reliable, with a good flow. But the spring on White Mountain, three miles from the trailhead, is fouled by the cattle that graze the area in summer and early fall.

There are good possible campsites from White Mountain to Barnaby Buttes, but backpackers should carry plenty of water.

The trail begins with a gentle descent to a broad saddle thick with grasses beneath the charred snags of the 1988 blaze. The trail ahead begins a moderate

HIKE 83   KETTLE CREST SOUTH TRAIL TO BARNABY BUTTES

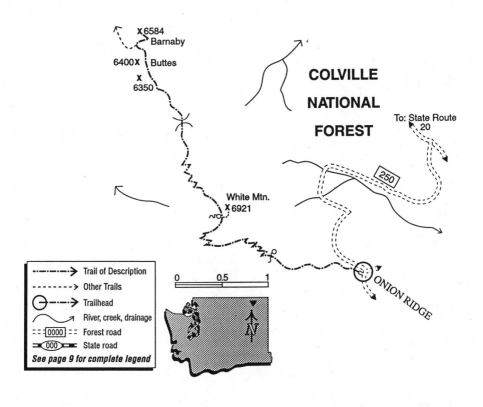

grade, climbing south-facing slopes and alternating from stands of Douglas fir and western larch to tall, blackened snags.

Views along the way follow the Kettle Range as its forested ridges fade into the distance far to the south on the Colville Indian Reservation.

After 1.3 miles, at the bend of the second switchback on the trail, you'll find a small spring fifty feet off the trail.

Presently, the trail begins switchbacking steadily upward, sometimes steeply, upon the south slopes of rocky White Mountain, looming boldly on the skyline ahead. Views are far-ranging from these open slopes, stretching from the Okanogan Cascades in the west to the valley of the Columbia River in the east.

After 2.6 miles, you surmount the summit ridge of White Mountain where the grade eases and encounter partially burned groves of subalpine fir just below the mountains's summit. At the three-mile point, a faint, unsigned path forks right (east), leading 0.2 mile to the 6,921-foot summit of White Mountain.

The trail ahead begins to descend, soon becoming muddy below a trickling, piped spring. After crossing the rocky slopes just north of White Mountain, the trail switchbacks steadily down the Kettle Crest to a broad, 6,000-foot saddle where the Barnaby Creek Trail joins the route from the east.

The Kettle Crest South Trail to Sherman Peak ascends through the ghostly remains of a burned forest. Ron Adkison photo.

Now the trail climbs moderately once again, alternating from green forest to groves of snags to a high saddle on the crest of Barnaby Buttes, 5.7 miles from the trailhead. Leave the Kettle Crest Trail here and follow the long-abandoned lookout access road as it climbs grassy slopes and passes groves of subalpine fir for 0.3 mile to the 6,534-foot knob that is the high point of Baranaby Buttes.

The vistas are panoramic from this former lookout site. Northward, the tall, conical peaks of Bald, Snow, and Sherman are in the foreground of the gentle summits of the northern Kettle Crest. Eastward, ranks of forested mountains stretch away to the Selkirks on the distant horizon. And westward are the eastern outliers of the Cascade Range, from the Sawtooth Range to the Okanogan Cascades.

There are several possible campsites for backpackers that carried adequate water on Barnaby Buttes—the only gentle, meadow-sloped mountain in the southern Kettle Crest.

Hikers should either retrace their steps to the trailhead from the buttes, or, if a car shuttle was arranged, continue north on the Kettle Crest Trail for another 7.4 miles to Sherman Pass. □

HIKE 84 *NORTHRUP CANYON NATURAL AREA*

General description: A 5.5-mile, round-trip day hike to a lake resting at the head of a basalt-rimmed canyon in the Grand Coulee country of east-central Washington.
Elevation gain and loss: +580 feet, -130 feet.
Trailhead elevation: 1,800 feet.
High point: 2,250 feet.
Maps: Steamboat Rock SE and Electric City 7.5-minute USGS quads.
Season: March through November.
Water availability: Carry an ample supply, no potable water en route.

Finding the trailhead: Follow State Route 155 south from Electric City for 6.5 miles or north from U.S. Highway 2 near Coulee City for 16.5 miles to eastbound Northrup Road, opposite the turnoff for a Steamboat Rock State Park rest area and Boat Launch 1. Follow this gravel road generally eastward, bearing right at three unsigned junctions. You'll reach the locked gate at the trailhead after 0.7 mile.

The hike: In the vast reaches of the Columbia Basin—that broad, arid land between the Rockies and the Cascades—the land is dominated by a plateau of basalt intermittently dissected by deep, narrow river canyons and many dry stream channels known as coulees. Travelers in the region often wonder how such an unusual landscape was sculpted.

Beginning in the Miocene epoch nearly fifteen million years ago, enormous quantities of molten basalt issued from a number of fissures in the earth's crust throughout eastern Washington and surrounding areas. This basalt buried everything in its path, including rivers, lakes, and lush, humid forests. A succession of these flood-like lava flows piled the basalt flow upon flow, reaching thicknesses of hundreds of feet. Along the Columbia and in the Grand Coulee, these layered lava flows are most noticeable.

Through time, the Cascade Range began uplifting west of the Columbia Basin. The climate began cooling and precipitation increased. Eventually, an ice age began, and vast sheets of ice flowed southward from Canada. A lobe of the Cordilleran Ice Sheet flowed southward through what is now the Okanogan Valley, temporarily damming the Columbia River and diverting it southward, where it began eroding a channel into the basalt-covered landscape.

But that was only the beginning. About 15,000 years ago another glacier, this one flowing southward from British Columbia into northern Idaho, dammed the Clark Fork River near present-day Sandpoint, Idaho. In doing so, it created Glacial Lake Missoula, a vast impoundment that backed up water far into western Montana. Geologists believe it was about the size of present-day Lake Ontario.

Periodically the ice dam burst, sending floodwaters unequalled in the geologic record across the basalt-covered Columbia Basin. Known as the Spokane Floods, the catastrophic emptying of Glacial Lake Missoula ocurred repeatedly—at least forty-one times, according to geologists. These floods scoured the landscape of eastern Washington into a vast system of now-dry stream channels, or coulees. The result is known as the "channeled scablands."

The largest of all these channels is the Grand Coulee, nearly fifty miles long, four miles wide, and 1,000 feet deep. After the Okanogan lobe of the ice sheet receded, the Columbia resumed its original course, transforming the Grand Coulee into a riverless scar across the basin.

Today, the north end of Grand Coulee lies under the waters of Banks Lake, just south of impressive Grand Coulee Dam, the largest such structure in the world. The waters of Franklin D. Roosevelt Lake, impounded by Grand Coulee Dam, are pumped into Banks Lake by a series of huge, powerful siphons. Canals then distribute this water far to the south and east to farmlands of the Columbia Basin Project. This vast, arid steppe was transformed almost overnight into one of the most productive agricultural areas of the Pacific Northwest.

Unfortunately for hikers, most of the Columbia Basin is privately owned, but one exception is the impressive, basalt-rimmed tributary canyon of the Grand Coulee through which this unique day hike will lead you. Northrup Canyon is like a Grand Coulee in miniature, and a trout-filled lake rests at its head.

This is a day-use-only area administrated by Steamboat Rock State Park. Carry plenty of water for this mostly dry hike.

From the locked gate in the shadow of Gibraltar Rock, follow the sagebrush-lined dirt road eastward. You'll soon reach the canyon bottom, where mosquitoes are troublesome during early summer. After hiking briefly through Douglas-firs, ponderosa pines, birches, and lush (for this region) streamside growth, you'll reach open ground where you'll have good views up the canyon. Precipitous basalt cliffs, dotted by ponderosa pines and Douglas-firs, rise abruptly north and south of it.

Nearly 0.75 mile from the trailhead, you'll pass two southbound tracks that lead to the site of an old homestead. A quarter of a mile later, the road circum-navigates a broad meadow, passing an area of exposed granite at its eastern edge. This rock is presumed to be part of the pre-basalt landscape re-exposed by the Spokane Floods.

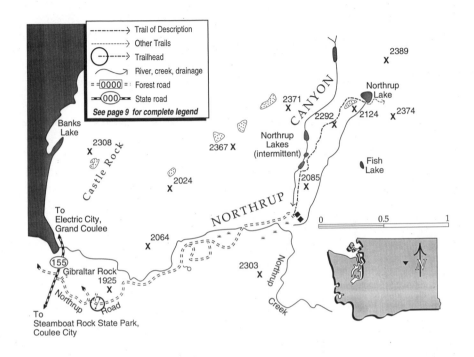

Shortly beyond is a jumble of columnar basalt along the streambed. When molten basalt cools at the surface, it often fractures into these interesting columns. Well-known examples include the Devil's Tower in Wyoming and the Devil's Postpile in California.

The road skirts another large meadow and reaches a private residence 1.5 miles from the trailhead. At this point, the canyon splits; the right fork cuts deep into the basalt toward the southeast (Northrup Creek), while the left fork continues its northeast course (Northrup Canyon).

The trail is hard to find here. Above the house, under a power line, is a long, narrow, abandoned chicken house. The very faint trail leads past the chicken house and up the canyon through sagebrush, Douglas-fir, and ponderosa pine. Beware of rattlesnakes.

Soon the route becomes easy to follow as it climbs moderately, winding among granite boulders and sparse forest. The trail passes a marshy pond after two miles. As it passes a above a second pond, it crosses a place where the older granite and the younger basalt meet. The latter dominates the trailside briefly ahead. The presence of wildflowers, grasses, and timber helps soften the appearance of an otherwise bleak landscape.

About a quarter of a mile beyond the two ponds, the trail climbs to a sparsely forested, granitic knoll. From here you'll get a nice glimpse into the inviting northern reaches of the canyon. Then the trail briefly negotiates the ridgeline separating the two forks of the canyon, passes a seasonal pond, and reaches 2,130-foot-high Northrup Lake, 2.75 miles from the trailhead.

This two-acre-plus lake harbors a hungry trout population that should keep anglers busy. It's encircled by cliffs of basalt, shaded by ponderosa pines and Douglas-firs, and bordered by lush riparian vegetation. A trail continues eastward beyond the lake.

After enjoying this unique hiking area for the day, retrace the route to the trailhead. □

HIKE 85 *HARTBAUER CREEK TO ABERCROMBIE MOUNTAIN*

General description: A moderate 6.4-mile, round-trip day hike to a remote alpine peak in northeastern Washington's Colville National Forest.
Elevation gain and loss: 2,308 feet.
Trailhead elevation: 5,000 feet.
High point: Abercrombie Mountain, 7,308 feet.
Maps: Abercrombie Mtn. 7.5-minute USGS quad; Colville National Forest map.
Season: July through early October.
Water availability: Carry an adequate supply, none is available after the first mile.

Finding the trailhead: Follow State Route 25 northeast along the Columbia River for 31.6 miles from Kettle Falls to Northport. Then turn right where a sign points to Deep Lake. Follow this paved county road 11.3 miles to a junction, and bear left toward Deep Lake. (The right fork leads twenty-five miles south to State Route 20, 1.5 miles east of Colville).

You'll reach Leadpoint after another seven miles. Turn right (southeast) there onto dirt-surfaced Silver Creek Road. Bear left after 0.6 mile, following the narrow, poor dirt road to the Colville National Forest boundary, where the road improves. Bear left again 0.4 mile from the forest boundary, where Road 70 forks right. You'll reach the end of maintained road after another two miles. Stay left. Ignore right-branching Road 250 after two more miles, and finally turn right onto Road 300, the Hartbauer Basin Road, after another 0.2 mile. This narrow and rutted dirt road leads 3.3 miles to its end at the trailhead.

The hike: A series of major north-south ridges extends eastward from the Columbia River in northeastern Washington, marching into the panhandle of Idaho. These are known as the Selkirk Mountains, the highest terrain east of the Cascades. At 7,308 feet, Abercrombie Mountain is the second highest peak in the Washington Selkirks. It offers a panoramic view of mountain ranges both near and far.

Three trails lead to Abercrombie, each offering a unique hiking experience. The route from Hartbauer Basin is the shortest, but the road to the trailhead is quite rough.

HIKE 85 · HARTBAUER CREEK TO ABERCROMBIE MOUNTAIN

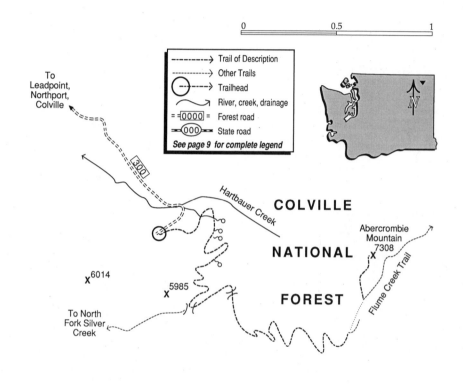

Carry plenty of drinking water for this mostly dry hike.

Your trek begins on an old, closed logging road. Soon you'll climb clearcut northwest slopes and cross numerous rivulets. Above looms the rounded summit of your destination. To the northwest, you may also get glimpses of distant summits of British Columbia's Christina Range.

After 1.2 miles of moderate ascent, the road ends and a trail quickly leads to a saddle, trail junction and register at 5,750 feet. The right-forking trail descends steadily for 4.2 miles to the North Fork Silver Creek Trailhead. Turn left and hike through subalpine fir and lodgepole pine to another saddle a quarter mile to the northeast.

Here the trail jogs south and climbs moderately upon burned-over, southwest slopes that are slowly being reforested by lodgepole pine. Bear grass, lupine, whortleberry, huckleberry, pearly everlasting, and yarrow offer trailside company as you proceed. Ever-expanding vistas will urge you upward toward their climax atop Abercrombie.

Near the crest, the trail passes through an area of weather-sculpted, multi-branched snags, remnants of the stunted timberline forest that once stood here.

A broad swath cut through timbered mountains, visible from many of northern Washington's trails, denotes the boundary between British Columbia, on the left, and Washington, on the right. Bob Arrington photo.

Amid these snags are young subalpine firs and whitebark and lodgepole pines—the next timberline forest.

When the trail crosses the ridge crest, you'll be treated to even more fantastic views.

Avoid a faint trail that heads northeast, and instead follow a cross-country route marked by cairns for a quarter mile north along the ridge. At that point the trail coming up from Flume Creek joins on the right (east). You need to turn left and pass by the last persistent but weather-tortured trees to the rocky summit (a former lookout site), where a breathtaking panorama unfolds.

The swath marking the international boundary is plainly visible, stretching westward through the forested mountains. Forming the western horizon is the Kettle River Range and, over the border to the northwest, the Christina Range.

A sliver of the Columbia River is visible below to the northwest. Beyond lie the towns of Grand Forks and Rossland, British Columbia, as well as a Canadian power plant. Numerous power lines can be seen snaking through that populated area. Distant, rugged peaks of the Selkirks are visible to the horizon in the north and northeast across the border.

To the east are the forested valley of the Pend Oreille River and beyond, the Salmo-Priest Wilderness. On the eastern horizon is a range of impressive granite crags—Idaho's Selkirk Crest.

When you've gotten your fill of this tremendous, geographically diverse view, retrace your steps to the trailhead. □

HIKE 86 *FOREST ROAD 2220 TO SOUTH SALMO RIVER*

General description: A 6.2-mile backpack to Washington's northeasternmost river, the South Salmo, featuring good fishing and the isolation of a deep canyon in the Salmo-Priest Wilderness.
Elevation gain and loss: -1,835 feet.
Trailhead elevation: 5,910 feet.
High point: Trailhead, 5,910 feet.
Low point: 4,075 feet.
Maps: Salmo Mountain (Washington-Idaho-British Columbia) 7.5-minute USGS quad; Colville National Forest map.
Season: July through early October.
Water availability: Abundant.

Finding the trailhead: Follow the directions given in Hike 87.

The hike: In many mountainous areas, canyons harbor climatic conditions very different from those of surrounding hillsides. Such is the case in the canyon of the South Salmo River, where a lush, inland rain forest is nurtured by abundant precipitation and a modicum of sunlight. This is one of only a few such rain forests in the northern Rocky Mountains.

Another unique feature of this trip into the Salmo-Priest Wilderness is the presence of grizzly bears, woodland caribou, and a host of other animals that

HIKE 86 *FOREST ROAD 2220 TO SOUTH SALMO RIVER*

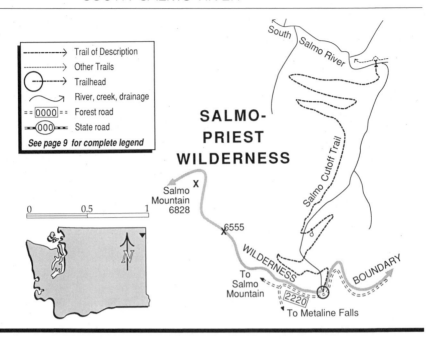

Trail of Description
Other Trails
Trailhead
River, creek, drainage
Forest road
State road
See page 9 for complete legend

SALMO-
PRIEST
WILDERNESS

Salmo Mountain 6828

6555

To Salmo Mountain

2220

To Metaline Falls

South Salmo River

Salmo Cutoff Trail

WILDERNESS

BOUNDARY

0   0.5   1

N

epitomize the wilderness experience. These denizens of the wildest country left in Washington find the old-growth forests of the Salmo-Priest region ideal for their survival. The abundant goatsbeard lichen clinging to trees on the shadier slopes are the preferred diet of the few woodland caribou who roam here. Recent transplants into the area are expected to bolster that caribou population.

The people of Washington have wisely chosen to protect this isolated corner of the state from encroachment by logging, roads, and other development. The result is 39,973 acres of prime wildlife habitat, as well as a hiker's heaven. North of the border in British Columbia, logging, power lines, and roads threaten the region, creeping right up to the international border. In Idaho, more than 40,000 acres adjacent to the Salmo-Priest have been proposed for wilderness status, including the wild and scenic Upper Priest River. But logging is a constant threat there as well.

This hike begins in subalpine forest and heads constantly downhill to a temperate rain forest on the South Salmo—a forest reminiscent of those found in the western Cascades. In fact, the climate along the South Salmo is very similar to that of the western Cascades, a remarkable fact when you consider that the Salmo-Priest Wilderness lies almost 250 miles from the ocean.

Trout fishing in the South Salmo can be productive for pan-sized cutthroats. Water is fairly abundant all the way to the river.

From the trailhead, you'll begin descending moderately through a north-slope forest of Englemann spruce and subalpine fir. You may see patches of snow well into early July.

The smooth trail crosses a small creek twice during the initial 0.75 mile. At times you'll get tree-framed glimpses northward beyond the nadir of the Salmo to a Canadian ridge that soars nearly 3,000 feet above the canyon. Notice the swath cut through the forest on the face of that ridge. It marks the international boundary.

As the trail descends below 5,500 feet, the subalpine forest is gradually replaced by western hemlock (uncommon east of the Cascades) and western redcedar, with a few scattered white pines as well. You'll cross the same small creek a third time after 1.5 miles, passing a small campsite on the opposite bank. Then you'll cross high above the west bank of the creek and into the Salmo Mountain Research Natural Area. This is land on which "various natural features are preserved in an undisturbed state solely for research and educational purposes."

Proceed steadily downward toward the South Salmo River under an increasingly shady canopy of hemlock and cedar, and you'll reach the log bridge across the river, 3.1 miles from the trailhead at an elevation of 4,075 feet. Good campsites lie nearby, shaded by moss-draped western redcedar and western hemlock. Understory plants are typical of a moist forest environment; they include ferns, bunchberry dogwood, and the elegant calypso orchid, which blooms in late spring.

Anglers can proceed upstream or down in search of cutthroat trout, a favorite pastime along the South Salmo.

If you want to extend your trip, you can make a rewarding eighteen-mile loop by following the trail upstream past numerous campsites. You'll re-enter subalpine forest before passing a spring and climbing to the dry divide separating the South Salmo from the Priest River. Snowy Top, rising to 7,572 feet, is a popular destination lying just north of the trail along the divide. Boundary Lake, at 6,178 feet, straddles the border between Idaho and British Columbia just a short distance northwest. It, too, is a popular destination.

The loop returns to the trailhead via a protracted but view-filled ridge walk. Keep in mind that water is nonexistent along the ridge; you'll either need to pack a supply, go before all the snow melts in early July, or simply hike through to the South Salmo or Boundary Lake, the only reliable water sources en route. ☐

HIKE 87 *FOREST ROAD 2220 TO SHEDROOF MOUNTAIN*

General description: A moderate 7.4-mile, round-trip day hike to a superb Salmo-Priest Wilderness viewpoint in northeastern Washington's Selkirk Mountains.
Elevation gain and loss: +1,025 feet, -170 feet.
Trailhead elevation: 5,910 feet.
High point: Shedroof Mountain, 6,764 feet.
Maps: Salmo Mtn. 7.5-minute USGS quad; Colville National Forest map.
Season: July through September.
Water availability: None available.

Finding the trailhead: From State Route 31 just south of Ione, turn east onto paved county road (Road 9345) where a sign points to Sullivan Lake. Drive past the deep, 3.5-mile-long lake to a junction with eastbound Forest Road 22,

12.6 miles from the highway. (This junction can also be reached by driving 6.5 miles north then east from Metaline Falls and following Sullivan Lake signs.)

Turn east onto Forest Road 22 where a sign points to Salmo Mountain and Priest Lake. This good gravel road follows the course of Sullivan Creek and reaches a junction with northbound Forest Road 2220 after six miles. South bound Forest Road 22 forks right here, leading to Pass Creek Pass and Nordman, Idaho. Bear left at this four-way junction and follow Forest Road 2220, ignoring numerous signed spur roads, to a ridgetop junction with left-forking Forest Road 270, which leads to a tremendous vista atop Salmo Mountain, 18.25 miles from the county road. Bear right here and proceed 0.3 mile to the roadend at the Salmo Pass Trailhead. Hike 86 also begins here.

The hike: The Salmo-Priest Wilderness encompasses 39,973 acres of the wildest country in Washington. This horseshoe-shaped region protects a western divide, much of which was burned over around the turn of the century, and an eastern divide featuring old-growth forests of subalpine fir and Englemann spruce. The northern portion of the wilderness protects the headwaters of the South Salmo River, a tributary of the Pend Oreille River.

This country epitomizes what the western United States was like before Europeans arrived and began altering the land to suit their needs.

Old-growth forests (such as those present in this part of the Selkirks) form a fragile and complex ecosystem. Wildlife biologists estimate that at least one-fifth of all forest animals depend either partially or totally upon old-growth forests for survival. Grizzly bears and woodland caribou are among such dependent wildlife in the Salmo-Priest country. Sightings of moose and wolverine have also been reported.

With logging and other development taking place immediately to the east (in Idaho) and north (in British Columbia), the possibility exists that these animals may become increasingly dependent upon this wild area for their continued existence. For now, however, it seems that the caribou herd only occasionally ranges south from Canada into the Salmo-Priest. The Selkirk herd consists of approximately twenty-five animals, but more animals have been transplanted here recently in an attempt to increase the size of the herd in the United States.

Biologists estimate Washington's grizzly population at twenty-five to thirty animals, but these bears also range into adjacent areas of British Columbia and Idaho.

The presence of the grizzly and woodland caribou indicates the wildness of Washington's northeast corner, for these animals require the wildest of country in which to survive.

Hikers are discovering the Salmo-Priest, but certainly not in great numbers. High divides featuring broad vistas, cirque lakes, alpine meadows, old-growth forests (both subalpine and lowland), and a fishable river all combine to make an outing in this part of the Selkirks a memorable wildland experience.

These are the Northern Rockies, and they receive abundant precipitation, as much as eighty inches annually. Lying far east of the rain shadow cast by the Cascades, these mountains attract Pacific storms from the northwest during winter and thunderstorms from the south during summer. Because they are far inland from the moderating influence of the Pacific, they are much colder

HIKE 87 *FOREST ROAD 2220 TO SHEDROOF MOUNTAIN*

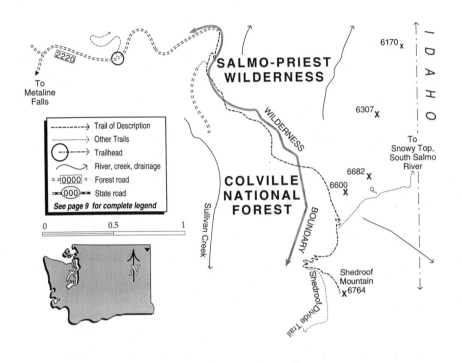

than the Cascades. This inland maritime climate has led to the development of flora unique to the Northern Rockies.

This pleasant day hike passes through an old-growth, subalpine forest on its way to a panoramic viewpoint. It's unlikely you'll see a grizzly or caribou, but they've surely been around.

This trail can be combined with the trail down to the South Salmo (see Hike 86) to form a rewarding eighteen-mile loop backpack, perhaps the most popular hike in the wilderness.

No water is available en route to Shedroof Mountain, so carry an ample supply.

From the trailhead, follow the closed road for one mile through a cool forest of spruce and fir to the beginning of the trail, after crossing into the Salmo-Priest Wilderness. Tree-framed views across the deep South Salmo drainage extend northward to 7,572-foot Snowy Top, 1.5 miles inside Idaho and 0.75 mile south of the Canadian border.

After a brief 0.2 mile from the end of the closed road, a spur trail joins your route from the southwest atop a 6,050-foot saddle. Ignore it.

Soon the trail begins a traverse upon southwest-facing slopes, temporarily leaving the wilderness. Views along this stretch are impressive, including the open slopes and glacial cirques of Crowell Ridge, the western arm of the Salmo-Priest horseshoe. Gypsy Peak crowns that ridge. Reaching to 7,309 feet, it's the highest point in the state east of the Cascades.

After 2.8 miles of pleasant hiking through timberline forests and across slopes carpeted in bear grass, the route descends to a 6,320-foot saddle and a junction. The northeast-bound trail traverses the divide between the Salmo and Priest rivers toward Snowy Top before descending into the valley of the South Salmo—a rewarding, diverse eighteen-mile loop trip.

To reach Shedroof Mountain, take the right fork, the Shedroof Divide Trail. This lightly used trail contours through the forest to a series of moderately steep switchbacks, attaining a ridgetop after half a mile. Turn left here onto the unmaintained path leading southeastward up the ridge for 0.4 mile to the 6,764-foot summit of Shedroof Mountain. En route, you'll have to slow to a snail's pace as you climb up and over one blown-down subalpine fir after another.

The open, bear-grass-decorated peak was once the site of a lookout tower, as you'll be able to see by the remaining concrete foundation.

The view is magnificent. You'll be able to see the Crowell Ridge on the western skyline and Idaho's jagged Selkirk Crest on the eastern one. The valley of the Priest River lies below to the east, and Upper Priest Lake and a sliver of Priest Lake are also visible in the southeast.

A few miles north, Snowy Top dominates the scene, and beyond are mountains of British Columbia, separated from you by miles of mountainous terrain and an imaginary, political boundary. Even Mount Spokane peeks above other nearby mountains, far to the south. □

HIKE 88 PASS CREEK PASS TO GRASSY TOP MOUNTAIN

General description: An easy 7.6-mile, round-trip day hike, leading through subalpine forests to a grassy viewpoint in the Selkirk Mountains inside the Colville National Forest.
Elevation gain and loss: +920 feet, -50 feet.
Trailhead elevation: 5,375 feet.
High point: Grassy Top Mountain, 6,253 feet.
Maps: Pass Creek 7.5-minute USGS quad; Colville National Forest map.
Season: Late June through early October.
Water availability: None.

Finding the trailhead: Follow directions given in Hike 87 to the junction of Forest Roads 22 and 2220, six miles from the county road, and turn right, staying on Road 22. Follow this narrow, sometimes steep, and winding dirt road for another 7.8 miles to Pass Creek Pass and park here. The signed Grassy Top Trail begins 0.1 mile west of the pass.

The hike: The hike from Pass Creek Pass to Grassy Top will lead you through old-growth, subalpine forests to—you guessed it—a grassy mountaintop where panoramas of northeastern Washington, northern Idaho, and southern British Columbia unfold.

Washington's Selkirk Mountains consist of two major divides rising east and west of the Pend Oreille River valley. The eastern divide along the Idaho border contains the wildest country in Washington, home to moose, grizzly bears, and a small band of woodland caribou that occasionally ranges southward from the mountains of southeastern British Columbia.

Old-growth forests are a chief component of the woodland caribou's habitat. These forests are protected north of Pass Creek Pass within the 41,335-acre Salmo-Priest Wilderness, but south of the pass logging roads and clearcuts threaten this crucial habitat.

The woodland caribou is the most endangered large mammal in the nation; only about twenty-five have been spotted here. But the transplant of twenty-four animals from British Columbia in 1987 should help increase the numbers of the Selkirk herd. These animals were radio-tagged and released in the Selkirks, where they split into two herds. One herd has reportedly found a home on Round Top Mountain, only one mile north of Pass Creek Pass in the Salmo-Priest Wilderness.

Other transplants are planned, and biologists hope they will eventually help remove the woodland caribou from the list of endangered species.

No water is available along this ridgetop hike, so carry an ample supply.

The trail begins 0.1 mile west of the pass and quickly descends to a porcupine-gnawed register box and a right-forking trail. Bear left. The main trail traverses north and then west on slopes blanketed by a mixed forest of Engelmann spruce, subalpine fir, lodgepole and white pine, western larch, and Douglas-fir.

The easy and scenic hike to aptly named Grassy Top Mountain is a fine choice for a rewarding day hike, even for families with small children. Ron Adkison photo.

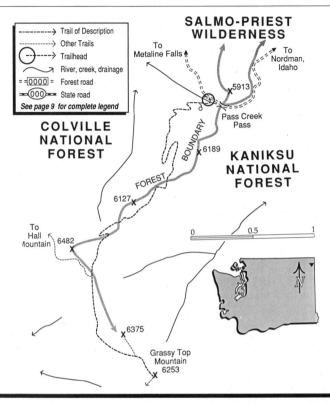

You will reach the main divide after 1.5 miles of hiking in subalpine forest. For the next mile, you'll alternate between east and west slopes before reaching a junction with the Hall Mountain Trail. Hall Mountain, five miles to the west, is home to a band of bighorn sheep.

Beyond the junction, the trail continues south along west slopes. Soon it breaks out of the timber onto grassy slopes and passes scattered timberline trees. Some trailside pines have been stripped of bark by porcupines in search of the nutritious cambium layer between the bark and the sapwood. Porcupines seem to prefer pines, since the bark of nearby subalpine firs remains intact.

Broad views both south and west will accompany you along these open slopes. You'll be able to see the Kettle River Range to the west and isolated Abercrombie Mountain to the northwest. After an easy mile from the previous junction, the trail reaches a saddle at 6,200 feet. A trail here forks left, climbing northward along the crest for 0.2 mile to Peak 6375, where vistas surpassing those obtained from Grassy Top can be enjoyed.

But to reach the pleasant, flat, grassy summit of Grassy Top, bear right at the saddle and climb easily for 0.2 mile to the 6,253-foot mountain.

To the west, a wall of subalpine fir obscures your view, but to the east the view is glorious. In that direction you'll see the Priest River valley and the rugged Selkirk Crest of Idaho. To the north you can gaze along the Shedroof Divide to Snowy Top and beyond to distant Canadian peaks. □

HIKE 89 *PASS CREEK PASS TO HELMER MOUNTAIN*

General description: A 10.4-mile round trip day hike along the eastern ridge of the Salmo-Priest Wilderness in northeastern Washington, leading through subalpine forest to a grand vista that reaches into Idaho and British Columbia.
Elevation gain and loss: +1,925 feet; -530 feet.
Trailhead elevation: 5,400 feet.
High point: Helmer Mountain, 6,595 feet.
Maps: Pass Creek and Helmer Mountain 7.5-minute USGS quads; Colville National Forest map.
Season: Late June through early October.
Water availability: Small spring four miles from the trailhead.

Finding the trailhead: Follow directions given in Hike 88.

The hike: The eastern crest of the Selkirk Mountains in northeastern Washington forms a lofty divide from the town of Newport north to the Canadian border. The northernmost sixteen-mile segment of this crest—the Shedroof Divide—is protected within the boundaries of the Salmo-Priest Wilderness and an adjacent roadless area in Idaho. Seldom tread by hikers, the Shedroof Divide Trail north of Pass Creek Pass is more often traveled by mule deer, elk, and, occasionally, by grizzly bear, and woodland caribou.

The trail is narrow and overgrown in places but maintains a gentle to moderate grade and is easy to follow. Vistas en route are superb, stretching eastward to the glacier carved granite peaks of the Selkirk Crest in Idaho and northward to the mountainous wonderland of southeastern British Columbia.

Carry plenty of water; the spring at the four-mile point may not be flowing enough to refill a water bottle.

From Pass Creek Pass follow the dirt road eastward for 0.2 mile. A "trail" sign indicates the beginning of the trail on the left, or north, side of the road.

Climbing past a trail register and entering the Salmo-Priest Wilderness, the trail soon leads into fir forest and winds gently upward toward the foot of grassy Round Top Mountain. After 0.9 mile from the road, ignore a left-forking abandoned trail. Instead, bear right, climbing moderately around the wildflower-speckled slopes of Round Top. After re-entering fir forest on the mountain's north slope, the trail descends moderately to the ridge below, where a pleasant 1.5 mile walk begins just west of the ridge's crest.

After strolling about 0.75 mile along the ridge, you enter a ghost forest of silver-grey snags, the result of the 600-acre Ace Creek Fire of 1987, when winds spread a slash fire into the forests of the Salmo-Priest.

Cresting the ridge just south of 6,590-foot Mankato Mountain, the trail begins a gentle descent contouring through virgin forest. The grassy south slopes of Helmer Mountain loom boldly just one mile ahead.

At the foot of Helmer Mountain, the trail curves east past a small spring; just beyond the spring a small campsite lies south of the trail. The trail ahead switchbacks once while climbing moderately up the south slope of Helmer, among beargrass, huckleberry patches, and groves of subalpine fir.

Curving around the west slope of the mountain just below an unnamed

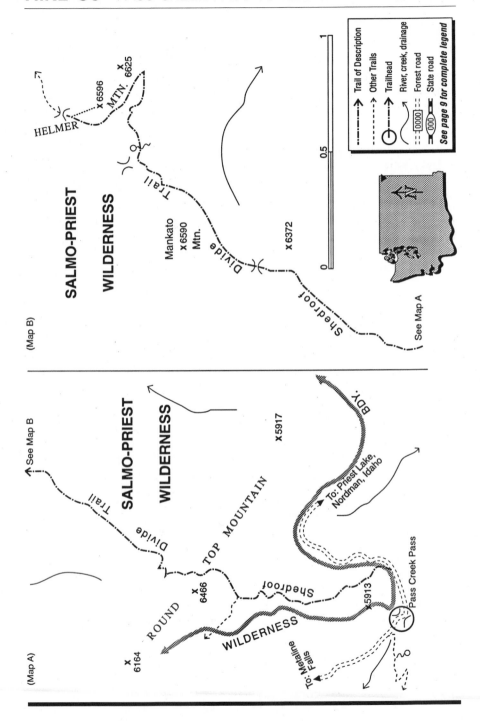

(Map B)

SALMO-PRIEST
WILDERNESS

HELMER MTN.
x 6596
x 6625

Mankato
x 6590
Mtn.

Divide

Trail

Shedroot

x 6372

See Map A

Trail of Description
Other Trails
Trailhead
River, creek, drainage
10000 Forest road
000 State road

See page 9 for complete legend

0   0.5   1

(Map A)

See Map B

SALMO-PRIEST
WILDERNESS

Divide

Trail

ROUND TOP MOUNTAIN

x 5917

x 6466

x 6164

Shedroot

WILDERNESS

x 5913

To: Metaline
Falls

Pass Creek Pass

To: Priest Lake,
Nordman, Idaho

BDY.

Views from Helmer Mountain are grand and expansive. Ron Adkison photo.

summit (6,596 feet), whitebark pine joins the fir forest; stroll ahead on the gently climbing trail to a 6,491-foot saddle, 5.1 miles from the trailhead.

The south summit of Helmer Mountain (6,596 feet) is more open and offers the finest vista. To get there, climb the ridge through fir forest and thickets of menziesia for 250 yards to the small summit.

Eastward lies part of Upper Priest Lake, resting at the foot of Idaho's rugged Selkirk Crest. Northward the Shedroof Divide foregrounds a tremendous panorama of lofty peaks stretching to the horizon in British Columbia.

After enjoying the fabulous views from Helmer Mountain, retrace the route to the trailhead. □

HIKE 90 *SMITH GAP TO MOUNT KIT CARSON*

General description: A 3.9-mile semi-loop day hike to a fine vista point only an hour's drive from Spokane in Mount Spokane State Park.
Elevation gain and loss: 1,171 feet.
Trailhead elevation: 4,100 feet.
High point: Mount Kit Carson, 5,271 feet.
Maps: Mount Spokane 15-minute USGS quad (trail not shown on quad); Mount Spokane State Park brochure and map.
Season: Mid-July through mid-October.
Water availability: No water en route.

Finding the trailhead: Drive ten miles north of Spokane on U.S. Highway 2 to eastbound State Route 206, indicated by a Mount Spokane State Park sign. Follow this winding, paved road for 16.8 miles to the Mount Kit Carson Loop

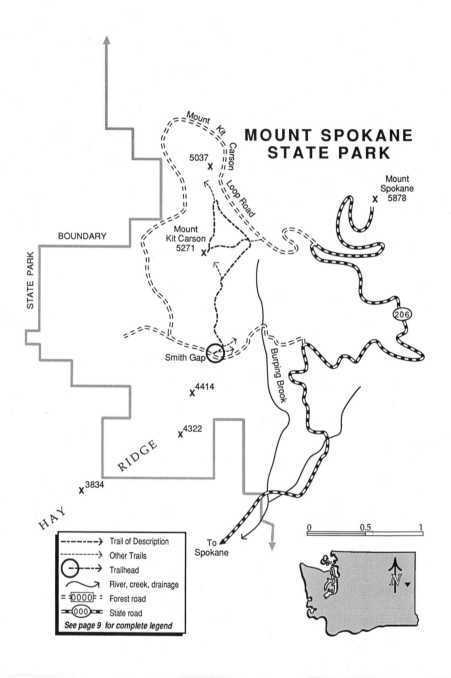

MOUNT SPOKANE
STATE PARK

5037
X

Mount
Spokane
5878
X

BOUNDARY

STATE PARK

Mount
Kit Carson
5271
X

Burping Brook

206

Smith Gap

X 4414

X 4322

RIDGE

X 3834

HAY

To
Spokane

0   0.5   1

------→ Trail of Description
- - - -→ Other Trails
◯- -→ Trailhead
⌇⌇⌇↘ River, creek, drainage
= 0000 = Forest road
- (000) - State road
See page 9 for complete legend

N

Road and bear left. This dirt road leads 1.2 miles past several shady picnic areas to Smith Gap. The obvious trail (unmarked except for a "No vehicles allowed". sign) begins on the north side of the road.

The hike: Spokane residents are fortunate to live in the Rocky Mountains, where enormous opportunities to enjoy the outdoors lie nearby. Only an hour's drive from downtown Spokane, Mount Spokane State Park consists of a large dome of granite south of Washington's Selkirk Mountains and offers a variety of short trail walks. Here, hikers can briefly flee the pressures of city life to stroll in the mountains for a few hours or a day.

The short but rigorous hike to Mount Kit Carson offers a good workout and broad views of mountains, valleys, and Washington's second-largest city. Carry plenty of drinking water and realize that you might encounter mountain bikes along this trail. Keep an eye out for white-tailed deer. They're quite common in the area.

From Smith Gap, the wide, unmarked trail (all trails in the State Park are marked only with a "no vehicles allowed" sign) climbs quickly past two right-forking trails into a forest dominated by lodgepole pine. The dusty trail climbs steeply past a variety of understory plants, including Sitka alder, Douglas maple, mallow ninebark, spirea, Oregon grape, wild rose, huckleberry, bracken fern, ocean spray, thimbleberry, snowberry, and pearly everlasting.

After 0.75 mile of relentless climbing, the trail levels off on a grassy spur ridge emanating from Mount Kit Carson. Ignore a faint path forking left, and traverse east-facing slopes under a canopy of Douglas-fir, western larch, and lodgepole pine to a junction 1.25 miles from Smith Gap. The right fork quickly leads to the Mount Kit Carson Loop Road. Turn left at the junction and then fork right almost immediately, heading northwest under a shady forest canopy dominated by lodgepole pine, with an understory of huckleberry, bear grass, and menziesia.

This nearly level trail reaches a junction after half a mile, where you should turn left. The trail then climbs moderately through a thick stand of lodgepole pines to the summit ridge and another junction half a mile later. Bear right, quite soon attaining the exfoliating granite crown of 5,271-foot Mount Kit Carson, where a superb vista unfolds.

Westward lies a patchwork of forest and rangeland, stretching to the timbered ridges of the westernmost reaches of the Northern Rockies. Southward, the mountains steadily descend into the valley of the Spokane River, with its cities and sprawling suburbs. A continuous mountainscape extends eastward to the crest of the Bitterroot Range, straddling the border between Idaho and Montana. The dome-like summit of Mount Spokane dominates the skyline a mere 1.5 miles to the east, cluttered with radio transmitters and other works of man.

From the summit, hike back down the trail to the previously mentioned junction and bear right, hiking northeastward along the grassy ridge. Then descend through timber for 0.4 mile to the junction with the trail to Mount Kit Carson Loop Road. From here, turn right and retrace the steep and dusty route to Smith Gap. □

THE HIKER'S CHECK LIST

Have you ever hiked into the backcountry and discovered that you forgot some essential items? Before setting out, make your own checklist, based on the ideas below, to make sure you don't face such a dilemma again.

Clothing
Dependable rain parka
Rain pants
Wind garment
Thermal underwear
  (wool or
  polypropylene
  are best)
Shorts or long pants
Wool cap or balaclava
Hat
Wool shirt or sweater
Jacket or parka
  (fiberpile is excellent)
Extra socks
Underwear
Lightweight shirt(s)
Bandana(s)
Mittens or gloves
Belt

Footwear
Sturdy, comfortable
  footwear
Lightweight camp shoes

Bedding
Sleeping bag
Foam pad or air
  mattress
Ground sheet (plastic or
  nylon)
Dependable tent

Hauling
Day pack or backpack

Cooking
One-quart water
  container (plastic)
One-gallon water
  container for camp
  use (collapsible)
Backpack stove and
  extra fuel
Aluminum foil (as
  windscreen for
  backpack stove or
  candle holder)
Cooking pots
Spoon and fork
Pot scrubber
Matches in waterproof
  container

Food and drink
Enough food, plus a
  little extra

Photography
Camera and film

Miscellaneous
Sunglasses
Maps and a compass
Toilet paper
Pocketknife
Sunscreen
Good insect repellent
Lip balm
Flashlight with good
  batteries and a
  spare bulb
Candle(s)
First-aid kit
Survival kit
Small garden trowel or
  shovel
Water filter or
  purification tablets
Plastic bags (for trash)
Soap
Towel
Toothbrush
Fishing license
Fishing rod, reel, lures,
  flies, etc.
Binoculars
Waterproof covering
  for pack
Watch
Sewing kit

FOR MORE INFORMATION

Hikers who need additional information about the hiking areas in this guide should contact the following administrative agencies:

Hikes 1, 2, and 3: Pomeroy Ranger District, Route 1, Box 53-F, Pomeroy, WA 99347, (509) 843-1891; or Forest Supervisor, Umatilla National Forest, 2517 SW Hailey Ave., Pendleton, OR 97801, (503) 276-3811.

Hike 4: Bureau of Land Management, Spokane District Office, E. 4217 Main Ave., Spokane, WA 99202, (509) 456-2570.

Hike 5: State of Washington Department of Wildlife, Region 3 HQ, 2802 Fruitvale Blvd., Yakima, WA 98902; or State of Washington Department of Game, 600 N. Capitol Way GJ-11, Olympia, WA 98504, (206) 753-5700.

Hike 6: Ginkgo Petrified Forest State Park, Vantage, WA 98950.

For more information on hikes in Gifford Pinchot National Forest, contact Forest Supervisor, Gifford Pinchot National Forest, 500 W. 12th St., Vancouver, WA 98660, (206) 696-7500, or the appropriate ranger district:

Hikes 7 and 8: Wind River Ranger District, Carson, WA 98610, (509) 427-5645.

Hikes 9, 10, 11, 16, and 17: Mount Adams Ranger District, 2455 Highway 141, Trout Lake, WA 98650, (509) 395-2501.

Hikes 12 and 13: Mount St. Helens National Volcanic Monument, Route 1, Box 369, Amboy, WA 98601, (206) 247-5473; or Mount St. Helens Visitor Center, 3029 Spirit Lake Hwy., Castle Rock, WA 98611.

Hikes 14, 15, 19, and 20: Randle Ranger District, Randle, WA 98377, (206) 497-7565.

Hikes 18, 21, and 22: Packwood Ranger District, 13068 U.S. Highway 12, Packwood, WA 98361, (206) 494-5515.

Hikes 23, 24, 25, 26, 27, 28, and 29: Superintendent, Mount Rainier National Park, Tahoma Woods, Star Route, Ashford, WA 98304, (206) 569-2211; or National Park Service Outdoor Recreation Information Center, 1018 First Ave., Seattle, WA 98104, (206) 442-0170.

For more information on hikes in Wenatchee National Forest, contact Forest Supervisor, Wenatchee National Forest, P.O. Box 811, Wenatchee, WA 98801, (509) 662-4335, or the appropriate ranger district:

Hikes 23, 30, and 31: Naches Ranger District, 10061 Highway 12, Naches, WA 98937, (509) 653-2205.

Hikes 42 and 44: Leavenworth Ranger District, 600 Sherbourne, Leavenworth, WA 98826, (509) 782-1413.

Hikes 43 and 45: Cle Elum Ranger District, W. Second, Cle Elum, WA 98922, (509) 674-4411.

Hikes 48, 49, and 50: Lake Wenatchee Ranger District, 22976 Highway 207, Leavenworth, WA 98826, (509) 763-3103.

Hike 51: Entiat Ranger District, P.O. Box 476, Entiat, WA 98822, (509) 784-1511.

Hike 52: Chelan Ranger District, P.O. Box 189, Chelan, WA 98816, (509) 682-2576.

For information about hikes in Olympic National Forest, contact the Forest

Supervisor, Olympic National Forest, P.O. Box 2288, Olympia, WA 98507 (206) 753-9534, or the appropriate ranger district:

Hikes 32 and 33: Quinault Ranger Station, Quinault, WA 98575, (206) 288-2525.

Hike 41: Quilcene Ranger Station, P.O. Box 280, Quilcene, WA 98376, (206) 765-3368.

Hike 42: Hood Canal Ranger Station, P.O. Box 68, Hoodsport, WA 98548, (206) 877-5254.

Hikes 34, 35, 36, 37, 38, 39, and 40: Park Superintendent, Olympic National Park, 600 E. Park Ave., Port Angeles, WA 98362, (206) 452-4501.

For information about hikes in Mount Baker-Snoqualmie National Forest, contact Forest Supervisor, Mount Baker-Snoqualmie National Forest, Supervisor's Office, 21905 64th Ave. W., Mountlake Terrace, WA 98043, (206) 775-9702; or the Forest Service/National Park Service Outdoor Recreation Information Office, 1018 First Ave., Seattle, WA 98104, (206) 442-0170; or the appropriate ranger district:

Hike 46: North Bend Ranger District, P.O. Box AA, North Bend, WA 98045, (206) 888-1421.

Hike 47: Skykomish Ranger District, P.O. Box 305, Skykomish, WA 98288, (206) 677-2414.

Hikes 53 and 54: Darrington Ranger District, 1405 Emmens St., Darrington, WA 98241, (206) 436-1155.

Hikes 60, 61, 62, 63, and 64: Mount Baker Ranger District, 2105 Highway 20, Sedro-Woolley, WA 98284, (206) 856-5700.

Hikes 56, 62, 65, 66, and 67: Park Superintendent, North Cascades National Park, 2105 Highway 20, Sedro-Woolley, WA 98284, (206) 856-5700.

Hikes 57 and 58: Moran State Park, Star Route, Box 22, Eastbound, WA 98245, (206) 376-2326. For ferry information, contact Washington State Ferries, Seattle Ferry Terminal, Seattle, WA 98104, (206) 464-6400.

Hikes 59: Washington Department of Natural Resources, Public Lands Building, Olympia, WA 98504 (206) 753-5327.

For information about hikes in Okanogan National Forest, contact Forest Supervisor, Okanogan National Forest, P.O. Box 950, Okanogan, WA 98840, (509) 442-2704, or contact the appropriate ranger district:

Hikes 68, 69, 70, 71, 72, 73, 74, 75, and 76: Winthrop Ranger District, P.O. Box 579, Winthrop, WA 98862, (509) 996-2266.

Hike 77: Twisp Ranger District, P.O. Box 188, Twisp, WA 98856, (509) 997-2131.

Hike 78: Tonasket Ranger District, P.O. Box 466, Tonasket, WA 98855, (509) 486-2186.

For more information about hikes in Colville National Forest, contact Forest Supervisor, Colville National Forest, 695 S. Main, Federal Building, Colville, WA 99114, (509) 684-3711, or contact the appropriate ranger district:

Hike 79: Republic Ranger District, P.O. Box 468, Republic, WA 99166, (509) 775-3305.

Hike 79, 80, 81, 82, and 83: Kettle Falls Ranger District, 255 W. 11th, Kettle Falls, WA 99141, (509) 738-6111.

Hike 84: Steamboat Rock State Park, P.O. Box 370, Electric City, WA 99123.

Hike 85: Colville Ranger District, 755 S. Main, Colville, WA 99114, (509) 684-4557.

Hikes 86, 87, 88, and 89: Sullivan Lake Ranger District, 12641 Sullivan Lake Road, Metaline Falls, WA 99153, (509) 446-2681.

Hike 90: Mount Spokane State Park, North 26107 Mount Spokane Park Drive, Mead, WA 99021.

ABOUT THE AUTHOR

Ron Adkison has been exploring wildlands and studying the natural environment of the West for many years. He has walked each hike in this guide to provide precise, firsthand information about not only the trails but features and processes of ecological interest as well. Adkison, the author of *The Hiker's Guide to California*, lives with his wife and two children near Whitehall, Montana, where they raise llamas and sheep.

Out here—there's no one to ask directions

...except your **FALCON**GUIDE.

HIKING NOTES